Printed in the USA

Serbian Language:

101 Serbian Verbs

BY ANTONIJE ILIC

Contents

Introduction to Serbian Verbs Forms   1

To Accept – прѝхватити - prihvatiti   9

To Admit – прѝзнати - priznati   11

To Answer – одговòрити - odgovoriti   13

To Appear – изглéдати - izgledati   15

To Ask - пѝтати – pitati   17

To Be - бѝти – biti   19

To Be Able To – мòћи - moći   21

To Become – пòстати - postati   23

To Begin – пòчети – početi   25

To Break – слòмити – slomiti   27

To Breathe - дѝсати – disati   29

To Buy - кýпити – kupiti   31

To Call – пòзвати – pozvati   33

Can – ỳмети – umeti   35

To Choose – изàбрати – izabrati   37

To Close – затвòрити - zatvoriti   39

To Come - дóћи – doći   41

To Cook - кỳвати – kuvati   43

To Cry - плàкати – plakati   45

To Dance - плéсати   47

To Decide - одлýчити – odlučiti   49

To Decrease - смàњити – smanjiti   51

To Die – ỳмрети – umreti   53

To Do – òбавити – obaviti   55

To Drink - пѝти - piti   57

To Drive – во̀зити – voziti 59

To Eat - jе̏сти – jesti 61

To Enter - у́ћи – ući 63

To Exit - изáћи – izaći 65

To Explain - objа́снити – objasniti 67

To Fall – па̏сти – pasti 69

To Feel – о̀сећати – osećati 71

To Fight – бо̀рити се – boriti se 73

To Find - нáћи – naći 75

To Finish – завр̀шити – završiti 77

To Fly – лѐтети – leteti 79

To Forget – забо̀равити – zaboraviti 81

To Get Up – у̀стати – ustati 83

To Give - да̏ти – dati 85

To Go – и̏ћи – ići 87

To Happen - де̏сити се – desiti se 89

To Have – и̏мати – imati 91

To Hear - чу̏ти - čuti 93

To Help – помо̀ћи – pomoći 95

To Hold – др̀жати – držati 97

To Increase – повѐћати – povećati 99

To Introduce – прѐдставити – pradstaviti 101

To Invite – по̀звати – pozvati 103

To Kill – у̀бити – ubiti 105

To Kiss - пољу́бити – poljubiti 107

To Know - зна̏ти – znati 109

To Laugh - смѐјати се – smejati se 111

To Learn - у̀чити – učiti 113

To Lie Down – лѐћи - leći 115

To Like – вòлети – voleti 117

To Listen - слȳшати – slušati 119

To Live - жѝвети – živeti 121

To Lose – изгу̀бити – izgubiti 123

To Love - обожа́вати – obožavati 125

To Meet - срȅсти се - sresti se 127

To Need - трȇбати – trebati 129

To Notice - приме́тити – primetiti 131

To Open – отвòрити – otvoriti 133

To Play - ѝграти се - igrati se 135

To Put - ста̏вити – staviti 137

To Read – чѝтати – čitati 139

To Receive - при́мити – primiti 141

To Remember – сȅћати се - sećati se 143

To Repeat – понòвити – ponoviti 145

To Return - вра́тити се – vratiti se 147

To Run – тр̀чати – trčati 149

To Say – рȅћи – reći 151

To Scream - при́снути – vrisnuti 153

To See - вѝдети – videti 155

To Seem – чѝнити се - činiti se 157

To Sell – прòдати – prodati 159

To Send – пòслати – poslati 161

To Show - пока́зати – pokazati 163

To Sing - пȅвати – pevati 165

To Sit Down - сȅсти – sesti 167

To Sleep - спа́вати – spavati 169

To Smile - осме́хнути се – osmehnuti se 171

To Speak - при́чати - pričati 173

To Stand – стòјати – stojati   175

To Start – запòчети - započeti   177

To Stay – òстати – ostati   179

To Take – у̀зети – uzeti   181

To Talk – говòрити – govoriti   183

To Teach - подучáвати – podučavati   185

To Think - мѝслити – misliti   187

To Touch – дотàћи – dotaći   189

To Travel – путòвати – putovati   191

To Understand – разу̀мети – razumeti   193

To Use - корѝстити – koristiti   195

To Wait - чѐкати – čekati   197

To Walk - шéтати – šetati   199

To Want – жѐлети – želeti   201

To Watch - глѐдати – gledati   203

To Win - побéдити – pobediti   205

To Work - рáдити – raditi   207

To Write - пѝсати - pisati   209

Introduction to Serbian Verb Forms

In contrast to modern English, which is a weakly inflected language, Serbian has a high degree of inflection. That means that Serbian language makes extensive use of affixes for different grammatical categories such as tense, aspect, mood, voice, gender or number. Therefore Serbian verbs conjugate in many ways. More specifically, in the English sentence "We will sing", the word "sing" is not inflected in any way, whereas the Serbian equivalent, expressed as a one-word sentence "pevaćemo", contains the suffix "ćemo", designating a specific tense (future), number (plural) and person (first).

All Slavic languages have complex and varied verb forms, and Serbian is no exception. Serbian language has as many as 14 verb forms. There are **nine finite verb forms** and **five non-finite** ones. Most finite verb forms are formed by inflection, meaning that the verb is modified according to tense, aspect, person, number, gender or mood. The finite forms can broadly be categorized according to tenses and the mood. There are seven tenses in Serbian: present, perfect, future I, future II, aorist, imperfect and pluperfect. The Imperfect and Pluperfect tenses have a very limited use in daily speech and are considered to be old-fashioned and archaic. The grammatical mood is expressed with the Imperative and Conditional. As for the non-finite verb forms, there is one infinitive, two adjectival participles (active and passive) and two adverbial participles (present and past). Serbian also has two voices – active and passive.

Verbal Aspect

Another important property of Serbian verbs is their aspect. It can be either perfective or imperfective. The perfective aspect of a verb expresses a completed action, while the imperfective indicates an action that is incomplete, ongoing or iterative. Unlike English, which uses different tenses for completed and continuous actions, Serbian verbs have the aspect built into the verb itself. For example, the sentence "She read the book" indicates that the action was finished. On the other hand, "She was reading the book" expresses a progressive action. In Serbian, perfective verbs are usually formed from their imperfective counterparts and prefixes:

"Она је прочитала књигу" (perfective aspect, completed action)
Ona je pročitala knjigu.

"Она је читала књигу" (imperfective aspect, ongoing or iterative action).
Ona je čitala knjigu.

As seen, the imperfective verb "прочитати" (read – as a completed action) is formed by adding the prefix "про" to the otherwise imperfective verb "читати" (read – as a progressive action).

Therefore, Serbian verbs often come in pairs, bearing the same meaning, but signifying a different aspect. When learning Serbian, one should learn both verb forms for different aspects.

Non-finite Verb Forms

As mentioned earlier, there are five non-finite verb forms in Serbian.

1. **Infinitive** is a dictionary form of the verb. All Serbian infinitives end in -ти or –ћи. Unlike English infinitives, that can indicate certain grammatical categories such as voice, tense or aspect (e.g. to be making, to have been made), Serbian infinitives cannot be inflected or marked in any way. On the other hand, the infinitive stem in Serbian is used for formation of several tenses. If the infinitive ends in –ти, the infinitive stem is formed by removing the ending.
   For example: кувати (kuvati) (to cook) - infinitive
   кува (kuva) – infinitive stem
   If the infinitive ends in –ћи or –сти, the infinitive stem is formed by using the first person singular of the verb in the Aorist without the ending -ox
   For example: пећи (to bake) - infinitive
   пекох (pekoh) – 1st person singular of the Aorist
   пек (pek) – infinitive stem

2. **Active adjectival participle** is used for the formation of complex verb tenses such as Future Tense I, Paste Tense (Perfect), Pluperfect and Conditional. It is inflected for gender and number and it is formed by adding the following endings to the infinitive stem:

Gender	Singular	Plural
Feminine	-ла	-ле
Masculine	-о	-ли
Neuter	-ло	-ла

For example: радити (raditi) (to work) – infinitive
ради (radi) – infinitive stem
радила (radila) – active adjectival participle for feminine gender singular

3. **Passive adjectival participle** is used for the formation of the Passive Voice. Therefore, it can be used only for transitive verbs. It is also inflected both for gender and number. It is formed by adding the following suffixes to the infinitive stem:

Gender	Singular	Plural
Feminine	-на, -ена,-вена, -та	-не, -ене, -вене, -те
Masculine	-н, -ен, -вен, -т	-ни, -ени, -вени, -ти
Neuter	-но, -ено, -вено, -то	-на, -ена, -вена, -та

For example: радити (raditi) (to work) – infinitive
рађени (rađeni) – passive adjectival participle for masculine gender plural

4. **Present adverbial participle** (or the present verbal adverb) refers to an action which is happening simultaneously with another action or an action that is immediately preceding or

following an event. In a sentence it usually serves as an adverbial modifier for manner. It is formed by adding the ending –ħи to the 3rd person plural of the Present Tense.

For example: певају (pevaju) (They are singing/They sing) – 3rd person plural of the Present Tense verb "певати" (pevati) (to sing)

певајући (pevajući) – present adverbial participle

5. **Past adverbial participle** (or the past verbal adverb) refers to a past action happening before the action expressed by the predicate of a sentence. It is usually used as an adverbial modifier for manner or time. Past adverbial participles are formed by the infinitive stem of perfective verbs and the ending –вши/авши.

For example: видети (videti) (to see) – infinitive

виде (vide) – infinitive stem

видевши (videvši) – past adverbial participle

Finite Verb Forms
a. Tenses

The Present Tense is used to describe:

a. a habitual or repetitive action: _Возим бицикл сваки дан.Vozim bicikl svaki dan. (I ride my bicycle every day)_

b. an action happening at the moment of speaking: _Погледај! Пада киша. Pogledaj! Pada kiša. (Look! It's raining),_

c. or for future events: _Сутра идем на час француског. Sutra idem na čas francuskog. (I'm taking a French class tomorrow)_

Formation: the infinitive stem/the present tense stem + three main sets of endings.

Person	Singular	Plural
1st	-им, -ам, -ем	-имо, -амо, -емо
2nd	-иш, -аш, -еш	-ите, ате, ете
3rd	-и, -а, -е	-е, -ајy, -у

Person	Verb ending in –им учити – to learn		Verb ending in –ам певати – to sing		Verb ending in –ем прати – to wash	
1st	учим	учимо	певам	певамо	перем	перемо
2nd	учиш	учите	певаш	певате	переш	перете
3rd	учи	уче	пева	певају	пере	перу

3

The Past Tense (Perfect Tense) is the most used tense form in Serbian when speaking about past events. It is used to describe an action happening in the past that can be either ongoing or completed. The Past Tense uses both perfective and imperfective verbs, thus replacing the Aorist and Imperfective in the Serbian vernacular.

Jуче сам купио овај капут. Juče sam kupio ovaj kaput. I bought this coat yesterday.

Formation: short form of the Present Tense of the verb "бити"(biti) (to be) + active adjectival participle

Verb "радити" – to work		
Person	**Singular**	**Plural**
1st	Ја сам радио/радила	Ми смо радили/радиле
2nd	Ти си радио/радила	Ви сте радили/радиле
3rd	Он/Она је радио/радила	Они/Оне су радили/радиле

Note: Ја,ти, он/она, ми, ви, они (ja, ti, on/ona, mi, vi, oni) are personal pronouns corresponding to I, you, he/she, we, you, they.

Serbian past tense is also inflected for gender; therefore the form "радила" (radila) indicates that the subject is female, whereas the form "радио" (radio) indicates a male subject.

The Aorist is a past tense that can be formed only with perfective verbs and is usually used for actions that have just been completed. Nowadays, due to its archaic tone, it is rarely used and is often replaced by the Past Tense.

Изгубих кључеве од кола. Izgubih ključeva od kola. I have just lost my car keys.

Formation: the infinitive stem + two sets of endings

Person	Singular	Plural
1st	-х, -ох	-смо, -осмо
2nd	--, -е	-сте, -осте
3rd	--, -е	-ше, -оше

Person	Infinitive ending in **-ти** погледати - to watch		Infinitive ending in **–сти** or **-ħи** пасти - to fall	
1st	погледах	погледасмо	падох	падосмо
2nd	погледа	погледасте	паде	падосте
3rd	погледа	погледаше	паде	падоше

The Imperfect is a past tense designating an action that lasted for some time. Since the emphasis is on duration of an action, only imperfective verbs are used in this tense. The usage of the Imperfect is almost exclusively limited to literature and the narrative mode, as it is considered to be rather archaic and outdated.

Играсмо се као деца. Igrasmo se као deca. We used to play when we were kids.

Formation: the infinitive stem + three sets of endings

Person	Singular	Plural
1st	-ах, -јах, -ијах	-асмо, -јасмо, -ијасмо
2nd	-аше, -јаше, -ијаше	-асте, -јасте, -ијасте
3rd	-аше, -јаше, -ијаху	-аху, -јаху, -ијаху

Person	Infinitive stem ending in **–a** кувати – to cook		Infinitive stem ending in a vowel **other than –a** чути – to hear		Infinitive ending in **–сти** or **–ħи** пећи – to bake	
1st	кувах	кувасмо	чујах	чујасмо	пецијах	пецијасмо
2nd	куваше	кувасте	чујаше	чујасте	пецијаше	пецијасте
3rd	куваше	куваху	чујаше	чујаху	пецијаше	пецијаху

The Pluperfect Tense is used to describe an action that happened before a past event. In modern Serbian it is rarely used and it usually gives way to the Paste Tense.

Кад је Марко стигао, они су већ били отишли. Kad je Marko stigao, oni su već bili otišli. When Mark arrived, they had already left.

Formation: past tense of the verb "бити" (biti) (to be) (or more rarely imperfect of the verb "бити") + active adjectival participle.

Verb "радити" – to work		
Person	**Singular**	**Plural**
1st	Ја сам био/била радио/радила	Ми смо били/биле радили/радиле
2nd	Ти си био/била радио/радила	Ви сте били/биле радили/радиле
3rd	Он/Она је био/била радио/радила	Они/Оне су били/биле радили/радиле

Note: The Past Tense of the verb "бити" is also inflected for gender, the forms био/били (bio/bili) signifying the masculine gender, and била/биле (bila/bile) the feminine gender.

Future Tense I is used for an action or occurrence that is about to take place in the future.

Сутра ћу купити нове ципеле. Sutra ću kupiti nove cipele. I will buy a pair of new shoes tomorrow.

Formation: a. short form of the Present Tense of the verb "хтети"(hteti) + infinitive verb form

b. infinitive stem + short form of the Present Tense of the verb "хтети" (hteti)

a.

Verb "ићи" – to go		
Person	**Singular**	**Plural**
1st	Ја ћу ићи	Ми ћемо ићи
2nd	Ти ћеш ићи	Ви ћете ићи
3rd	Он/Она/Оно ће ићи	Они/Оне ће ићи

Note: the forms "ћу, ћеш, ће, ћемо, ћете, ће" (ću, ćeš, će, ćemo, ćete, će) are the short forms of the verb "хтети" (hteti) (to want).

b.

Person	Infinitive ending in -**ћи** Verb "ићи" - to go		Infinitive ending in -**ти** Verb "трчати" – to run	
1st	ићи ћу	ићи ћемо	трчаћу	трчаћемо
2nd	ићи ћеш	ићи ћете	трчаћеш	трчаћете
3rd	ићи ће	ићи ће	трчаће	трчаће

Note: if the infinitive ends in "ћи", the verb "хтети" is written as a separate word.

If the infinitive ends in "ти", the infinitive stem and verb "хтети" are written as a single word.

The Future Tense II describes an action that will take part in the future before another future action. Therefore, it is used only in complex sentences, as a part of a subordinate clause. On the other hand, the Future I is used in the main clause of such sentences. The Future II can also be replaced with the Present Tense in subordinate clauses.

Када будем завршила, позваћу те. Kada budem završila, pozvaću te. When I'm done, I'll call you.

Formation: present tense of the verb "бити"(biti) (to be) + active adjectival participle

Verb "радити" – to work		
Person	**Singular**	**Plural**
1st	будем радио/радила	будемо радили/радиле
2nd	будеш радио/радила	будете радили/радиле
3rd	буде радио/радила	буду радили/радиле

Note: the forms "будем, будеш, буде, будемо, будете, буду" (budem, budeš, bude, budemo, budete, budu) are the present tense forms of the verb "бити" (biti) (to be).

b. The Mood

The Imperative is a grammatical mood that expresses the speaker's command, wish, request, permission, prohibition or plea. It can only be formed in the second person singular and the first and second person plural.

Престани да вичеш! Prestani da vičeš! Stop shouting!

Formation: the present tense verb stem for the 3rd person plural + the endings presented below:

Person	Singular	Plural
1st	--	-имо, -jмо
2nd	-и, -j	-ите, -jте
3rd	--	--

Verb "скочити" – to jump		
Person	Singular	Plural
1st	--	скочимо
2nd	скочи	скочите
3rd	--	--

The Conditional is a grammatical mood that expresses a possibility of something happening. It also shows the speaker's attitude towards an action or ocurrence.

Кад <u>бих имао</u> времена и новца, <u>путовао бих</u> по свету. Kad <u>bih imao</u> vremena i novca, <u>putovao bih</u> po svetu. If I <u>had</u> the time and money, I <u>would travel</u> the world.

Formation: the aorist of the verb (to be) + active adjectival participle

Verb "доћи"—to come		
Person	**Singular**	**Plural**
1ˢᵗ	бих дошла/дошао	бисмо дошле/дошли
2ⁿᵈ	би дошла/дошао	бисте дошле/дошли
3ʳᵈ	би дошла/дошао	би дошле/дошли

Note: the forms "бих, би, би, бисмо, бисте, би" (bih, bi, bi, bismo, biste, bi) are the aorist forms of the verb "бити" (biti) (to be).

To Accept – прихватити - prihvatiti

	Present (Презент)	Future I (Футур први)	Future II (Футур други)
1st per	Ја прихватам Ja prihvatam	Ја ћу прихватити/Прихватићу Ja ću prihvatiti/Prihvatiću	Ја будем прихватио/прихватила Ja budem prihvatio/prihvatila
2nd per	Ти прихваташ Ti prihvataš	Ти ћеш прихватити/Прихватићеш Ti ćeš prihvatiti/Prihvatićeš	Ти будеш прихватио/прихватила Ti budeš prihvatio/prihvatila
3rd per (M)	Он прихвата On prihvata	Он ће прихватити/Прихватиће On će prihvatiti/Prihvatiće	Он буде прихватио On bude prihvatio
3rd per (F)	Она прихвата Ona prihvata	Она ће прихватити/Прихватиће Ona će prihvatiti/Prihvatiće	Она буде прихватила Ona bude prihvatila
3rd per (N)	Оно прихвата Ono prihvata	Оно ће прихватити/Прихватиће Ono će prihvatiti/Prihvatiće	Оно буде прихватило Ono bude prihvatilo
1st per pl	Ми прихватамо Mi prihvatamo	Ми ћемо прихватити/Прихватићемо Mi ćemo prihvatiti/Prihvatićemo	Ми будемо прихватили/прихватиле Mi budemo prihvatili/prihvatile
2nd per pl	Ви прихватате Vi prihvatate	Ви ћете прихватити/Прихватићете Vi ćete prihvatiti/Prihvatićete	Ви будете прихватили/прихватиле Vi budete prihvatili/prihvatile
3rd per pl	Они/Оне прихватају Oni/One prihvataju	Они/Оне ће прихватити/Прихватиће Oni/One će prihvatiti/Prihvatiće	Они/Оне буду прихватили/прихватиле Oni/One budu prihvatili/prihvatile

	Past Tense (Перфект)	Pluperfect (Плусквамперфект)	Conditional (Потенцијал)
1st per	Ја сам прихватио Ja sam prihvatio	Ја сам био прихватио Ja sam bio prihvatio	Ја бих прихватио Ja bih prihvatio
2nd per	Ти си прихватио Ti si prihvatio	Ти си био прихватио Ti si bio prihvatio	Ти би прихватио Ti bi prihvatio
3rd per (M)	Он је прихватио On je prihvatio	Он је био прихватио On je bio prihvatio	Он би прихватио On bi prihvatio
3rd per (F)	Она је прихватила Ona je prihvatila	Она је била прихватила Ona je bila prihvatila	Она би прихватила Ona bi prihvatila
3rd per (N)	Оно је прихватило Ono je prihvatilo	Оно је било прихватило Ono je bilo prihvatilo	Оно би прихватило Ono bi prihvatilo
1st per pl	Ми смо прихватили Mi smo prihvatili	Ми смо били прихватили Mi smo bili prihvatili	Ми бисмо прихватили Mi bismo prihvatili
2nd per pl	Ви сте прихватили Vi ste prihvatili	Ви сте били прихватили Vi ste bili prihvatili	Ви бисте прихватили Vi biste prihvatili
3rd per pl	Они су прихватили Oni su prihvatili	Они су били прихватили Oni su bili prihvatili	Они би прихватили Oni bi prihvatili

	Imperative (Императив)
2nd per sg	(Ти) прихвати (Ti) prihvati
1st per pl	(Ми) прихватимо (Mi) prihvatimo
2nd per pl	(Ви) прихватите (Vi) prihvatite

Non-finite Forms

Infinitive (Инфинитив)	прихва̀тити **pri**hvatiti
Present Adverbial Participle (Глаголски прилог садашњи)	--
Past Adverbial Participle (Глаголски прилог прошли)	прихва̀тивши **pri**hvativši

	Active Adjectival Participle (Глаголски придев радни)		Passive Adjectival Participle (Глаголски придев трпни)	
Gender	Singular	Plural	Singular	Plural
Feminine	прихва̀тила **pri**hvatila	прихва̀тиле **pri**hvatile	прихва̄ћена **pri**hvaćena	прихва̄ћене **pri**hvaćene
Masculine	прихва̀тио **pri**hvatio	прихва̀тили **pri**hvatili	прихва̄ћен **pri**hvaćen	прихва̄ћени **pri**hvaćeni
Neuter	прихва̀тило **pri**hvatilo	прихва̀тила **pri**hvatila	прихва̄ћено **pri**hvaćeno	прихва̄ћена **pri**hvaćena

To Admit – признати - priznati

	Present (Презент)	Future I (Футур први)	Future II (Футур други)
1st per	Ja признајем Ja **priz**najem	Ja ћу признати/ Признаћу Ja ću **priz**nati/**Priz**naću	Ja будем признао/признала Ja budem **priz**nao/**priz**nala
2nd per	Ти признајеш Ti **priz**naješ	Ти ћеш признати/Признаћеш Ti ćeš **priz**nati/**Priz**naćeš	Ти будеш признао/признала Ti budeš **priz**nao/**priz**nala
3rd per (M)	Он признаје On **priz**naje	Он ће признати/Признаће On će **priz**nati/**Priz**naće	Он буде признао On bude **priz**nao
3rd per (F)	Она признаје Ona **priz**naje	Она ће признати/Признаће Ona će **priz**nati/**Priz**naće	Она буде признала Ona bude **priz**nala
3rd per (N)	Оно признаје Ono **priz**naje	Оно ће признати/Признаће Ono će **priz**nati/**Priz**naće	Оно буде признало Ono bude **priz**nalo
1st per pl	Ми признајемо Mi **priz**najemo	Ми ћемо признати/Признаћемо Mi ćemo **priz**nati/**Priz**naćemo	Ми будемо признали/признале Mi budemo **priz**nali/**priz**nale
2nd per pl	Ви признајете Vi **priz**najete	Ви ћете признати/Признаћете Vi ćete **priz**nati/**Priz**naćete	Ви будете признали/признале Vi budete **priz**nali/**priz**nale
3rd per pl	Они/Оне признају Oni/One **priz**naju	Они/Оне ће признати/Признаће Oni/One će **priz**nati/**Priz**naće	Они/Оне буду признали/признале Oni/One budu **priz**nali/**priz**nale

	Past Tense (Перфект)	Pluperfect (Плусквамперфект)	Conditional (Потенцијал)
1st per	Ja сам признао Ja sam **priz**nao	Ja сам био признао Ja sam bio **priz**nao	Ja бих признао Ja bih **priz**nao
2nd per	Ти си признао Ti si **priz**nao	Ти си био признао Ti si bio **priz**nao	Ти би признао Ti bi **priz**nao
3rd per (M)	Он је признао On je **priz**nao	Он је био признао On je bio **priz**nao	Он би признао On bi **priz**nao
3rd per (F)	Она је признала Ona je **priz**nala	Она је била признала Ona je bila **priz**nala	Она би признала Ona bi **priz**nala
3rd per (N)	Оно је признало Ono je **priz**nalo	Оно је било признало Ono je bilo **priz**nalo	Оно би признало Ono bi **priz**nalo
1st per pl	Ми смо признали Mi smo **priz**nali	Ми смо били признали Mi smo bili **priz**nali	Ми бисмо признали Mi bismo **priz**nali
2nd per pl	Ви сте признали Vi ste **priz**nali	Ви сте били признали Vi ste bili **priz**nali	Ви бисте признали Vi biste **priz**nali
3rd per pl	Они су признали Oni su **priz**nali	Они су били признали Oni su bili **priz**nali	Они би признали Oni bi **priz**nali

	Imperative (Императив)
2nd per sg	(Ти) признај (Ti) **priz**naj
1st per pl	(Ми) признајмо (Mi) **priz**najmo
2nd per pl	(Ви) признајте (Vi) **priz**najte

Non-finite Forms

Infinitive (Инфинитив)	при̏знати **pri**znati
Present Adverbial Participle (Глаголски прилог садашњи)	при̏знају̀ћи **pri**znajući
Past Adverbial Participle (Глаголски прилог прошли)	при̏знавши **pri**znavši

	Active Adjectival Participle (Глаголски придев радни)		Passive Adjectival Participle (Глаголски придев трпни)	
Gender	Singular	Plural	Singular	Plural
Feminine	при̏знала **pri**znala	при̏знале **pri**znale	при̏зната **pri**znata	при̏знате **pri**znate
Masculine	при̏знао **pri**znao	при̏знали **pri**znali	при̏знат **pri**znat	при̏знати **pri**znati
Neuter	при̏знало **pri**znalo	при̏знала **pri**znala	при̏знато **pri**znato	при̏зната **pri**znata

To Answer – одговòрити - odgovoriti

	Present (Презент)	Future I (Футур први)	Future II (Футур други)
1st per	Ja одгòворим Ja odgovorim	Ja ћу одговòрити/Одговòрићу Ja ću odgovoriti/Odgovoriću	Ja будем одговòрио/одговòрила Ja budem odgovorio/odgovorila
2nd per	Ти одгòвориш Ti odgovoriš	Ти ћеш одговòрити/Одговòрићеш Ti ćeš odgovoriti/Odgovorićeš	Ти будеш одговòрио/одговòрила Ti budeš odgovorio/odgovorila
3rd per (M)	Он одгòвори On odgovori	Он ће одговòрити/Одговòриће On će odgovoriti/Odgovoriće	Он буде одговòрио On bude odgovorio
3rd per (F)	Она одгòвори Ona odgovori	Она ће одговòрити/Одговòриће Ona će odgovoriti/Odgovoriće	Она буде одговòрила Ona bude odgovorila
3rd per (N)	Оно одгòвори Ono odgovori	Оно ће одговòрити/Одговòриће Ono će odgovoriti/Odgovoriće	Оно буде одговòрило Ono bude odgovorilo
1st per pl	Ми одгòворимо Mi odgovorimo	Ми ћемо одговòрити/Одговòрићемо Mi ćemo odgovoriti/Odgovorićemo	Ми будемо одговòрили/одговòриле Mi budemo odgovorili/odgovorile
2nd per pl	Ви одгòворите Vi odgovorite	Ви ћете одговòрити/Одговòрићете Vi ćete odgovoriti/Odgovorićete	Ви будете одговòрили/одговòриле Vi budete odgovorili/odgovorile
3rd per pl	Они/Оне одгòворе Oni/One odgovore	Они/Оне ће одговòрити/Одговòриће Oni/One će odgovoriti/Odgovoriće	Они/Оне буду одговòрили/одговòриле Oni/One budu odgovorili/odgovorile

	Past Tense (Перфект)	Pluperfect (Плусквамперфект)	Conditional (Потенцијал)
1st per	Ja сам одговòрио Ja sam odgovorio	Ja сам био одговòрио Ja sam bio odgovorio	Ja бих одговòрио Ja bih odgovorio
2nd per	Ти си одговòрио Ti si odgovorio	Ти си био одговòрио Ti si bio odgovorio	Ти би одговòрио Ti bi odgovorio
3rd per (M)	Он је одговòрио On je odgovorio	Он је био одговòрио On je bio odgovorio	Он би одговòрио On bi odgovorio
3rd per (F)	Она је одговòрила Ona je odgovorila	Она је била одговòрила Ona je bila odgovorila	Она би одговòрила Ona bi odgovorila
3rd per (N)	Оно је одговòрило Ono je odgovorilo	Оно је било одговòрило Ono je bilo odgovorilo	Оно би одговòрило Ono bi odgovorilo
1st per pl	Ми смо одговòрили Mi smo odgovorili	Ми смо били одговòрили Mi smo bili odgovorili	Ми бисмо одговòрили Mi bismo odgovorili
2nd per pl	Ви сте одговòрили Vi ste odgovorili	Ви сте били одговòрили Vi ste bili odgovorili	Ви бисте одговòрили Vi biste odgovorili
3rd per pl	Они су одговòрили Oni su odgovorili	Они су били одговòрили Oni su bili odgovorili	Они би одговòрили Oni bi odgovorili

	Imperative (Императив)
2nd per sg	(Ти) одговòри (Ti) odgovori
1st per pl	(Ми) одговòримо (Mi) odgovorimo

2nd per pl	(Ви) одгово̀рите
	(Vi) odgo**vo**rite

Non-finite Forms

Infinitive (Инфинитив)	одгово̀рити
	odgo**vo**riti
Present Adverbial Participle (Глаголски прилог садашњи)	--
Past Adverbial Participle (Глаголски прилог прошли)	одгово̀ривши
	odgo**vo**rivši

	Active Adjectival Participle (Глаголски придев радни)		Passive Adjectival Participle (Глаголски придев трпни)	
Gender	Singular	Plural	Singular	Plural
Feminine	одгово̀рила	одгово̀риле	одго̀ворена	одго̀ворене
	odgo**vo**rila	odgo**vo**rile	od**go**vorena	od**go**vorene
Masculine	одгово̀рио	одгово̀рили	одго̀ворен	одго̀ворени
	odgo**vo**rio	odgo**vo**rili	od**go**voren	od**go**voreni
Neuter	одгово̀рило	одгово̀рила	одго̀ворено	одго̀ворена
	odgo**vo**rilo	odgo**vo**rila	od**go**voreno	od**go**vorena

To Appear – изгле́дати - izgledati

	Present (Презент)	Future I (Футур први)	Future II (Футур други)
1st per	Ја изгле́дам Ja izgledam	Ја ћу изгле́дати/Изгле́даћу Ja ću izgledati/Izgledaću	Ја будем изгле́дао/изгле́дала Ja budem izgledao/izgledala
2nd per	Ти изгле́даш Ti izgledaš	Ти ћеш изгле́дати/Изгле́даћеш Ti ćeš izgledati/Izgledaćeš	Ти будеш изгле́дао/изгле́дала Ti budeš izgledao/izgledala
3rd per (M)	Он изгле́да On izgleda	Он ће изгле́дати/Изгле́даће On će izgledati/Izgledaće	Он буде изгле́дао On bude izgledao
3rd per (F)	Она изгле́да Ona izgleda	Она ће изгле́дати/Изгле́даће Ona će izgledati/Izgledaće	Она буде изгле́дала Ona bude izgledala
3rd per (N)	Оно изгле́да Ono izgleda	Оно ће изгле́дати/Изгле́даће Ono će izgledati/Izgledaće	Оно буде изгле́дало Ono bude izgledalo
1st per pl	Ми изгле́дамо Mi izgledamo	Ми ћемо изгле́дати/Изгле́даћемо Mi ćemo izgledati/Izgledaćemo	Ми будемо изгле́дали/изгле́дале Mi budemo izgledali/izgledale
2nd per pl	Ви изгле́дате Vi izgledate	Ви ћете изгле́дати/Изгле́даћете Vi ćete izgledati/Izgledaćete	Ви будете изгле́дали/изгле́дале Vi budete izgledali/izgledale
3rd per pl	Они/Оне изгле́дају Oni/One izgledaju	Они/Оне ће изгле́дати/Изгле́даће Oni/One će izgledati/Izgledaće	Они/Оне буду изгле́дали/изгле́дале Oni/One budu izgledali/izgledale

	Past Tense (Перфект)	Pluperfect (Плусквамперфект)	Conditional (Потенцијал)
1st per	Ја сам изгле́дао Ja sam izgledao	Ја сам био изгле́дао Ja sam bio izgledao	Ја бих изгле́дао Ja bih izgledao
2nd per	Ти си изгле́дао Ti si izgledao	Ти си био изгле́дао Ti si bio izgledao	Ти би изгле́дао Ti bi izgledao
3rd per (M)	Он је изгле́дао On je izgledao	Он је био изгле́дао On je bio izgledao	Он би изгле́дао On bi izgledao
3rd per (F)	Она је изгле́дала Ona je izgledala	Она је била изгле́дала Ona je bila izgledala	Она би изгле́дала Ona bi izgledala
3rd per (N)	Оно је изгле́дало Ono je izgledalo	Оно је било изгле́дало Ono je bilo izgledalo	Оно би изгле́дало Ono bi izgledalo
1st per pl	Ми смо изгле́дали Mi smo izgledali	Ми смо били изгле́дали Mi smo bili izgledali	Ми бисмо изгле́дали Mi bismo izgledali
2nd per pl	Ви сте изгле́дали Vi ste izgledali	Ви сте били изгле́дали Vi ste bili izgledali	Ви бисте изгле́дали Vi biste izgledali
3rd per pl	Они су изгле́дали Oni su izgledali	Они су били изгле́дали Oni su bili izgledali	Они би изгле́дали Oni bi izgledali

	Imperative (Императив)
2nd per sg	(Ти) изгледај (Ti) izgledaj
1st per pl	(Ми) изгледајмо (Mi) izgledajmo
2nd per pl	(Ви) изгледајте (Vi) izgledajte

Non-finite Forms

Infinitive (Инфинитив)	изгле́дати izgledati
Present Adverbial Participle (Глаголски прилог садашњи)	изгле́дајући izgledajući
Past Adverbial Participle (Глаголски прилог прошли)	--

	Active Adjectival Participle (Глаголски придев радни)		Passive Adjectival Participle (Глаголски придев трпни)	
Gender	Singular	Plural	Singular	Plural
Feminine	изгле́дала izgledala	изгле́дале izgledale	--	--
Masculine	изгле́дао izgledao	изгле́дали izgledali	--	--
Neuter	изгле́дало izgledalo	изгле́дала izgledala	--	--

To Ask - пѝтати - pitati

	Present (Презент)	Future I (Футур први)	Future II (Футур други)
1st per	Ja пѝтам Ja **pi**tam	Ja ћу пѝтати/Пѝтаћу Ja ću **pi**tati/**Pi**taću	Ja будем пѝтао/пѝтала Ja budem **pi**tao/**pi**tala
2nd per	Ти пѝташ Ti **pi**taš	Ти ћеш пѝтати/Пѝтаћеш Ti ćeš **pi**tati/**Pi**taćeš	Ти будеш пѝтао/ пѝтала Ti budeš **pi**tao/**pi**tala
3rd per (M)	Он пѝта On **pi**ta	Он ће пѝтати/Пѝтаће On će **pi**tati/**Pi**taće	Он буде пѝтао On bude **pi**tao
3rd per (F)	Она пѝта Ona **pi**ta	Она ће пѝтати/Пѝтаће Ona će **pi**tati/**Pi**taće	Она буде пѝтала Ona bude **pi**tala
3rd per (N)	Оно пѝта Ono **pi**ta	Оно ће пѝтати/Пѝтаће Ono će **pi**tati/**Pi**taće	Оно буде пѝтало Ono bude **pi**talo
1st per pl	Ми пѝтамо Mi **pi**tamo	Ми ћемо пѝтати/Пѝтаћемо Mi ćemo **pi**tati/**Pi**taćemo	Ми будемо пѝтали/пѝтале Mi budemo **pi**tali/**pi**tale
2nd per pl	Ви пѝтате Vi **pi**tate	Ви ћете пѝтати/Пѝтаћете Vi ćete **pi**tati/**Pi**taćete	Ви будете пѝтали/пѝтале Vi budete **pi**tali/**pi**tale
3rd per pl	Они/Оне пѝтају Oni/One **pi**taju	Они/Оне ће пѝтати/Пѝтаће Oni/One će **pi**tati/**Pi**taće	Они/Оне буду пѝтали/пѝтале Oni/One budu **pi**tali/**pi**tale

	Past Tense (Перфект)	Pluperfect (Плусквамперфект)	Conditional (Потенцијал)
1st per	Ja сам пѝтао Ja sam **pi**tao	Ja сам био пѝтао Ja sam bio **pi**tao	Ja бих пѝтао Ja bih **pi**tao
2nd per	Ти си пѝтао Ti si **pi**tao	Ти си био пѝтао Ti si bio **pi**tao	Ти би пѝтао Ti bi **pi**tao
3rd per (M)	Он је пѝтао On je **pi**tao	Он је био пѝтао On je bio **pi**tao	Он би пѝтао On bi **pi**tao
3rd per (F)	Она је пѝтала Ona je **pi**tala	Она је била пѝтала Ona je bila **pi**tala	Она би пѝтала Ona bi **pi**tala
3rd per (N)	Оно је пѝтало Ono je **pi**talo	Оно је било пѝтало Ono je bilo **pi**talo	Оно би пѝтало Ono bi **pi**talo
1st per pl	Ми смо пѝтали Mi smo **pi**tali	Ми смо били пѝтали Mi smo bili **pi**tali	Ми бисмо пѝтали Mi bismo **pi**tali
2nd per pl	Ви сте пѝтали Vi ste **pi**tali	Ви сте били пѝтали Vi ste bili **pi**tali	Ви бисте пѝтали Vi biste **pi**tali
3rd per pl	Они су пѝтали Oni su **pi**tali	Они су били пѝтали Oni su bili **pi**tali	Они би пѝтали Oni bi **pi**tali

	Imperative (Императив)
2nd per sg	(Ти) пи́тај (Ti) **pi**taj
1st per pl	(Ми) пи́тајмо (Mi) **pi**tajmo
2nd per pl	(Ви) пи́тајте (Vi) **pi**tajte

Non-finite Forms

Infinitive (Инфинитив)	пи́тати **pi**tati
Present Adverbial Participle (Глаголски прилог садашњи)	пи́тајући **pi**tajući
Past Adverbial Participle (Глаголски прилог прошли)	--

	Active Adjectival Participle (Глаголски придев радни)		Passive Adjectival Participle (Глаголски придев трпни)	
Gender	Singular	Plural	Singular	Plural
Feminine	пи́тала **pi**tala	пи́тале **pi**tale	пи́тана **pi**tana	пи́тане **pi**tane
Masculine	пи́тао **pi**tao	пи́тали **pi**tali	пи́тан **pi**tan	пи́тани **pi**tani
Neuter	пи́тало **pi**talo	пи́тала **pi**tala	пи́тано **pi**tano	пи́тана **pi**tana

To Be - бити - biti

	Present (Презент)	Future I (Футур први)	Future II (Футур други)
1st per	Ja бу̏дем Ja **bu**dem	Ja ћу би̏ти/Би̏ћу Ja ću **bi**ti/**Bi**ću	Ja будем би̏о/би́ла Ja budem **bi**o/**bi**la
2nd per	Ти бу̏деш Ti **bu**deš	Ти ћеш би̏ти/Би̏ћеш Ti ćeš **bi**ti/**Bi**ćeš	Ти будеш би̏о/би́ла Ti budeš **bi**o/**bi**la
3rd per (M)	Он бу̏де On **bu**de	Он ће би̏ти/Би̏ће On će **bi**ti/**Bi**će	Он буде би̏о On bude **bi**o
3rd per (F)	Она бу̏де Ona **bu**de	Она ће би̏ти/Би̏ће Ona će **bi**ti/**Bi**će	Она буде би́ла Ona bude **bi**la
3rd per (N)	Оно бу̏де Ono **bu**de	Оно ће би̏ти/Би̏ће Ono će **bi**ti/**Bi**će	Оно буде би́ло Ono bude **bi**lo
1st per pl	Ми бу̏демо Mi **bu**demo	Ми ћемо би̏ти/Би̏ћемо Mi ćemo **bi**ti/**Bi**ćemo	Ми будемо би́ли/би́ле Mi budemo **bi**li/**bi**le
2nd per pl	Ви бу̏дете Vi **bu**dete	Ви ћете би̏ти/Би̏ћете Vi ćete **bi**ti/**Bi**ćete	Ви будете би́ли/би́ле Vi budete **bi**li/**bi**le
3rd per pl	Они/Оне бу̏ду Oni/One **bu**du	Они/Оне ће би̏ти/Би̏ће Oni/One će **bi**ti/**Bi**će	Они/Оне буду би́ли/би́ле Oni/One budu **bi**li/**bi**le

	Past Tense (Перфект)	Pluperfect (Плусквамперфект)	Conditional (Потенцијал)
1st per	Ja сам би̏о Ja sam **bi**o	--	Ja бих би̏о Ja bih **bi**o
2nd per	Ти си би̏о Ti si **bi**o		Ти би би̏о Ti bi **bi**o
3rd per (M)	Он је би̏о On je **bi**o		Он би би̏о On bi **bi**o
3rd per (F)	Она је би́ла Ona je **bi**la		Она би би́ла Ona bi **bi**la
3rd per (N)	Оно је би́ло Ono je **bi**lo		Оно би би́ло Ono bi **bi**lo
1st per pl	Ми смо би́ли Mi smo **bi**li		Ми бисмо би́ли Mi bismo **bi**li
2nd per pl	Ви сте би́ли Vi ste **bi**li		Ви бисте би́ли Vi biste **bi**li
3rd per pl	Они су би́ли Oni su **bi**li		Они би би́ли Oni bi **bi**li

	Imperative (Императив)
2nd per sg	(Ти) бу̏ди (Ti) **bu**di
1st per pl	(Ми) бу̏димо (Mi) **bu**dimo

2nd per pl	(Ви) бу̏дите
	(Vi) **bu**dite

Non-finite Forms

Infinitive (Инфинитив)	би̏ти
	biti
Present Adverbial Participle (Глаголски прилог садашњи)	--
Past Adverbial Participle (Глаголски прилог прошли)	--

	Active Adjectival Participle (Глаголски придев радни)		Passive Adjectival Participle (Глаголски придев трпни)	
Gender	Singular	Plural	Singular	Plural
Feminine	би́ла	би́ле	--	--
	bila	**bi**le		
Masculine	би̏о	би́ли	--	--
	bio	**bi**li		
Neuter	би́ло	би́ла	--	--
	bilo	**bi**la		

To Be Able To – мо̀ћи - moći

	Present (Презент)	Future I (Футур први)	Future II (Футур други)
1st per	Ја мо̀гу Ja mogu	Ја ћу мо̀ћи/Мо̀ћи ћу Ja ću moći/Moći ću	Ја будем мо̀гао/мо̀гла Ja budem mogao/mogla
2nd per	Ти мо̀жеш Ti možeš	Ти ћеш мо̀ћи/Мо̀ћи ћеш Ti ćeš moći/Moći ćeš	Ти будеш мо̀гао/мо̀гла Ti budeš mogao/mogla
3rd per (M)	Он мо̀же On može	Он ће мо̀ћи/Мо̀ћи ће On će moći/Moći će	Он буде мо̀гао On bude mogao
3rd per (F)	Она мо̀же Ona može	Она ће мо̀ћи/Мо̀ћи ће Ona će moći/Moći će	Она буде мо̀гла Ona bude mogla
3rd per (N)	Оно мо̀же Ono može	Оно ће мо̀ћи/Мо̀ћи ће Ono će moći/Moći će	Оно буде мо̀гло Ono bude moglo
1st per pl	Ми мо̀жемо Mi možemo	Ми ћемо мо̀ћи/Мо̀ћи ћемо Mi ćemo moći/Moći ćemo	Ми будемо мо̀гли/мо̀гле Mi budemo mogli/mogle
2nd per pl	Ви мо̀жете Vi možete	Ви ћете мо̀ћи/Мо̀ћи ћете Vi ćete moći/Moći ćete	Ви будете мо̀гли/мо̀гле Vi budete mogli/mogle
3rd per pl	Они/Оне мо̀гу Oni/One mogu	Они/Оне ће мо̀ћи/Мо̀ћи ће Oni/One će moći/Moći će	Они/Оне буду мо̀гли/мо̀гле Oni/One budu mogli/mogle

	Past Tense (Перфект)	Pluperfect (Плусквамперфект)	Conditional (Потенцијал)
1st per	Ја сам мо̀гао Ja sam mogao	Ја сам био мо̀гао Ja sam bio mogao	Ја бих мо̀гао Ja bih mogao
2nd per	Ти си мо̀гао Ti si mogao	Ти си био мо̀гао Ti si bio mogao	Ти би мо̀гао Ti bi mogao
3rd per (M)	Он је мо̀гао On je mogao	Он је био мо̀гао On je bio mogao	Он би мо̀гао On bi mogao
3rd per (F)	Она је мо̀гла Ona je mogla	Она је била мо̀гла Ona je bila mogla	Она би мо̀гла Ona bi mogla
3rd per (N)	Оно је мо̀гло Ono je moglo	Оно је било мо̀гло Ono je bilo moglo	Оно би мо̀гло Ono bi moglo
1st per pl	Ми смо мо̀гли Mi smo mogli	Ми смо били мо̀гли Mi smo bili mogli	Ми бисмо мо̀гли Mi bismo mogli
2nd per pl	Ви сте мо̀гли Vi ste mogli	Ви сте били мо̀гли Vi ste bili mogli	Ви бисте мо̀гли Vi biste mogli
3rd per pl	Они су мо̀гли Oni su mogli	Они су били мо̀гли Oni su bili mogli	Они би мо̀гли Oni/One bi mogli

	Imperative (Императив)
2nd per sg	(Ти) --
1st per pl	(Ми) --
2nd per pl	(Ви) --

Non-finite Forms

Infinitive (Инфинитив)	мо̀ћи **mo**ći
Present Adverbial Participle (Глаголски прилог садашњи)	--
Past Adverbial Participle (Глаголски прилог прошли)	мо̀гавши **mo**gavši

	Active Adjectival Participle (Глаголски придев радни)		Passive Adjectival Participle (Глаголски придев трпни)	
Gender	Singular	Plural	Singular	Plural
Feminine	мо̀гла **mo**gla	мо̀гле **mo**gle	--	--
Masculine	мо̀гао **mo**gao	мо̀гли **mo**gli	--	--
Neuter	мо̀гло **mo**glo	мо̀гла **mo**gla	--	--

To Become – пòстати - postati

	Present (Презент)	Future I (Футур први)	Future II (Футур други)
1st per	Ja пòстајем Ja **po**stajem	Ja ћу пòстати/Пòстаћу Ja ću **po**stati/**Po**staću	Ja будем пòстао/пòстала Ja budem **po**stao/**po**stala
2nd per	Ти пòстајеш Ti **po**staješ	Ти ћеш пòстати/Пòстаћеш Ti ćeš **po**stati/**Po**staćeš	Ти будеш пòстао/пòстала Ti budeš **po**stao/**po**stala
3rd per (M)	Он пòстаје On **po**staje	Он ће пòстати/Пòстаће On će **po**stati/**Po**staće	Он буде пòстао On bude **po**stao
3rd per (F)	Она пòстаје Ona **po**staje	Она ће пòстати/Пòстаће Ona će **po**stati/**Po**staće	Она буде пòстала Ona bude **po**stala
3rd per (N)	Оно пòстаје Ono **po**staje	Оно ће пòстати/Пòстаће Ono će **po**stati/**Po**staće	Оно буде пòстало Ono bude **po**stalo
1st per pl	Ми пòстајемо Mi **po**stajemo	Ми ћемо пòстати/Пòстаћемо Mi ćemo **po**stati/**Po**staćemo	Ми будемо пòстали/пòстале Mi budemo **po**stali/**po**stale
2nd per pl	Ви пòстајете Vi **po**stajete	Ви ћете пòстати/Пòстаћете Vi ćete **po**stati/**Po**staćete	Ви будете пòстали/пòстале Vi budete **po**stali/**po**stale
3rd per pl	Они/Оне пòстају Oni/One **po**staju	Они/Оне ће пòстати/Пòстаће Oni/One će **po**stati/**Po**staće	Они/Оне буду пòстали/пòстале Oni/One budu **po**stali/**po**stale

	Past Tense (Перфект)	Pluperfect (Плусквамперфект)	Conditional (Потенцијал)
1st per	Ja сам пòстао Ja sam **po**stao	Ja сам био пòстао Ja sam bio **po**stao	Ja бих пòстао Ja bih **po**stao
2nd per	Ти си пòстао Ti si **po**stao	Ти си био пòстао Ti si bio **po**stao	Ти би пòстао Ti bi **po**stao
3rd per (M)	Он је пòстао On je **po**stao	Он је био пòстао On je bio **po**stao	Он би пòстао On bi **po**stao
3rd per (F)	Она је пòстала Ona je **po**stala	Она је била пòстала Ona je bila **po**stala	Она би пòстала Ona bi **po**stala
3rd per (N)	Оно је пòстало Ono je **po**stalo	Оно је било пòстало Ono je bilo **po**stalo	Оно би пòстало Ono bi **po**stalo
1st per pl	Ми смо пòстали Mi smo **po**stali	Ми смо били пòстали Mi smo bili **po**stali	Ми бисмо пòстали Mi bismo **po**stali
2nd per pl	Ви сте пòстали Vi ste **po**stali	Ви сте били пòстали Vi ste bili **po**stali	Ви бисте пòстали Vi biste **po**stali
3rd per pl	Они су пòстали Oni su **po**stali	Они су били пòстали Oni su bili **po**stali	Они би пòстали Oni bi **po**stali

	Imperative (Императив)
2nd per sg	(Ти) пòстани (Ti) **po**stani
1st per pl	(Ми) пòстанимо (Mi) **po**stanimo

2nd per pl	(Ви) по̀станите (Vi) **po**stani**te**

Non-finite Forms

Infinitive (Инфинитив)	по̀стати **po**stati
Present Adverbial Participle (Глаголски прилог садашњи)	по̀стајући **po**stajući
Past Adverbial Participle (Глаголски прилог прошли)	по̀ставши **po**stavši

Gender	Active Adjectival Participle (Глаголски придев радни)		Passive Adjectival Participle (Глаголски придев трпни)	
	Singular	Plural	Singular	Plural
Feminine	по̀стала **po**stala	по̀стале **po**stale	--	--
Masculine	по̀стао **po**stao	по̀стали **po**stali	--	--
Neuter	по̀стало **po**stalo	по̀стала **po**stala	--	--

To Begin – по̀чети - početi

	Present (Презент)	Future I (Футур први)	Future II (Футур други)
1st per	Ja по̀чињем Ja **počinjem**	Ja ћу почети/По̀чећу Ja ću **početi/Počeću**	Ja будем по̀чео/по̀чела Ja budem **počeo/počela**
2nd per	Ти по̀чињеш Ti **počinješ**	Ти ћеш почети/По̀чећеш Ti ćeš **početi/Počećeš**	Ти будеш по̀чео/ по̀чела Ti budeš **počeo/ počela**
3rd per (M)	Он по̀чиње On **počinje**	Он ће почети/По̀чеће On će **početi/Počeće**	Он буде по̀чео On bude **počeo**
3rd per (F)	Она по̀чиње Ona **počinje**	Она ће почети/По̀чеће Ona će **početi/Počeće**	Она буде по̀чела Ona bude **počela**
3rd per (N)	Оно по̀чиње Ono **počinje**	Оно ће почети/По̀чеће Ono će **početi/Počeće**	Оно буде по̀чело Ono bude **počelo**
1st per pl	Ми по̀чињемо Mi **počinjemo**	Ми ћемо почети/По̀чећемо Mi ćemo **početi/Počećemo**	Ми будемо по̀чели/по̀челе Mi budemo **počeli/počele**
2nd per pl	Ви по̀чињете Vi **počinjete**	Ви ћете почети/По̀чећете Vi ćete **početi/Počećete**	Ви будете по̀чели/по̀челе Vi budete **počeli/počele**
3rd per pl	Они/Оне по̀чињу Oni/One **počinju**	Они/Оне ће почети/По̀чеће Oni/One će **početi/Počeće**	Они/Оне буду по̀чели/по̀челе Oni/One budu **počeli/počele**

	Past Tense (Перфект)	Pluperfect (Плусквамперфект)	Conditional (Потенцијал)
1st per	Ja сам по̀чео Ja sam **počeo**	Ja сам био по̀чео Ja sam bio **počeo**	Ja бих по̀чео Ja bih **počeo**
2nd per	Ти си по̀чео Ti si **počeo**	Ти си био по̀чео Ti si bio **počeo**	Ти би по̀чео Ti bi **počeo**
3rd per (M)	Он је по̀чео On je **počeo**	Он је био по̀чео On je bio **počeo**	Он би по̀чео On bi **počeo**
3rd per (F)	Она је по̀чела Ona je **počela**	Она је била по̀чела Ona je bila **počela**	Она би по̀чела Ona bi **počela**
3rd per (N)	Оно је по̀чело Ono je **počelo**	Оно је било по̀чело Ono je bilo **počelo**	Оно би по̀чело Ono bi **počelo**
1st per pl	Ми смо по̀чели Mi smo **počeli**	Ми смо били по̀чели Mi smo bili **počeli**	Ми бисмо по̀чели Mi bismo **počeli**
2nd per pl	Ви сте по̀чели Vi ste **počeli**	Ви сте били по̀чели Vi ste bili **počeli**	Ви бисте по̀чели Vi biste **počeli**
3rd per pl	Они су по̀чели Oni su **počeli**	Они су били по̀чели Oni su bili **počeli**	Они би по̀чели Oni bi **počeli**

	Imperative (Императив)
2nd per sg	(Ти) по̀чни (Ti) **počni**
1st per pl	(Ми) по̀чнимо (Mi) **počnimo**
2nd per pl	(Ви) по̀чните (Vi) **počnite**

Non-finite Forms

Infinitive (Инфинитив)	по̀чети **po**četi
Present Adverbial Participle (Глаголски прилог садашњи)	по̀чињући **po**činjući
Past Adverbial Participle (Глаголски прилог прошли)	по̀чевши **po**čevši

	Active Adjectival Participle (Глаголски придев радни)		Passive Adjectival Participle (Глаголски придев трпни)	
Gender	Singular	Plural	Singular	Plural
Feminine	по̀чела **po**čela	по̀челе **po**čele	по̀чета **po**četa	по̀чете **po**čete
Masculine	по̀чео **po**čeo	по̀чели **po**čeli	по̀чет **po**čet	по̀чети **po**četi
Neuter	по̀чело **po**čelo	по̀чела **po**čela	по̀чето **po**četo	по̀чета **po**četa

To Break – сло̀мити - slomiti

	Present (Презент)	Future I (Футур први)	Future II (Футур други)
1st per	Ja сло̀мим Ja **slo**mim	Ja ћу сло̀мити/Сло̀мићу Ja ću **slo**miti/**Slo**miću	Ja будем сло̀мио/сло̀мила Ja budem **slo**mio/**slo**mila
2nd per	Ти сло̀миш Ti **slo**miš	Ти ћеш сло̀мити/Сло̀мићеш Ti ćeš **slo**miti/**Slo**mićeš	Ти будеш сло̀мио/сло̀мила Ti budeš **slo**mio/**slo**mila
3rd per (M)	Он сло̀ми On **slo**mi	Он ће сло̀мити/Сло̀миће On će **slo**miti/**Slo**miće	Он буде сло̀мио On bude **slo**mio
3rd per (F)	Она сло̀ми Ona **slo**mi	Она ће сло̀мити/Сло̀миће Ona će **slo**miti/**Slo**miće	Она буде сло̀мила Ona bude **slo**mila
3rd per (N)	Оно сло̀ми Ono **slo**mi	Оно ће сло̀мити/Сло̀миће Ono će **slo**miti/**Slo**miće	Оно буде сло̀мило Ono bude **slo**milo
1st per pl	Ми сло̀мимо Mi **slo**mimo	Ми ћемо сло̀мити/Сло̀мићемо Mi ćemo **slo**miti/**Slo**mićemo	Ми будемо сло̀мили/сло̀миле Mi budemo **slo**mili/**slo**mile
2nd per pl	Ви сло̀мите Vi **slo**mite	Ви ћете сло̀мити/Сло̀мићете Vi ćete **slo**miti/**Slo**mićete	Ви будете сло̀мили/сло̀миле Vi budete **slo**mili/**slo**mile
3rd per pl	Они/Оне сло̀ме Oni/One **slo**me	Они/Оне ће сло̀мити/Сло̀миће Oni/One će **slo**miti/**Slo**miće	Они/Оне буду сло̀мили/сло̀миле Oni/One budu **slo**mili/**slo**mile

	Past Tense (Перфект)	Pluperfect (Плусквамперфект)	Conditional (Потенцијал)
1st per	Ja сам сло̀мио Ja sam **slo**mio	Ja сам био сло̀мио Ja sam bio **slo**mio	Ja бих сло̀мио Ja bih **slo**mio
2nd per	Ти си сло̀мио Ti si **slo**mio	Ти си био сло̀мио Ti si bio **slo**mio	Ти би сло̀мио Ti bi **slo**mio
3rd per (M)	Он је сло̀мио On je **slo**mio	Он је био сло̀мио On je bio **slo**mio	Он би сло̀мио On bi **slo**mio
3rd per (F)	Она је сло̀мила Ona je **slo**mila	Она је била сло̀мила Ona je bila **slo**mila	Она би сло̀мила Ona bi **slo**mila
3rd per (N)	Оно је сло̀мило Ono je **slo**milo	Оно је било сло̀мило Ono je bilo **slo**milo	Оно би сло̀мило Ono bi **slo**milo
1st per pl	Ми смо сло̀мили Mi smo **slo**mili	Ми смо били сло̀мили Mi smo bili **slo**mili	Ми бисмо сло̀мили Mi bismo **slo**mili
2nd per pl	Ви сте сло̀мили Vi ste **slo**mili	Ви сте били сло̀мили Vi ste bili **slo**mili	Ви бисте сло̀мили Vi biste **slo**mili
3rd per pl	Они су сло̀мили Oni su **slo**mili	Они су били сло̀мили Oni su bili **slo**mili	Они би сло̀мили Oni bi **slo**mili

	Imperative (Императив)
2nd per sg	(Ти) сло̀ми (Ti) **slo**mi
1st per pl	(Ми) сло̀мимо (Mi) **slo**mimo
2nd per pl	(Ви) сло̀мите (Vi) **slo**mite

Non-finite Forms

Infinitive (Инфинитив)	сло̀мити **slo**miti
Present Adverbial Participle (Глаголски прилог садашњи)	--
Past Adverbial Participle (Глаголски прилог прошли)	сло̀мивши **slo**mivši

	Active Adjectival Participle (Глаголски придев радни)		Passive Adjectival Participle (Глаголски придев трпни)	
Gender	Singular	Plural	Singular	Plural
Feminine	сло̀мила **slo**mila	сло̀миле **slo**mile	сло̏мљена **slo**mljena	сло̏мљене **slo**mljene
Masculine	сло̀мио **slo**mio	сло̀мили **slo**mili	сло̏мљен **slo**mljen	сло̏мљени **slo**mljeni
Neuter	сло̀мило **slo**milo	сло̀мила **slo**mila	сло̏мљено **slo**mljeno	сло̏мљена **slo**mljena

To Breathe - ди́сати - disati

	Present (Презент)	Future I (Футур први)	Future II (Футур други)
1st per	Ja ди́шем Ja **di**šem	Ja ћу ди́сати/Ди́саћу Ja ću **di**sati/**Di**saću	Ja будем ди́сао/ди́сала Ja budem **di**sao/**di**sala
2nd per	Ти ди́шеш Ti **di**šeš	Ти ћеш ди́сати/Ди́саћеш Ti ćeš **di**sati/**Di**saćeš	Ти будеш ди́сао/ди́сала Ti budeš **di**sao/**di**sala
3rd per (M)	Он ди́ше On **di**še	Он ће ди́сати/Ди́саће On će **di**sati/**Di**saće	Он буде ди́сао On bude **di**sao
3rd per (F)	Она ди́ше Ona **di**še	Она ће ди́сати/Ди́саће Ona će **di**sati/**Di**saće	Она буде ди́сала Ona bude **di**sala
3rd per (N)	Оно ди́ше Ono **di**še	Оно ће ди́сати/Ди́саће Ono će **di**sati/**Di**saće	Оно буде ди́сало Ono bude **di**salo
1st per pl	Ми ди́шемо Mi **di**šemo	Ми ћемо ди́сати/Ди́саћемо Mi ćemo **di**sati/**Di**saćemo	Ми будемо ди́сали/ди́сале Mi budemo **di**sali/**di**sale
2nd per pl	Ви ди́шете Vi **di**šete	Ви ћете ди́сати/ Ди́саћете Vi ćete **di**sati/ **Di**saćete	Ви будете ди́сали/ди́сале Vi budete **di**sali/**di**sale
3rd per pl	Они/Оне ди́шу Oni/One **di**šu	Они/Оне ће ди́сати/Ди́саће Oni/One će **di**sati/**Di**saće	Они/Оне буду ди́сали/ди́сале Oni/One budu **di**sali/**di**sale

	Past Tense (Перфект)	Pluperfect (Плусквамперфект)	Conditional (Потенцијал)
1st per	Ja сам ди́сао Ja sam **di**sao	Ja сам био ди́сао Ja sam bio **di**sao	Ja бих ди́сао Ja bih **di**sao
2nd per	Ти си ди́сао Ti si **di**sao	Ти си био ди́сао Ti si bio **di**sao	Ти би ди́сао Ti bi **di**sao
3rd per (M)	Он је ди́сао On je **di**sao	Он је био ди́сао On je bio **di**sao	Он би ди́сао On bi **di**sao
3rd per (F)	Она је ди́сала Ona je **di**sala	Она је била ди́сала Ona je bila **di**sala	Она би ди́сала Ona bi **di**sala
3rd per (N)	Оно је ди́сало Ono je **di**salo	Оно је било ди́сало Ono je bilo **di**salo	Оно би ди́сало Ono bi **di**salo
1st per pl	Ми смо ди́сали Mi smo **di**sali	Ми смо били ди́сали Mi smo bili **di**sali	Ми бисмо ди́сали Mi bismo **di**sali
2nd per pl	Ви сте ди́сали Vi ste **di**sali	Ви сте били ди́сали Vi ste bili **di**sali	Ви бисте ди́сали Vi biste **di**sali
3rd per pl	Они су ди́сали Oni su **di**sali	Они су били ди́сали Oni su bili **di**sali	Они би ди́сали Oni bi **di**sali

	Imperative (Императив)
2nd per sg	(Ти) ди́ши (Ti) **di**ši
1st per pl	(Ми) ди́шимо (Mi) **di**šimo

2nd per pl	(Ви) ди́шите
	(Vi) **di**šite

Non-finite Forms

Infinitive (Инфинитив)	ди́сати
	disati
Present Adverbial Participle (Глаголски прилог садашњи)	ди́шући
	dišući
Past Adverbial Participle (Глаголски прилог прошли)	--

	Active Adjectival Participle (Глаголски придев радни)		Passive Adjectival Participle (Глаголски придев трпни)	
Gender	Singular	Plural	Singular	Plural
Feminine	ди́сала	ди́сале	--	--
	disala	**di**sale		
Masculine	ди́сао	ди́сали	--	--
	disao	**di**sali		
Neuter	ди́сало	ди́сала	--	--
	disalo	**di**sala		

To Buy - ку́пити - kupiti

	Present (Презент)	Future I (Футур први)	Future II (Футур други)
1st per	Ja ку́пим Ja **ku**pim	Ja ћу ку́пити/Ку́пићу Ja ћu **ku**piti/**Ku**pićи	Ja будем ку́пио/ку́пила Ja budem **ku**pio/**ku**pila
2nd per	Ти ку́пиш Ti **ku**piš	Ти ћеш ку́пити/Ку́пићеш Ti ćeš **ku**piti/**Ku**pićeš	Ти будеш ку́пио/ку́пила Ti budeš **ku**pio/**ku**pila
3rd per (M)	Он ку́пи On **ku**pi	Он ће ку́пити/ Ку́пиће On će **ku**piti/ **Ku**piće	Он буде ку́пио On bude **ku**pio
3rd per (F)	Она ку́пи Ona **ku**pi	Она ће ку́пити/ Ку́пиће Ona će **ku**piti/ **Ku**piće	Она буде ку́пила Ona bude **ku**pila
3rd per (N)	Оно ку́пи Ono **ku**pi	Оно ће ку́пити/Ку́пиће Ono će **ku**piti/**Ku**piće	Оно буде ку́пило Ono bude **ku**pilo
1st per pl	Ми ку́пимо Mi **ku**pimo	Ми ћемо ку́пити/Ку́пићемо Mi ćemo **ku**piti/**Ku**pićemo	Ми будемо ку́пили/ку́пиле Mi budemo **ku**pili/**ku**pile
2nd per pl	Ви ку́пите Vi **ku**pite	Ви ћете ку́пити/Ку́пићете Vi ćete **ku**piti/**Ku**pićete	Ви будете ку́пили/ку́пиле Vi budete **ku**pili/**ku**pile
3rd per pl	Они/Оне ку́пе Oni/One **ku**pe	Они/Оне ће ку́пити/Ку́пиће Oni/One će **ku**piti/**Ku**piće	Они/Оне буду ку́пили/ку́пиле Oni/One budu **ku**pili/**ku**pile

	Past Tense (Перфект)	Pluperfect (Плусквамперфект)	Conditional (Потенцијал)
1st per	Ja сам ку́пио Ja sam **ku**pio	Ja сам био ку́пио Ja sam bio **ku**pio	Ja бих ку́пио Ja bih **ku**pio
2nd per	Ти си ку́пио Ti si **ku**pio	Ти си био ку́пио Ti si bio **ku**pio	Ти би ку́пио Ti bi **ku**pio
3rd per (M)	Он је ку́пио On je **ku**pio	Он је био ку́пио On je bio **ku**pio	Он би ку́пио On bi **ku**pio
3rd per (F)	Она је ку́пила Ona je **ku**pila	Она је била ку́пила Ona je bila **ku**pila	Она би ку́пила Ona bi **ku**pila
3rd per (N)	Оно је ку́пило Ono je **ku**pilo	Оно је било ку́пило Ono je bilo **ku**pilo	Оно би ку́пило Ono bi **ku**pilo
1st per pl	Ми смо ку́пили Mi smo **ku**pili	Ми смо били ку́пили Mi smo bili **ku**pili	Ми бисмо ку́пили Mi bismo **ku**pili
2nd per pl	Ви сте ку́пили Vi ste **ku**pili	Ви сте били ку́пили Vi ste bili **ku**pili	Ви бисте ку́пили Vi biste **ku**pili
3rd per pl	Они су ку́пили Oni su **ku**pili	Они су били ку́пили Oni su bili **ku**pili	Они би ку́пили Oni bi **ku**pili

	Imperative (Императив)
2nd per sg	(Ти) ку́пи (Ti) **ku**pi
1st per pl	(Ми) ку́пимо (Mi) **ku**pimo
2nd per pl	(Ви) ку́пите (Vi) **ku**pite

Non-finite Forms

Infinitive (Инфинитив)	ку́пити **ku**piti
Present Adverbial Participle (Глаголски прилог садашњи)	--
Past Adverbial Participle (Глаголски прилог прошли)	ку́пивши **ku**pivši

	Active Adjectival Participle (Глаголски придев радни)		Passive Adjectival Participle (Глаголски придев трпни)	
Gender	Singular	Plural	Singular	Plural
Feminine	ку́пила **ku**pila	ку́пиле **ku**pile	ку́пљена **ku**pljena	ку́пљене **ku**pljene
Masculine	ку́пио **ku**pio	ку́пили **ku**pili	ку́пљен **ku**pljen	ку́пљени **ku**pljeni
Neuter	ку́пило **ku**pilo	ку́пила **ku**pila	ку́пљено **ku**pljeno	ку́пљена **ku**pljena

To Call – пȍзвати - pozvati

	Present (Презент)	Future I (Футур први)	Future II (Футур други)
1st per	Ja пȍзовем	Ja ћу пȍзвати/Пȍзваћу	Ja будем пȍзвао/пȍзвала
2nd per	Ja **po**zovem	Ja ћу **po**zvati/**Po**zvaću	Ja budem **po**zvao/**po**zvala
3rd per (M)	Ти пȍзовеш	Ти ћеш пȍзвати/Пȍзваћеш	Ти будеш пȍзвао/пȍзвала
	Ti **po**zoveš	Ti ćeš **po**zvati/**Po**zvaćeš	Ti budeš **po**zvao/**po**zvala
	Он пȍзове	Он ће пȍзвати/Пȍзваће	Он буде пȍзвао
3rd per (F)	On **po**zove	On će **po**zvati/**Po**zvaće	On bude **po**zvao
	Она пȍзове	Она ће пȍзвати/Пȍзваће	Она буде пȍзвала
3rd per (N)	Ona **po**zove	Ona će **po**zvati/**Po**zvaće	Ona bude **po**zvala
	Оно пȍзове	Оно ће пȍзвати/Пȍзваће	Оно буде пȍзвало
	Ono **po**zove	Ono će **po**zvati/**Po**zvaće	Ono bude **po**zvalo
1st per pl	Ми пȍзовемо	Ми ћемо пȍзвати/Пȍзваћемо	Ми будемо пȍзвали/пȍзвале
	Mi **po**zovemo	Mi ćemo **po**zvati/**Po**zvaćemo	Mi budemo **po**zvali/**po**zvale
2nd per pl	Ви пȍзовете	Ви ћете пȍзвати/Пȍзваћете	Ви будете пȍзвали/пȍзвале
	Vi **po**zovete	Vi ćete **po**zvati/**Po**zvaćete	Vi budete **po**zvali/**po**zvale
3rd per pl	Они/Оне пȍзову	Они/Оне ће пȍзвати/Пȍзваће	Они/Оне буду пȍзвали/пȍзвале
	Oni/One **po**zovu	Oni/One će **po**zvati/**Po**zvaće	Oni/One budu **po**zvali/**po**zvale

	Past Tense (Перфект)	Pluperfect (Плусквамперфект)	Conditional (Потенцијал)
1st per	Ja сам пȍзвао	Ja сам био пȍзвао	Ja бих пȍзвао
	Ja sam **po**zvao	Ja sam bio **po**zvao	Ja bih **po**zvao
2nd per	Ти си пȍзвао	Ти си био пȍзвао	Ти би пȍзвао
	Ti si **po**zvao	Ti si bio **po**zvao	Ti bi **po**zvao
3rd per (M)	Он је пȍзвао	Он је био пȍзвао	Он би пȍзвао
	On je **po**zvao	On je bio **po**zvao	On bi **po**zvao
3rd per (F)	Она је пȍзвала	Она је била пȍзвала	Она би пȍзвала
	Ona je **po**zvala	Ona je bila **po**zvala	Ona bi **po**zvala
3rd per (N)	Оно је пȍзвало	Оно је било пȍзвало	Оно би пȍзвало
	Ono je **po**zvalo	Ono je bilo **po**zvalo	Ono bi **po**zvalo
1st per pl	Ми смо пȍзвали	Ми смо били пȍзвали	Ми бисмо пȍзвали
	Mi smo **po**zvali	Mi smo bili **po**zvali	Mi bismo **po**zvali
2nd per pl	Ви сте пȍзвали	Ви сте били пȍзвали	Ви бисте пȍзвали
	Vi ste **po**zvali	Vi ste bili **po**zvali	Vi biste **po**zvali
3rd per pl	Они су пȍзвали	Они су били пȍзвали	Они би пȍзвали
	Oni su **po**zvali	Oni su bili **po**zvali	Oni bi **po**zvali

	Imperative (Императив)
2nd per sg	(Ти) позȍви
	(Ti) po**zo**vi
1st per pl	(Ми) позȍвимо
	(Mi) po**zo**vimo
2nd per pl	(Ви) позȍвите
	(Vi) po**zo**vite

Non-finite Forms

Infinitive (Инфинитив)	по̀звати **po**zvati
Present Adverbial Participle (Глаголски прилог садашњи)	пози́вајући **po**zivajući
Past Adverbial Participle (Глаголски прилог прошли)	по̀звавши **po**zvavši

	Active Adjectival Participle (Глаголски придев радни)		Passive Adjectival Participle (Глаголски придев трпни)	
Gender	Singular	Plural	Singular	Plural
Feminine	по̀звала **po**zvala	по̀звале **po**zvale	по̀звана **po**zvana	по̀зване **po**zvane
Masculine	по̀звао **po**zvao	по̀звали **po**zvali	по̀зван **po**zvan	по̀звани **po**zvani
Neuter	по̀звало **po**zvalo	по̀звала **po**zvala	по̀звано **po**zvano	по̀звана **po**zvana

Can – у̀мети - umeti

	Present (Презент)	Future I (Футур први)	Future II (Футур други)
1st per	Ja у̀мем / Ja **um**em	Ja ћу у̀мети/У̀ме̏ћу / Ja ћу **um**eti/**Um**ећу	Ja будем у̀мео/у̀мела / Ja budem **um**eo/**um**ela
2nd per	Ти у̀меш / Ti **um**eš	Ти ћеш у̀мети/У̀ме̏ћеш / Ti ћеš **um**eti/**Um**ећeš	Ти будеш у̀мео/у̀мела / Ti budeš **um**eo/**um**ela
3rd per (M)	Он у̀ме / On **um**e	Он ће у̀мети/ У̀ме̏ће / On ће **um**eti/ **Um**eће	Он буде у̀мео / On bude **um**eo
3rd per (F)	Она у̀ме / Ona **um**e	Она ће у̀мети/У̀ме̏ће / Ona ће **um**eti/**Um**eће	Она буде у̀мела / Ona bude **um**ela
3rd per (N)	Оно у̀ме / Ono **um**e	Оно ће у̀мети/У̀ме̏ће / Ono ће **um**eti/**Um**eће	Оно буде у̀мело / Ono bude **um**elo
1st per pl	Ми у̀мемо / Mi **um**emo	Ми ћемо у̀мети/У̀ме̏ћемо / Mi ћemo **um**eti/**Um**eћemo	Ми будемо у̀мели/у̀меле / Mi budemo **um**eli/**um**ele
2nd per pl	Ви у̀мете / Vi **um**ete	Ви ћете у̀мети/У̀ме̏ћете / Vi ћete **um**eti/**Um**eћete	Ви будете у̀мели/у̀меле / Vi budete **um**eli/**um**ele
3rd per pl	Они/Оне у̀мејy / Oni/One **um**eju	Они/Оне ће у̀мети/У̀ме̏ће / Oni/One ће **um**eti/**Um**eће	Они/Оне буду у̀мели/у̀меле / Oni/One budu **um**eli/**um**ele

	Past Tense (Перфект)	Pluperfect (Плусквамперфект)	Conditional (Потенцијал)
1st per	Ja сам у̀мео / Ja sam **um**eo	Ja сам био у̀мео / Ja sam bio **um**eo	Ja бих у̀мео / Ja bih **um**eo
2nd per	Ти си у̀мео / Ti si **um**eo	Ти си био у̀мео / Ti si bio **um**eo	Ти би у̀мео / Ti bi **um**eo
3rd per (M)	Он је у̀мео / On je **um**eo	Он је био у̀мео / On je bio **um**eo	Он би у̀мео / On bi **um**eo
3rd per (F)	Она је у̀мела / Ona je **um**ela	Она је била у̀мела / Ona je bila **um**ela	Она би у̀мела / Ona bi **um**ela
3rd per (N)	Оно је у̀мело / Ono je **um**elo	Оно је било у̀мело / Ono je bilo **um**elo	Оно би у̀мело / Ono bi **um**elo
1st per pl	Ми смо у̀мели / Mi smo **um**eli	Ми смо били у̀мели / Mi smo bili **um**eli	Ми бисмо у̀мели / Mi bismo **um**eli
2nd per pl	Ви сте у̀мели / Vi ste **um**eli	Ви сте били у̀мели / Vi ste bili **um**eli	Ви бисте у̀мели / Vi biste **um**eli
3rd per pl	Они су у̀мели / Oni su **um**eli	Они су били у̀мели / Oni su bili **um**eli	Они би у̀мели / Oni bi **um**eli

	Imperative (Императив)
2nd per sg	(Ти) --
1st per pl	(Ми) --
2nd per pl	(Ви) --

Non-finite Forms

Infinitive (Инфинитив)	ỳмети **um**eti
Present Adverbial Participle (Глаголски прилог садашњи)	ỳмејући **um**ejući
Past Adverbial Participle (Глаголски прилог прошли)	ỳмевши **um**evši

	Active Adjectival Participle (Глаголски придев радни)		Passive Adjectival Participle (Глаголски придев трпни)	
Gender	Singular	Plural	Singular	Plural
Feminine	ỳмела **um**ela	ỳмеле **um**ele	--	--
Masculine	ỳмео **um**eo	ỳмели **um**eli	--	--
Neuter	ỳмело **um**elo	ỳмела **um**ela	--	--

To Choose – изàбрати - izabrati

	Present (Презент)	Future I (Футур први)	Future II (Футур други)
1st per	Ja изàберем Ja izaberem	Ja ћу изàбрати/Изàбраћу Ja ću izabrati/Izabraću	Ja будем йзабрао/йзабрала Ja budem izabrao/izabrala
2nd per	Ти изàбереш Ti izabereš	Ти ћеш изàбрати/Изàбраћеш Ti ćeš izabrati/Izabraćeš	Ти будеш йзабрао/йзабрала Ti budeš izabrao/izabrala
3rd per (M)	Он изàбере On izabere	Он ће изàбрати/Изàбраће On će izabrati/Izabraće	Он буде йзабрао On bude izabrao
3rd per (F)	Она изàбере Ona izabere	Она ће изàбрати/Изàбраће Ona će izabrati/Izabraće	Она буде йзабрала Ona bude izabrala
3rd per (N)	Оно изàбере Ono izabere	Оно ће изàбрати/Изàбраће Ono će izabrati/Izabraće	Оно буде йзабрало Ono bude izabralo
1st per pl	Ми изàберемо Mi izaberemo	Ми ћемо изàбрати/Изàбраћемо Mi ćemo izabrati/Izabraćemo	Ми будемо йзабрали/йзабрале Mi budemo izabrali/izabrale
2nd per pl	Ви изàберете Vi izaberete	Ви ћете изàбрати/Изàбраћете Vi ćete izabrati/Izabraćete	Ви будете йзабрали/йзабрале Vi budete izabrali/izabrale
3rd per pl	Они/Оне изàберу Oni/One izaberu	Они/Оне ће изàбрати/Изàбраће Oni/One će izabrati/Izabraće	Они/Оне буду йзабрали/йзабрале Oni/One budu izabrali/izabrale

	Past Tense (Перфект)	Pluperfect (Плусквамперфект)	Conditional (Потенцијал)
1st per	Ja сам йзабрао Ja sam izabrao	Ja сам био йзабрао Ja sam bio izabrao	Ja бих йзабрао Ja bih izabrao
2nd per	Ти си йзабрао Ti si izabrao	Ти си био йзабрао Ti si bio izabrao	Ти би йзабрао Ti bi izabrao
3rd per (M)	Он је йзабрао On je izabrao	Он је био йзабрао On je bio izabrao	Он би йзабрао On bi izabrao
3rd per (F)	Она је йзабрала Ona je izabrala	Она је била йзабрала Ona je bila izabrala	Она би йзабрала Ona bi izabrala
3rd per (N)	Оно је йзабрало Ono je izabralo	Оно је било йзабрало Ono je bilo izabralo	Оно би йзабрало Ono bi izabralo
1st per pl	Ми смо йзабрали Mi smo izabrali	Ми смо били йзабрали Mi smo bili izabrali	Ми бисмо йзабрали Mi bismo izabrali
2nd per pl	Ви сте йзабрали Vi ste izabrali	Ви сте били йзабрали Vi ste bili izabrali	Ви бисте йзабрали Vi biste izabrali
3rd per pl	Они су йзабрали Oni su izabrali	Они су били йзабрали Oni su bili izabrali	Они би йзабрали Oni bi izabrali

	Imperative (Императив)
2nd per sg	(Ти) изабèри (Ti) izaberi
1st per pl	(Ми) изабèримо (Mi) izaberimo
2nd per pl	(Ви) изабèрите (Vi) izaberite

Non-finite Forms

Infinitive (Инфинитив)	изàбрати
	izabrati
Present Adverbial Participle (Глаголски прилог садашњи)	--
Past Adverbial Participle (Глаголски прилог прошли)	изàбравши
	izabravši

| | Active Adjectival Participle (Глаголски придев радни) | | Passive Adjectival Participle (Глаголски придев трпни) | |
Gender	Singular	Plural	Singular	Plural
Feminine	йзабрала	йзабрале	йзабрана	йзабране
	izabrala	izabrale	izabrana	izabrane
Masculine	йзабрао	йзабрали	йзабран	йзабрани
	izabrao	izabrali	izabran	izabrani
Neuter	йзабрало	йзабрала	йзабрано	йзабрана
	izabralo	izabrala	izabrano	izabrana

To Close – затво̀рити - zatvoriti

	Present (Презент)	Future I (Футур први)	Future II (Футур други)
1ˢᵗ per	Ja за̀творим Ja **za**tvorim	Ja ћу затво̀рити/Затво̀рићу Ja ću za**tvo**riti/Zat**vo**riću	Ja будем затво̀рио/затво̀рила Ja budem za**tvo**rio/za**tvo**rila
2ⁿᵈ per	Ти за̀твориш Ti **za**tvoriš	Ти ћеш затво̀рити/Затво̀рићеш Ti ćeš za**tvo**riti/Zat**vo**rićeš	Ти будеш затво̀рио/затво̀рила Ti budeš za**tvo**rio/za**tvo**rila
3ʳᵈ per (M)	Он за̀твори On **za**tvori	Он ће затво̀рити/Затво̀риће On će za**tvo**riti/Zat**vo**riće	Он буде затво̀рио On bude za**tvo**rio
3ʳᵈ per (F)	Она за̀твори Ona **za**tvori	Она ће затво̀рити/Затво̀риће Ona će za**tvo**riti/Zat**vo**riće	Она буде затво̀рила Ona bude za**tvo**rila
3ʳᵈ per (N)	Оно за̀твори Ono **za**tvori	Оно ће затво̀рити/Затво̀риће Ono će za**tvo**riti/Zat**vo**riće	Оно буде затво̀рило Ono bude za**tvo**rilo
1ˢᵗ per pl	Ми за̀творимо Mi **za**tvorimo	Ми ћемо затво̀рити/Затво̀рићемо Mi ćemo za**tvo**riti/Zat**vo**rićemo	Ми будемо затво̀рили/затво̀риле Mi budemo za**tvo**rili/za**tvo**rile
2ⁿᵈ per pl	Ви за̀творите Vi **za**tvorite	Ви ћете затво̀рити/Затво̀рићете Vi ćete za**tvo**riti/Zat**vo**rićete	Ви будете затво̀рили/затво̀риле Vi budete za**tvo**rili/za**tvo**rile
3ʳᵈ per pl	Они/Оне за̀творе Oni/One **za**tvore	Они/Оне ће затво̀рити/Затво̀риће Oni/One će za**tvo**riti/Zat**vo**riće	Они/Оне буду затво̀рили/затво̀риле Oni/One budu za**tvo**rili/za**tvo**rile

	Past Tense (Перфект)	Pluperfect (Плусквамперфект)	Conditional (Потенцијал)
1ˢᵗ per	Ja сам затво̀рио Ja sam za**tvo**rio	Ja сам био затво̀рио Ja sam bio za**tvo**rio	Ja бих затво̀рио Ja bih za**tvo**rio
2ⁿᵈ per	Ти си затво̀рио Ti si za**tvo**rio	Ти си био затво̀рио Ti si bio za**tvo**rio	Ти би затво̀рио Ti bi za**tvo**rio
3ʳᵈ per (M)	Он је затво̀рио On je za**tvo**rio	Он је био затво̀рио On je bio za**tvo**rio	Он би затво̀рио On bi za**tvo**rio
3ʳᵈ per (F)	Она је затво̀рила Ona je za**tvo**rila	Она је била затво̀рила Ona je bila za**tvo**rila	Она би затво̀рила Ona bi za**tvo**rila
3ʳᵈ per (N)	Оно је затво̀рило Ono je za**tvo**rilo	Оно је било затво̀рило Ono je bilo za**tvo**rilo	Оно би затво̀рило Ono bi za**tvo**rilo
1ˢᵗ per pl	Ми смо затво̀рили Mi smo za**tvo**rili	Ми смо били затво̀рили Mi smo bili za**tvo**rili	Ми бисмо затво̀рили Mi bismo za**tvo**rili
2ⁿᵈ per pl	Ви сте затво̀рили Vi ste za**tvo**rili	Ви сте били затво̀рили Vi ste bili za**tvo**rili	Ви бисте затво̀рили Vi biste za**tvo**rili
3ʳᵈ per pl	Они су затво̀рили Oni su za**tvo**rili	Они су били затво̀рили Oni su bili za**tvo**rili	Они би затво̀рили Oni bi za**tvo**rili

	Imperative (Императив)
2ⁿᵈ per sg	(Ти) затво̀ри (Ti) zat**vo**ri
1ˢᵗ per pl	(Ми) затво̀римо (Mi) za**tvo**rimo
2ⁿᵈ per pl	(Ви) затво̀рите (Vi) zat**vo**rite

Non-finite Forms

Infinitive (Инфинитив)	затвòрити zatvoriti
Present Adverbial Participle (Глаголски прилог садашњи)	--
Past Adverbial Participle (Глаголски прилог прошли)	затвòривши zatvorivši

	Active Adjectival Participle (Глаголски придев радни)		Passive Adjectival Participle (Глаголски придев трпни)	
Gender	Singular	Plural	Singular	Plural
Feminine	затвòрила zatvorila	затвòриле zatvorile	зàтворена zatvorena	зàтворене zatvorene
Masculine	затвòрио zatvorio	затвòрили zatvorili	зàтворен zatvoren	зàтворени zatvoreni
Neuter	затвòрило zatvorilo	затвòрила zatvorila	зàтворено zatvoreno	зàтворена zatvorena

To Come - дôħи - doći

	Present (Презент)	Future I (Футур први)	Future II (Футур други)
1st per	Ja дôħем Ja dođem	Ja ħy дôħи/Дôħи ħy Ja ću doći/Doći ću	Ja будем дòшao/дòшла Ja budem došao/došla
2nd per	Ти дôħеш Ti dođeš	Ти ħeш дôħи/Дôħи ħeш Ti ćeš doći/Doći ćeš	Ти будеш дòшao/дòшла Ti budeš došao/došla
3rd per (M)	Он дôħе On dođe	Он ħe дôħи/Дôħи ħe On će doći/Doći će	Он буде дòшao On bude došao
3rd per (F)	Она дôħе Ona dođe	Она ħe дôħи/Дôħи ħe Ona će doći/Doći će	Она буде дòшла Ona bude došla
3rd per (N)	Оно дôħе Ono dođe	Оно ħe дôħи/Дôħи ħe Ono će doći/Doći će	Оно буде дòшло Ono bude došlo
1st per pl	Ми дôħемо Mi dođemo	Ми ħeмo дôħи/Дôħи ħeмo Mi ćemo doći/Doći ćemo	Ми будемо дòшли/дòшле Mi budemo došli/došle
2nd per pl	Ви дôħете Vi dođete	Ви ħeтe дôħи/Дôħи ħeтe Vi ćete doći/Doći ćete	Ви будете дòшли/дòшле Vi budete došli/došle
3rd per pl	Они/Оне дôħy Oni/One dođu	Они/Оне ħe дôħи/Дôħи ħe Oni/One će doći/Doći će	Они/Оне буду дòшли/дòшле Oni/One budu došli/došle

	Past Tense (Перфект)	Pluperfect (Плусквамперфект)	Conditional (Потенцијал)
1st per	Ja сам дòшao Ja sam došao	Ja сам био дòшao Ja sam bio došao	Ja бих дòшao Ja bih došao
2nd per	Ти си дòшao Ti si došao	Ти си био дòшao Ti si bio došao	Ти би дòшao Ti bi došao
3rd per (M)	Он je дòшao On je došao	Он je био дòшao On je bio došao	Он би дòшao On bi došao
3rd per (F)	Она je дòшла Ona je došla	Она je била дòшла Ona je bila došla	Она би дòшла Ona bi došla
3rd per (N)	Оно je дòшло Ono je došlo	Оно je било дòшло Ono je bilo došlo	Оно би дòшло Ono bi došlo
1st per pl	Ми смо дòшли Mi smo došli	Ми смо били дòшли Mi smo bili došli	Ми бисмо дòшли Mi bismo došli
2nd per pl	Ви сте дòшли Vi ste došli	Ви сте били дòшли Vi ste bili došli	Ви бисте дòшли Vi biste došli
3rd per pl	Они су дòшли Oni su došli	Они су били дòшли Oni su bili došli	Они би дòшли Oni bi došli

	Imperative (Императив)
2nd per sg	(Ти) дôħи (Ti) dođi
1st per pl	(Ми) дôħимо (Mi) dođimo
2nd per pl	(Ви) дôħите (Vi) dođite

Non-finite Forms

Infinitive (Инфинитив)	до́ћи **do**ći
Present Adverbial Participle (Глаголски прилог садашњи)	--
Past Adverbial Participle (Глаголски прилог прошли)	до̀шавши **do**šavši

	Active Adjectival Participle (Глаголски придев радни)		Passive Adjectival Participle (Глаголски придев трпни)	
Gender	Singular	Plural	Singular	Plural
Feminine	до̀шла **do**šla	до̀шле **do**šle	--	--
Masculine	до̀шао **do**šao	до̀шли **do**šli	--	--
Neuter	до̀шло **do**šlo	до̀шла **do**šla	--	--

To Cook - ку̏вати - kuvati

	Present (Презент)	Future I (Футур први)	Future II (Футур други)
1st per	Ja ку̏вам Ja **ku**vam	Ja ћу ку̏вати/Ку̏ва̏ћу Ja ću **ku**vati/**Ku**vaću	Ja будем ку̏вао/ку̏вала Ja budem **ku**vao/**ku**vala
2nd per	Ти ку̏ваш Ti **ku**vaš	Ти ћеш ку̏вати/Ку̏ва̏ћеш Ti ćeš **ku**vati/**Ku**vaćeš	Ти будеш ку̏вао/ку̏вала Ti budeš **ku**vao/**ku**vala
3rd per (M)	Он ку̏ва On **ku**va	Он ће ку̏вати/Ку̏ва̏ће On će **ku**vati/**Ku**vaće	Он буде ку̏вао On bude **ku**vao
3rd per (F)	Она ку̏ва Ona **ku**va	Она ће ку̏вати/Ку̏ва̏ће Ona će **ku**vati/**Ku**vaće	Она буде ку̏вала Ona bude **ku**vala
3rd per (N)	Оно ку̏ва Ono **ku**va	Оно ће ку̏вати/Ку̏ва̏ће Ono će **ku**vati/**Ku**vaće	Оно буде ку̏вало Ono bude **ku**valo
1st per pl	Ми ку̏вамо Mi **ku**vamo	Ми ћемо ку̏вати/Ку̏ва̏ћемо Mi ćemo **ku**vati/**Ku**vaćemo	Ми будемо ку̏вали/ку̏вале Mi budemo **ku**vali/**ku**vale
2nd per pl	Ви ку̏вате Vi **ku**vate	Ви ћете ку̏вати/Ку̏ва̏ћете Vi ćete **ku**vati/**Ku**vaćete	Ви будете ку̏вали/ку̏вале Vi budete **ku**vali/**ku**vale
3rd per pl	Они/Оне ку̏вају Oni/One **ku**vaju	Они/Оне ће ку̏вати/Ку̏ва̏ће Oni/One će **ku**vati/**Ku**vaće	Они/Оне буду ку̏вали/ку̏вале Oni/One budu **ku**vali/**ku**vale

	Past Tense (Перфект)	Pluperfect (Плусквамперфект)	Conditional (Потенцијал)
1st per	Ja сам ку̏вао Ja sam **ku**vao	Ja сам био ку̏вао Ja sam bio **ku**vao	Ja бих ку̏вао Ja bih **ku**vao
2nd per	Ти си ку̏вао Ti si **ku**vao	Ти си био ку̏вао Ti si bio **ku**vao	Ти би ку̏вао Ti bi **ku**vao
3rd per (M)	Он је ку̏вао On je **ku**vao	Он је био ку̏вао On je bio **ku**vao	Он би ку̏вао On bi **ku**vao
3rd per (F)	Она је ку̏вала Ona je **ku**vala	Она је била ку̏вала Ona je bila **ku**vala	Она би ку̏вала Ona bi **ku**vala
3rd per (N)	Оно је ку̏вало Ono je **ku**valo	Оно је било ку̏вало Ono je bilo **ku**valo	Оно би ку̏вало Ono bi **ku**valo
1st per pl	Ми смо ку̏вали Mi smo **ku**vali	Ми смо били ку̏вали Mi smo bili **ku**vali	Ми бисмо ку̏вали Mi bismo **ku**vali
2nd per pl	Ви сте ку̏вали Vi ste **ku**vali	Ви сте били ку̏вали Vi ste bili **ku**vali	Ви бисте ку̏вали Vi biste **ku**vali
3rd per pl	Они су ку̏вали Oni su **ku**vali	Они су били ку̏вали Oni su bili **ku**vali	Они би ку̏вали Oni bi **ku**vali

	Imperative (Императив)
2nd per sg	(Ти) ку̏вај (Ti) **ku**vaj
1st per pl	(Ми) ку̏вајмо (Mi) **ku**vajmo

2nd per pl	(Ви) кӯвајте
	(Mi) **ku**vajte

Non-finite Forms

Infinitive (Инфинитив)	кӯвати
	kuvati
Present Adverbial Participle (Глаголски прилог садашњи)	кӯвајући
	kuvajući
Past Adverbial Participle (Глаголски прилог прошли)	--

	Active Adjectival Participle (Глаголски придев радни)		Passive Adjectival Participle (Глаголски придев трпни)	
Gender	Singular	Plural	Singular	Plural
Feminine	кӯвала	кӯвале	кӯвана	кӯване
	kuvala	**ku**vale	**ku**vana	**ku**vane
Masculine	кӯвао	кӯвали	кӯван	кӯвани
	kuvao	**ku**vali	**ku**van	**ku**van
Neuter	кӯвало	кӯвала	кӯвано	кӯвана
	kuvalo	**ku**vala	**ku**vano	**ku**vana

To Cry - плакати - plakati

	Present (Презент)	Future I (Футур први)	Future II (Футур други)
1st per	Ja плачем Ja **plač**em	Ja ћу плакати/Плакаћу Ja ću **pla**kati/**Pla**kaću	Ja будем плакао/плакала Ja budem **pla**kao/**pla**kala
2nd per	Ти плачеш Ti **plač**eš	Ти ћеш плакати/Плакаћеш Ti ćeš **pla**kati/**Pla**kaćeš	Ти будеш плакао/плакала Ti budeš **pla**kao/**pla**kala
3rd per (M)	Он плаче On **pla**če	Он ће плакати/Плакаће On će **pla**kati/**Pla**kaće	Он буде плакао On bude **pla**kao
3rd per (F)	Она плаче Ona **pla**če	Она ће плакати/Плакаће Ona će **pla**kati/**Pla**kaće	Она буде плакала Ona bude **pla**kala
3rd per (N)	Оно плаче Ono **pla**če	Оно ће плакати/Плакаће Ono će **pla**kati/**Pla**kaće	Оно буде плакало Ono bude **pla**kalo
1st per pl	Ми плачемо Mi **pla**čemo	Ми ћемо плакати/Плакаћемо Mi ćemo **pla**kati/**Pla**kaćemo	Ми будемо плакали/плакале Mi budemo **pla**kali/**pla**kale
2nd per pl	Ви плачете Vi **pla**čete	Ви ћете плакати/Плакаћете Vi ćete **pla**kati/**Pla**kaćete	Ви будете плакали/плакале Vi budete **pla**kali/**pla**kale
3rd per pl	Они/Оне плачу Oni/One **pla**ču	Они/Оне ће плакати/Плакаће Oni/One će **pla**kati/**Pla**kaće	Они/Оне буду плакали/плакале Oni/One budu **pla**kali/**pla**kale

	Past Tense (Перфект)	Pluperfect (Плусквамперфект)	Conditional (Потенцијал)
1st per	Ja сам плакао Ja sam **pla**kao	Ja сам био плакао Ja sam bio **pla**kao	Ja бих плакао Ja bih **pla**kao
2nd per	Ти си плакао Ti si **pla**kao	Ти си био плакао Ti si bio **pla**kao	Ти би плакао Ti bi **pla**kao
3rd per (M)	Он је плакао On je **pla**kao	Он је био плакао On je bio **pla**kao	Он би плакао On bi **pla**kao
3rd per (F)	Она је плакала Ona je **pla**kala	Она је била плакала Ona je bila **pla**kala	Она би плакала Ona bi **pla**kala
3rd per (N)	Оно је плакало Ono je **pla**kalo	Оно је било плакало Ono je bilo **pla**kalo	Оно би плакало Ono bi **pla**kalo
1st per pl	Ми смо плакали Mi smo **pla**kali	Ми смо били плакали Mi smo bili **pla**kali	Ми бисмо плакали Mi bismo **pla**kali
2nd per pl	Ви сте плакали Vi ste **pla**kali	Ви сте били плакали Vi ste bili **pla**kali	Ви бисте плакали Vi biste **pla**kali
3rd per pl	Они су плакали Oni su **pla**kali	Они су били плакали Oni su bili **pla**kali	Они би плакали Oni bi **pla**kali

	Imperative (Императив)
2nd per sg	(Ти) плачи (Ti) **pla**či
1st per pl	(Ми) плачимо (Mi) **pla**čimo
2nd per pl	(Ви) плачите (Vi) **pla**čite

Non-finite Forms

Infinitive (Инфинитив)	пла̏кати **pla**kati
Present Adverbial Participle (Глаголски прилог садашњи)	пла̏чӯћи **pla**čući
Past Adverbial Participle (Глаголски прилог прошли)	--

	Active Adjectival Participle (Глаголски придев радни)		Passive Adjectival Participle (Глаголски придев трпни)	
Gender	Singular	Plural	Singular	Plural
Feminine	пла̏кала **pla**kala	пла̏кале **pla**kale	--	--
Masculine	пла̏као **pla**kao	пла̏кали **pla**kali	--	--
Neuter	пла̏кало **pla**kalo	пла̏кала **pla**kala	--	--

To Dance - плѐсати

	Present (Презент)	Future I (Футур први)	Future II (Футур други)
1st per	Ja плѐшем Ja **ple**šem	Ja ћу плѐсати/Плѐсаћу Ja ću **ple**sati/**Ple**saću	Ja будем плѐсао/плѐсала Ja budem **ple**sao/**ple**sala
2nd per	Ти плѐшеш Ti **ple**šeš	Ти ћеш плѐсати/Плѐсаћеш Ti ćeš **ple**sati/**Ple**saćeš	Ти будеш плѐсао/плѐсала Ti budeš **ple**sao/**ple**sala
3rd per (M)	Он плѐше On **ple**še	Он ће плѐсати/Плѐсаће On će **ple**sati/**Ple**saće	Он буде плѐсао On bude **ple**sao
3rd per (F)	Она плѐше Ona **ple**še	Она ће плѐсати/Плѐсаће Ona će **ple**sati/**Ple**saće	Она буде плѐсала Ona bude **ple**sala
3rd per (N)	Оно плѐше Ono **ple**še	Оно ће плѐсати/Плѐсаће Ono će **ple**sati/**Ple**saće	Оно буде плѐсало Ono bude **ple**salo
1st per pl	Ми плѐшемо Mi **ple**šemo	Ми ћемо плѐсати/Плѐсаћемо Mi ćemo **ple**sati/**Ple**saćemo	Ми будемо плѐсали/плѐсале Mi budemo **ple**sali/**ple**sale
2nd per pl	Ви плѐшете Vi **ple**šete	Ви ћете плѐсати/Плѐсаћете Vi ćete **ple**sati/**Ple**saćete	Ви будете плѐсали/плѐсале Vi budete **ple**sali/**ple**sale
3rd per pl	Они/Оне плѐшу Oni/One **ple**šu	Они/Оне ће плѐсати/Плѐсаће Oni/One će **ple**sati/**Ple**saće	Они/Оне буду плѐсали/плѐсале Oni/One budu **ple**sali/**ple**sale

	Past Tense (Перфект)	Pluperfect (Плусквамперфект)	Conditional (Потенцијал)
1st per	Ja сам плѐсао Ja sam **ple**sao	Ja сам био плѐсао Ja sam bio **ple**sao	Ja бих плѐсао Ja bih **ple**sao
2nd per	Ти си плѐсао Ti si **ple**sao	Ти си био плѐсао Ti si bio **ple**sao	Ти би плѐсао Ti bi **ple**sao
3rd per (M)	Он је плѐсао On je **ple**sao	Он је био плѐсао On je bio **ple**sao	Он би плѐсао On bi **ple**sao
3rd per (F)	Она је плѐсала Ona je **ple**sala	Она је била плѐсала Ona je bila **ple**sala	Она би плѐсала Ona bi **ple**sala
3rd per (N)	Оно је плѐсало Ono je **ple**salo	Оно је било плѐсало Ono je bilo **ple**salo	Оно би плѐсало Ono bi **ple**salo
1st per pl	Ми смо плѐсали Mi smo **ple**sali	Ми смо били плѐсали Mi smo bili **ple**sali	Ми бисмо плѐсали Mi bismo **ple**sali
2nd per pl	Ви сте плѐсали Vi ste **ple**sali	Ви сте били плѐсали Vi ste bili **ple**sali	Ви бисте плѐсали Vi biste **ple**sali
3rd per pl	Они су плѐсали Oni su **ple**sali	Они су били плѐсали Oni su bili **ple**sali	Они би плѐсали Oni bi **ple**sali

	Imperative (Императив)
2nd per sg	(Ти) плѐши (Ti) **ple**ši
1st per pl	(Ми) плѐшимо (Mi) **ple**šimo

2nd per pl	(Ви) пле́шите
	(Vi) **ple**šite

Non-finite Forms

Infinitive (Инфинитив)	пле́сати
	plesati
Present Adverbial Participle (Глаголски прилог садашњи)	пле́шући
	plešući
Past Adverbial Participle (Глаголски прилог прошли)	--

	Active Adjectival Participle (Глаголски придев радни)		Passive Adjectival Participle (Глаголски придев трпни)	
Gender	Singular	Plural	Singular	Plural
Feminine	пле́сала	пле́сале	--	--
	plesala	**ple**sale		
Masculine	пле́сао	пле́сали	--	--
	plesao	**ple**sali		
Neuter	пле́сало	пле́сала	--	--
	plesalo	**ple**sala		

To Decide - одлу́чити – odlučiti

	Present (Презент)	Future I (Футур први)	Future II (Футур други)
1st per	Ja о̀длучим Ja **od**lučim	Ja ћу одлу́чити/Одлу́чићу Ja ću **od**lučiti/Odlučiću	Ja будем одлу́чио/одлу́чила Ja budem **od**lučio/odlučila
2nd per	Ти о̀длучиш Ti **od**lučiš	Ти ћеш одлу́чити/Одлу́чићеш Ti ćeš **od**lučiti/Odlučićeš	Ти будеш одлу́чио/одлу́чила Ti budeš **od**lučio/odlučila
3rd per (M)	Он о̀длучи On **od**luči	Он ће одлу́чити/Одлу́чиће On će **od**lučiti/Odlučiće	Он буде одлу́чио On bude **od**lučio
3rd per (F)	Она о̀длучи Ona **od**luči	Она ће одлу́чити/Одлу́чиће Ona će **od**lučiti/Odlučiće	Она буде одлу́чила Ona bude **od**lučila
3rd per (N)	Оно о̀длучи Ono **od**luči	Оно ће одлу́чити/Одлу́чиће Ono će **od**lučiti/Odlučiće	Оно буде одлу́чило Ono bude **od**lučilo
1st per pl	Ми о̀длучимо Mi **od**lučimo	Ми ћемо одлу́чити/Одлу́чићемо Mi ćemo **od**lučiti/Odlučićemo	Ми будемо одлу́чили/одлу́чиле Mi budemo **od**lučili/odlučile
2nd per pl	Ви о̀длучите Vi **od**lučite	Ви ћете одлу́чити/Одлу́чићете Vi ćete **od**lučiti/Odlučićete	Ви будете одлу́чили/одлу́чиле Vi budete **od**lučili/odlučile
3rd per pl	Они/Оне о̀длуче Oni/One **od**luče	Они/Оне ће одлу́чити/ Одлу́чиће Oni/One ће **od**lučiti/ Odlučiće	Они/Оне буду одлу́чили/одлу́чиле Oni/One budu **od**lučili/odlučile

	Past Tense (Перфект)	Pluperfect (Плусквамперфект)	Conditional (Потенцијал)
1st per	Ja сам одлу́чио Ja sam **od**lučio	Ja сам био одлу́чио Ja sam bio **od**lučio	Ja бих одлу́чио Ja bih **od**lučio
2nd per	Ти си одлу́чио Ti si **od**lučio	Ти си био одлу́чио Ti si bio **od**lučio	Ти би одлу́чио Ti bi **od**lučio
3rd per (M)	Он је одлу́чио On je **od**lučio	Он је био одлу́чио On je bio **od**lučio	Он би одлу́чио On bi **od**lučio
3rd per (F)	Она је одлу́чила Ona je **od**lučila	Она је била одлу́чила Ona je bila **od**lučila	Она би одлу́чила Ona bi **od**lučila
3rd per (N)	Оно је одлу́чило Ono je **od**lučilo	Оно је било одлу́чило Ono je bilo **od**lučilo	Оно би одлу́чило Ono bi **od**lučilo
1st per pl	Ми смо одлу́чили Mi smo **od**lučili	Ми смо били одлу́чили Mi smo bili **od**lučili	Ми бисмо одлу́чили Mi bismo **od**lučili
2nd per pl	Ви сте одлу́чили Vi ste **od**lučili	Ви сте били одлу́чили Vi ste bili **od**lučili	Ви бисте одлу́чили Vi biste **od**lučili
3rd per pl	Они су одлу́чили Oni su **od**lučili	Они су били одлу́чили Oni su bili **od**lučili	Они би одлу́чили Oni bi **od**lučili

	Imperative (Императив)
2nd per sg	(Ти) одлу́чи (Ti) **od**luči
1st per pl	(Ми) одлу́чимо (Mi) **od**lučimo
2nd per pl	(Ви) одлу́чите (Vi) **od**lučite

Non-finite Forms

Infinitive (Инфинитив)	одлу́чити od**lu**čiti
Present Adverbial Participle (Глаголски прилог садашњи)	одлу̀чу̀јући od**lu**čujući
Past Adverbial Participle (Глаголски прилог прошли)	одлу́чивши od**lu**čivši

	Active Adjectival Participle (Глаголски придев радни)		Passive Adjectival Participle (Глаголски придев трпни)	
Gender	Singular	Plural	Singular	Plural
Feminine	одлу́чила od**lu**čila	одлу́чиле od**lu**čile	о̀длучена od**lu**čena	о̀длучене od**lu**čene
Masculine	одлу́чио od**lu**čio	одлу́чили od**lu**čili	о̀длучен od**lu**čen	о̀длучени od**lu**čeni
Neuter	одлу́чило od**lu**čilo	одлу́чила od**lu**čila	о̀длучено od**lu**čeno	о̀длучена od**lu**čena

To Decrease - смáњити - smanjiti

	Present (Презент)	Future I (Футур први)	Future II (Футур други)
1st per	Ja смáњим Ja **sma**njim	Ja ћу смáњити/Смáњићу Ja ću **sma**njiti/**Sma**njiću	Ja будем смáњио/смáњила Ja budem **sma**njio/**sma**njila
2nd per	Ти смáњиш Ti **sma**njiš	Ти ћеш смáњити/Смáњићеш Ti ćeš **sma**njiti/**Sma**njićeš	Ти будеш смáњио/смáњила Ti budeš **sma**njio/**sma**njila
3rd per (M)	Он смáњи On **sma**nji	Он ће смáњити/Смáњиће On će **sma**njiti/**Sma**njiće	Он буде смáњио On bude **sma**njio
3rd per (F)	Она смáњи Ona **sma**nji	Она ће смáњити/Смáњиће Ona će **sma**njiti/**Sma**njiće	Она буде смáњила Ona bude **sma**njila
3rd per (N)	Оно смáњи Ono **sma**nji	Оно ће смáњити/Смáњиће Ono će **sma**njiti/**Sma**njiće	Оно буде смáњило Ono bude **sma**njilo
1st per pl	Ми смáњимо Mi **sma**njimo	Ми ћемо смáњити/Смáњићемо Mi ćemo **sma**njiti/**Sma**njićemo	Ми будемо смáњили/смáњиле Mi budemo **sma**njili/**sma**njile
2nd per pl	Ви смáњите Vi **sma**njite	Ви ћете смáњити/Смáњићете Vi ćete **sma**njiti/**Sma**njićete	Ви будете смáњили/смáњиле Vi budete **sma**njili/**sma**njile
3rd per pl	Они/Оне смáње Oni/One **sma**nje	Они/Оне ће смáњити/Смáњиће Oni/One će **sma**njiti/**Sma**njiće	Они/Оне буду смáњили/смáњиле Oni/One budu **sma**njili/**sma**njile

	Past Tense (Перфект)	Pluperfect (Плусквамперфект)	Conditional (Потенцијал)
1st per	Ja сам смáњио Ja sam **sma**njio	Ja сам био смáњио Ja sam bio **sma**njio	Ja бих смáњио Ja bih **sma**njio
2nd per	Ти си смáњио Ti si **sma**njio	Ти си био смáњио Ti si bio **sma**njio	Ти би смáњио Ti bi **sma**njio
3rd per (M)	Он је смáњио On je **sma**njio	Он је био смáњио On je bio **sma**njio	Он би смáњио On bi **sma**njio
3rd per (F)	Она је смáњила Ona je **sma**njila	Она је била смáњила Ona je bila **sma**njila	Она би смáњила Ona bi **sma**njila
3rd per (N)	Оно је смáњило Ono je **sma**njilo	Оно је било смáњило Ono je bilo **sma**njilo	Оно би смáњило Ono bi **sma**njilo
1st per pl	Ми смо смáњили Mi smo **sma**njili	Ми смо били смáњили Mi smo bili **sma**njili	Ми бисмо смáњили Mi bismo **sma**njili
2nd per pl	Ви сте смáњили Vi ste **sma**njili	Ви сте били смáњили Vi ste bili **sma**njili	Ви бисте смáњили Vi biste **sma**njili
3rd per pl	Они су смáњили Oni su **sma**njili	Они су били смáњили Oni su bili **sma**njili	Они би смáњили Oni bi **sma**njili

	Imperative (Императив)
2nd per sg	(Ти) смáњи (Ti) **sma**nji
1st per pl	(Ми) смáњимо (Mi) **sma**njimo

2nd per pl	(Ви) смáњите
	(Vi) **sma**njite

Non-finite Forms

Infinitive (Инфинитив)	смáњити
	smanjiti
Present Adverbial Participle (Глаголски прилог садашњи)	--
Past Adverbial Participle (Глаголски прилог прошли)	смáњивши
	smanjivši

	Active Adjectival Participle (Глаголски придев радни)		Passive Adjectival Participle (Глаголски придев трпни)	
Gender	Singular	Plural	Singular	Plural
Feminine	смáњила	смáњиле	смâњена	смâњене
	smanjila	**sma**njile	**sma**njena	**sma**njene
Masculine	смáњио	смáњили	смâњен	смâњени
	smanjio	**sma**njili	**sma**njen	**sma**njeni
Neuter	смáњило	смáњила	смâњено	смâњена
	smanjilo	**sma**njila	**sma**njeno	**sma**njena

To Die – у̀мрети - umreti

	Present (Презент)	Future I (Футур први)	Future II (Футур други)
1st per	Ja у̀мрем / Ja umrem	Ja ћу у̀мрети/У̀мрећу / Ja ću umreti/Umreću	Ja будем у̀мро/у̀мрла / Ja budem umro/umrla
2nd per	Ти у̀мреш / Ti umreš	Ти ћеш у̀мрети/У̀мрећеш / Ti ćeš umreti/Umrećeš	Ти будеш у̀мро/у̀мрла / Ti budeš umro/umrla
3rd per (M)	Он у̀мре / On umre	Он ће у̀мрети/У̀мреће / On će umreti/Umreće	Он буде у̀мро / On bude umro
3rd per (F)	Она у̀мре / Ona umre	Она ће у̀мрети/У̀мреће / Ona će umreti/Umreće	Она буде у̀мрла / Ona bude umrla
3rd per (N)	Оно у̀мре / Ono umre	Оно ће у̀мрети/У̀мреће / Ono će umreti/Umreće	Оно буде у̀мрло / Ono bude umrlo
1st per pl	Ми у̀мремо / Mi umremo	Ми ћемо у̀мрети/У̀мрећемо / Mi ćemo umreti/Umrećemo	Ми будемо у̀мрли/у̀мрле / Mi budemo umrli/umrle
2nd per pl	Ви у̀мрете / Vi umrete	Ви ћете у̀мрети/У̀мрећете / Vi ćete umreti/Umrećete	Ви будете у̀мрли/у̀мрле / Vi budete umrli/umrle
3rd per pl	Они/Оне у̀мру / Oni/One umru	Они/Оне ће у̀мрети/У̀мреће / Oni/One će umreti/Umreće	Они/Оне буду у̀мрли/у̀мрле / Oni/One budu umrli/umrle

	Past Tense (Перфект)	Pluperfect (Плусквамперфект)	Conditional (Потенцијал)
1st per	Ja сам у̀мро / Ja sam umro	Ja сам био у̀мро / Ja sam bio umro	Ja бих у̀мро / Ja bih umro
2nd per	Ти си у̀мро / Ti si umro	Ти си био у̀мро / Ti si bio umro	Ти би у̀мро / Ti bi umro
3rd per (M)	Он је у̀мро / On je umro	Он је био у̀мро / On je bio umro	Он би у̀мро / On bi umro
3rd per (F)	Она је у̀мрла / Ona je umrla	Она је била у̀мрла / Ona je bila umrla	Она би у̀мрла / Ona bi umrla
3rd per (N)	Оно је у̀мрло / Ono je umrlo	Оно је било у̀мрло / Ono je bilo umrlo	Оно би у̀мрло / Ono bi umrlo
1st per pl	Ми смо у̀мрли / Mi smo umrli	Ми смо били у̀мрли / Mi smo bili umrli	Ми бисмо у̀мрли / Mi bismo umrli
2nd per pl	Ви сте у̀мрли / Vi ste umrli	Ви сте били у̀мрли / Vi ste bili umrli	Ви бисте у̀мрли / Vi biste umrli
3rd per pl	Они су у̀мрли / Oni su umrli	Они су били у̀мрли / Oni su bili umrli	Они би у̀мрли / Oni bi umrli

	Imperative (Императив)
2nd per sg	(Ти) у̀мри / (Ti) umri
1st per pl	(Ми) у̀мримо / (Mi) umrimo
2nd per pl	(Ви) у̀мрите / (Vi) umrite

Non-finite Forms

Infinitive (Инфинитив)	у̏мрети **u**mreti
Present Adverbial Participle (Глаголски прилог садашњи)	--
Past Adverbial Participle (Глаголски прилог прошли)	у̏мревши **u**mrevši

	Active Adjectival Participle (Глаголски придев радни)		Passive Adjectival Participle (Глаголски придев трпни)	
Gender	Singular	Plural	Singular	Plural
Feminine	у̏мрла **u**mrla	у̏мрле **u**mrle	--	--
Masculine	у̏мро **u**mro	у̏мрли **u**mrli	--	--
Neuter	у̏мрло **u**mrlo	у̏мрла **u**mrla	--	--

To Do – òбавити - obaviti

	Present (Презент)	Future I (Футур први)	Future II (Футур други)
1st per	Ja òбавим Ja obavim	Ja ћу òбавити/Òбавићу Ja ću obaviti/Obaviću	Ja будем òбавио/òбавила Ja budem obavio/obavila
2nd per	Ти òбавиш Ti obaviš	Ти ћеш òбавити/Òбавићеш Ti ćeš obaviti/Obavićeš	Ти будеш òбавио/òбавила Ti budeš obavio/obavila
3rd per (M)	Он òбави On obavi	Он ће òбавити/Òбавиће On će obaviti/Obaviće	Он буде òбавио On bude obavio
3rd per (F)	Она òбави Ona obavi	Она ће òбавити/Òбавиће Ona će obaviti/Obaviće	Она буде òбавила Ona bude obavila
3rd per (N)	Оно òбави Ono obavi	Оно ће òбавити/Òбавиће Ono će obaviti/Obaviće	Оно буде òбавило Ono bude obavilo
1st per pl	Ми òбавимо Mi obavimo	Ми ћемо òбавити/Òбавићемо Mi ćemo obaviti/Obavićemo	Ми будемо òбавили/òбавиле Mi budemo obavili/obavile
2nd per pl	Ви òбавите Vi obavite	Ви ћете òбавити/Òбавићете Vi ćete obaviti/Obavićete	Ви будете òбавили/òбавиле Vi budete obavili/obavile
3rd per pl	Они/Оне òбаве Oni/One obave	Они/Оне ће òбавити/Òбавиће Oni/One će obaviti/Obaviće	Они/Оне буду òбавили/òбавиле Oni/One budu obavili/obavile

	Past Tense (Перфект)	Pluperfect (Плусквамперфект)	Conditional (Потенцијал)
1st per	Ja сам òбавио Ja sam obavio	Ja сам био òбавио Ja sam bio obavio	Ja бих òбавио Ja bih obavio
2nd per	Ти си òбавио Ti si obavio	Ти си био òбавио Ti si bio obavio	Ти би òбавио Ti bi obavio
3rd per (M)	Он је òбавио On je obavio	Он је био òбавио On je bio obavio	Он би òбавио On bi obavio
3rd per (F)	Она је òбавила Ona je obavila	Она је била òбавила Ona je bila obavila	Она би òбавила Ona bi obavila
3rd per (N)	Оно је òбавило Ono je obavilo	Оно је било òбавило Ono je bilo obavilo	Оно би òбавило Ono bi obavilo
1st per pl	Ми смо òбавили Mi smo obavili	Ми смо били òбавили Mi smo bili obavili	Ми бисмо òбавили Mi bismo obavili
2nd per pl	Ви сте òбавили Vi ste obavili	Ви сте били òбавили Vi ste bili obavili	Ви бисте òбавили Vi biste obavili
3rd per pl	Они су òбавили Oni su obavili	Они су били òбавили Oni su bili obavili	Они би òбавили Oni bi obavili

	Imperative (Императив)
2nd per sg	(Ти) òбави (Ti) obavi
1st per pl	(Ми) òбавимо (Mi) obavimo
2nd per pl	(Ви) òбавите (Vi) obavite

Non-finite Forms

Infinitive (Инфинитив)	òбавити **o**baviti
Present Adverbial Participle (Глаголски прилог садашњи)	--
Past Adverbial Participle (Глаголски прилог прошли)	òбавивши **o**bavivši

	Active Adjectival Participle (Глаголски придев радни)		Passive Adjectival Participle (Глаголски придев трпни)	
Gender	Singular	Plural	Singular	Plural
Feminine	òбавила **o**bavila	òбавиле **o**bavile	òбавњена **o**bavljena	òбавњене **o**bavljene
Masculine	òбавио **o**bavio	òбавили **o**bavili	òбавњен **o**bavljen	òбавњени **o**bavljeni
Neuter	òбавило **o**bavilo	òбавила **o**bavila	òбавњено **o**bavljeno	òбавњена **o**bavljena

To Drink - пи̏ти - piti

	Present (Презент)	Future I (Футур први)	Future II (Футур други)
1st per	Ja пи̏јем Ja **pi**jem	Ja ћу пи̏ти/Пи̏ћу Ja ću **piti/Pi**ću	Ja будем пи̏о/пи́ла Ja budem **pio/pi**la
2nd per	Ти пи̏јеш Ti **pi**ješ	Ти ћеш пи̏тиПи̏ћеш Ti ćeš **piti/Pi**ćeš	Ти будеш пи̏о/пи́ла Ti budeš **pio/pi**la
3rd per (M)	Он пи̏је On **pi**je	Он ће пи̏ти/Пи̏ће On će **piti/Pi**će	Он буде пи̏о On bude **pio**
3rd per (F)	Она пи̏је Ona **pi**je	Она ће пи̏ти/Пи̏ће Ona će **piti/Pi**će	Она буде пи́ла Ona bude **pi**la
3rd per (N)	Оно пи̏је Ono **pi**je	Оно ће пи̏ти/Пи̏ће Ono će **piti/Pi**će	Оно буде пи̏ло Ono bude **pi**lo
1st per pl	Ми пи̏јемо Mi **pi**jemo	Ми ћемо пи̏ти/Пи̏ћемо Mi ćemo **piti/Pi**ćemo	Ми будемо пи́ли/пи́ле Mi budemo **pili/pi**le
2nd per pl	Ви пи̏јете Vi **pi**jete	Ви ћете пи̏ти/Пи̏ћете Vi ćete **piti/Pi**ćete	Ви будете пи́ли/пи́ле Vi budete **pili/pi**le
3rd per pl	Они/Оне пи̏ју Oni/One **pi**ju	Они/Оне ће пи̏ти/Пи̏ће Oni/One će **piti/Pi**će	Они/Оне буду пи́ли/пи́ле Oni/One budu **pili/pi**le

	Past Tense (Перфект)	Pluperfect (Плусквамперфект)	Conditional (Потенцијал)
1st per	Ja сам пи̏о Ja sam **pio**	Ja сам био пи̏о Ja sam bio **pio**	Ja бих пи̏о Ja bih **pio**
2nd per	Ти си пи̏о Ti si **pio**	Ти си био пи̏о Ti si bio **pio**	Ти би пи̏о Ti bi **pio**
3rd per (M)	Он је пи̏о On je **pio**	Он је био пи̏о On je bio **pio**	Он би пи̏о On bi **pio**
3rd per (F)	Она је пи́ла Ona je **pi**la	Она је била пи́ла Ona je bila **pila**	Она би пи́ла Ona bi **pi**la
3rd per (N)	Оно је пи̏ло Ono je **pi**lo	Оно је било пи̏ло Ono je bilo **pilo**	Оно би пи̏ло Ono bi **pi**lo
1st per pl	Ми смо пи́ли Mi smo **pi**li	Ми смо били пи́ли Mi smo bili **pili**	Ми бисмо пи́ли Mi bismo **pili**
2nd per pl	Ви сте пи́ли Vi ste **pi**li	Ви сте били пи́ли Vi ste bili **pili**	Ви бисте пи́ли Vi biste **pili**
3rd per pl	Они су пи́ли Oni su **pi**li	Они су били пи́ли Oni su bili **pili**	Они би пи́ли Oni bi **pili**

	Imperative (Императив)
2nd per sg	(Ти) пи̏ј (Ti) pij
1st per pl	(Ми) пи̏јмо (Mi) **pi**jmo

2nd per pl	(Ви) пи̑јте (Vi) **pi**jte

Non-finite Forms

Infinitive (Инфинитив)	пи̏ти **pi**ti
Present Adverbial Participle (Глаголски прилог садашњи)	пи̏ју̀ћи **pi**jući
Past Adverbial Participle (Глаголски прилог прошли)	--

	Active Adjectival Participle (Глаголски придев радни)		Passive Adjectival Participle (Глаголски придев трпни)	
Gender	Singular	Plural	Singular	Plural
Feminine	пи́ла **pi**la	пи́ле **pi**le	--	--
Masculine	пи̏о **pi**o	пи́ли **pi**li	--	--
Neuter	пи́ло **pi**lo	пи́ла **pi**la	--	--

To Drive – вòзити - voziti

	Present (Презент)	Future I (Футур први)	Future II (Футур други)
1st per	Ja вòзим Ja vozim	Ja ћу возѝти/Вòзићу Ja ću voziti/Vozićú	Ja будем вòзио/вòзила Ja budem vozio/vozila
2nd per	Ти вòзиш Ti voziš	Ти ћеш возѝти/Вòзићеш Ti ćeš voziti/Vozićeš	Ти будеш вòзио/вòзила Ti budeš vozio/vozila
3rd per (M)	Он вòзи On vozi	Он ће возѝти/Вòзиће On će voziti/Voziće	Он буде вòзио On bude vozio
3rd per (F)	Она вòзи Ona vozi	Она ће возѝти/Вòзиће Ona će voziti/Voziće	Она буде вòзила Ona bude vozila
	Оно вòзи Ono vozi	Оно ће возѝти/Вòзиће Ono će voziti/Voziće	Оно буде вòзило Ono bude vozilo
3rd per (N) 1st per pl	Ми вòзимо Mi vozimo	Ми ћемо возѝти/Вòзићемо Mi ćemo voziti/Vozićemo	Ми будемо вòзили/вòзиле Mi budemo vozili/vozile
2nd per pl	Ви вòзите Vi vozite	Ви ћете возѝти/Вòзићете Vi ćete voziti/Vozićete	Ви будете вòзили/вòзиле Vi budete vozili/vozile
3rd per pl	Они/Оне вòзе Oni/One voze	Они/Оне ће возѝти/Вòзиће Oni/One će voziti/Voziće	Они/Оне буду вòзили/вòзиле Oni/One budu vozili/vozile

	Past Tense (Перфект)	Pluperfect (Плусквамперфект)	Conditional (Потенцијал)
1st per	Ja сам вòзио Ja sam vozio	Ja сам био вòзио Ja sam bio vozio	Ja бих вòзио Ja bih vozio
2nd per	Ти си вòзио Ti si vozio	Ти си био вòзио Ti si bio vozio	Ти би вòзио Ti bi vozio
3rd per (M)	Он је вòзио On je vozio	Он је био вòзио On je bio vozio	Он би вòзио On bi vozio
3rd per (F)	Она је вòзила Ona je vozila	Она је била вòзила Ona je bila vozila	Она би вòзила Ona bi vozila
3rd per (N)	Оно је вòзило Ono je vozilo	Оно је било вòзило Ono je bilo vozilo	Оно би вòзило Ono bi vozilo
1st per pl	Ми смо вòзили Mi smo vozili	Ми смо били вòзили Mi smo bili vozili	Ми бисмо вòзили Mi bismo vozili
2nd per pl	Ви сте вòзили Vi ste vozili	Ви сте били вòзили Vi ste bili vozili	Ви бисте вòзили Vi biste vozili
3rd per pl	Они су вòзили Oni su vozili	Они су били вòзили Oni su bili vozili	Они би вòзили Oni bi vozili

	Imperative (Императив)
2nd per sg	(Ти) вòзи (Ti) vozi
1st per pl	(Ми) вòзимо (Mi) vozimo

2nd per pl	(Ви) во̀зите
	(Vi) **vo**zite

Non-finite Forms

Infinitive (Инфинитив)	во̀зити
	voziti
Present Adverbial Participle (Глаголски прилог садашњи)	во̀зећи
	vozeći
Past Adverbial Participle (Глаголски прилог прошли)	--

	Active Adjectival Participle (Глаголски придев радни)		Passive Adjectival Participle (Глаголски придев трпни)	
Gender	Singular	Plural	Singular	Plural
Feminine	во̀зила	во̀зиле	во̏жена	во̏жене
	vozila	**vo**zile	**vo**žena	**vo**žene
Masculine	во̀зио	во̀зили	во̏жен	во̏жени
	vozio	**vo**zili	**vo**žen	**vo**ženi
Neuter	во̀зило	во̀зила	во̏жено	во̏жена
	vozilo	**vo**zila	**vo**ženo	**vo**žena

To Eat - jȅсти - jesti

	Present (Презент)	Future I (Футур први)	Future II (Футур други)
1st per	Ja jèдем / Ja **jedem**	Ja ћу jȅсти/Jȅшћу / Ja ću **jesti**/**Ješću**	Ja будем jȅо/jȅла / Ja budem **je**o/**je**la
2nd per	Ти jèдеш / Ti **jedeš**	Ти ћеш jȅсти/Jȅшћеш / Ti ćeš **jesti**/**Ješćeš**	Ти будеш jȅо/jȅла / Ti budeš **je**o/**je**la
3rd per (M)	Он jèде / On **jede**	Он ће jȅсти/Jȅшће / On će **jesti**/**Ješće**	Он буде jȅо / On bude **je**o
3rd per (F)	Она jèде / Ona **jede**	Она ће jȅсти/Jȅшће / Ona će **jesti**/**Ješće**	Она буде jȅла / Ona bude **je**la
3rd per (N)	Оно jèде / Ono **jede**	Оно ће jȅсти/Jȅшће / Ono će **jesti**/**Ješće**	Оно буде jȅло / Ono bude **je**lo
1st per pl	Ми jèдемо / Mi **jedemo**	Ми ћемо jȅсти/Jȅшћемо / Mi ćemo **jesti**/**Ješćemo**	Ми будемо jȅли/jȅле / Mi budemo **je**li/**je**le
2nd per pl	Ви jèдете / Vi **jedete**	Ви ћете jȅсти/Jȅшћете / Vi ćete **jesti**/**Ješćete**	Ви будете jȅли/jȅле / Vi budete **je**li/**je**le
3rd per pl	Они/Оне jèду / Oni/One **jedu**	Они/Оне ће jȅсти/Jȅшће / Oni/One će **jesti**/**Ješće**	Они/Оне буду jȅли/jȅле / Oni/One budu **je**li/**je**le

	Past Tense (Перфект)	Pluperfect (Плусквамперфект)	Conditional (Потенцијал)
1st per	Ja сам jȅо / Ja sam **je**o	Ja сам био jȅо / Ja sam bio **je**o	Ja бих jȅо / Ja bih **je**o
2nd per	Ти си jȅо / Ti si **je**o	Ти си био jȅо / Ti si bio **je**o	Ти би jȅо / Ti bi **je**o
3rd per (M)	Он је jȅо / On je **je**o	Он је био jȅо / On je bio **je**o	Он би jȅо / On bi **je**o
3rd per (F)	Она је jȅла / Ona je **je**la	Она је била jȅла / Ona je bila **je**la	Она би jȅла / Ona bi **je**la
3rd per (N)	Оно је jȅло / Ono je **je**lo	Оно је било jȅло / Ono je bilo **je**lo	Оно би jȅло / Ono bi **je**lo
1st per pl	Ми смо jȅли / Mi smo **je**li	Ми смо били jȅли / Mi smo bili **je**li	Ми бисмо jȅли / Mi bismo **je**li
2nd per pl	Ви сте jȅли / Vi ste **je**li	Ви сте били jȅли / Vi ste bili **je**li	Ви бисте jȅли / Vi biste **je**li
3rd per pl	Они су jȅли / Oni su **je**li	Они су били jȅли / Oni su bili **je**li	Они би jȅли / Oni bi **je**li

	Imperative (Императив)
2nd per sg	(Ти) jèди / (Ti) **jedi**
1st per pl	(Ми) jèдимо / (Mi) **jedimo**

2nd per pl	(Ви) једѝте
	(Vi) **je**dite

Non-finite Forms

Infinitive (Инфинитив)	jȅсти
	jesti
Present Adverbial Participle (Глаголски прилог садашњи)	jèдуħи
	jedući
Past Adverbial Participle (Глаголски прилог прошли)	--

	Active Adjectival Participle (Глаголски придев радни)		Passive Adjectival Participle (Глаголски придев трпни)	
Gender	Singular	Plural	Singular	Plural
Feminine	jȅла	jȅле	jèдена	jèдене
	jela	**je**le	**je**dena	**je**dene
Masculine	jȅо	jȅли	jèден	jèдени
	jeo	**je**li	**je**den	**je**deni
Neuter	jȅло	jȅла	jèдено	jèдена
	jelo	**je**la	**je**deno	**je**dena

To Enter - ýħи - ući

	Present (Презент)	Future I (Футур први)	Future II (Футур други)
1st per	Ja ýħем / Ja uđem	Ja ħy ýħи/Ýħи ħy / Ja ću ući/Ući ću	Ja будем ỳшao/ỳшла / Ja budem ušao/ušla
2nd per	Ти ýħеш / Ti uđeš	Ти ħeш ýħи/Ýħи ħeш / Ti ćeš ući/Ući ćeš	Ти будеш ỳшao/ỳшла / Ti budeš ušao/ušla
3rd per (M)	Он ýħе / On uđe	Он ħe ýħи/Ýħи ħe / On će ući/Ući će	Он буде ỳшao / On bude ušao
3rd per (F)	Она ýħе / Ona uđe	Она ħe ýħи/Ýħи ħe / Ona će ući/Ući će	Она буде ỳшла / Ona bude ušla
3rd per (N)	Оно ýħе / Ono uđe	Оно ħe ýħи/Ýħи ħe / Ono će ući/Ući će	Оно буде ỳшло / Ono bude ušlo
1st per pl	Ми ýħемо / Mi uđemo	Ми ħemo ýħи/Ýħи ħemo / Mi ćemo ući/Ući ćemo	Ми будемо ỳшли/ỳшле / Mi budemo ušli/ušle
2nd per pl	Ви ýħете / Vi uđete	Ви ħете ýħи/Ýħи ħете / Vi ćete ući/Ući ćete	Ви будете ỳшли/ỳшле / Vi budete ušli/ušle
3rd per pl	Они/Оне ýħy / Oni/One uđu	Они/Оне ħe ýħи/Ýħи ħe / Oni/One će ući/Ući će	Они/Оне буду ỳшли/ỳшле / Oni/One budu ušli/ušle

	Past Tense (Перфект)	Pluperfect (Плусквамперфект)	Conditional (Потенцијал)
1st per	Ja сам ỳшao / Ja sam ušao	Ja сам био ỳшao / Ja sam bio ušao	Ja бих ỳшao / Ja bih ušao
2nd per	Ти си ỳшao / Ti si ušao	Ти си био ỳшao / Ti si bio ušao	Ти би ỳшao / Ti bi ušao
3rd per (M)	Он је ỳшao / On je ušao	Он је био ỳшao / On je bio ušao	Он би ỳшao / On bi ušao
3rd per (F)	Она је ỳшла / Ona je ušla	Она је била ỳшла / Ona je bila ušla	Она би ỳшла / Ona bi ušla
3rd per (N)	Оно је ỳшло / Ono je ušlo	Оно је било ỳшло / Ono je bilo ušlo	Оно би ỳшло / Ono bi ušlo
1st per pl	Ми смо ỳшли / Mi smo ušli	Ми смо били ỳшли / Mi smo bili ušli	Ми бисмо ỳшли / Mi bismo ušli
2nd per pl	Ви сте ỳшли / Vi ste ušli	Ви сте били ỳшли / Vi ste bili ušli	Ви бисте ỳшли / Vi biste ušli
3rd per pl	Они су ỳшли / Oni su ušli	Они су били ỳшли / Oni su bili ušli	Они би ỳшли / Oni bi ušli

	Imperative (Императив)
2nd per sg	(Ти) ýħи / (Ti) uđi
1st per pl	(Ми) ýħимо / (Mi) uđimo

2nd per pl	(Ви) у̀ђите
	(Vi) u**đ**ite

Non-finite Forms

Infinitive (Инфинитив)	у́ђи
	u**ć**i
Present Adverbial Participle (Глаголски прилог садашњи)	--
Past Adverbial Participle (Глаголски прилог прошли)	у̀шавши
	u**š**avši

	Active Adjectival Participle (Глаголски придев радни)		Passive Adjectival Participle (Глаголски придев трпни)	
Gender	Singular	Plural	Singular	Plural
Feminine	у̀шла	у̀шле	--	--
	u**š**la	u**š**le		
Masculine	у̀шао	у̀шли	--	--
	u**š**ao	u**š**li		
Neuter	у̀шло	у̀шла	--	--
	u**š**lo	u**š**la		

To Exit - изáћи - izaći

	Present (Презент)	Future I (Футур први)	Future II (Футур други)
1st per	Ja изáђем Ja izađem	Ja ћу изáћи/Изáћи ћу Ja ću izaći/Izaći ću	Ja будем изашао/изашла Ja budem izašao/izašla
2nd per	Ти изáђеш Ti izađeš	Ти ћеш изáћи/Изáћи ћеш Ti ćeš izaći/Izaći ćeš	Ти будеш изашао/изашла Ti budeš izašao/izašla
3rd per (M)	Он изáђе On izađe	Он ће изáћи/Изáћи ће On će izaći/Izaći će	Он буде изашао On bude izašao
3rd per (F)	Она изáђе Ona izađe	Она ће изáћи/Изáћи ће Ona će izaći/Izaći će	Она буде изашла Ona bude izašla
3rd per (N)	Оно изáђе Ono izađe	Оно ће изáћи/Изáћи ће Ono će izaći/Izaći će	Оно буде изашло Ono bude izašlo
1st per pl	Ми изáђемо Mi izađemo	Ми ћемо изáћи/Изáћи ћемо Mi ćemo izaći/Izaći ćemo	Ми будемо изашли/изашле Mi budemo izašli/izašle
2nd per pl	Ви изáђете Vi izađete	Ви ћете изáћи/ Изáћи ћете Vi ćete izaći/ Izaći ćete	Ви будете изашли/изашле Vi budete izašli/izašle
3rd per pl	Они/Оне изáђу Oni/One izađu	Они/Оне ће изáћи/Изáћи ће Oni/One će izaći/Izaći će	Они/Оне буду изашли/изашле Vi budete izašli/izašle

	Past Tense (Перфект)	Pluperfect (Плусквамперфект)	Conditional (Потенцијал)
1st per	Ja сам изашао Ja sam izašao	Ja сам био изашао Ja sam bio izašao	Ja бих изашао Ja bih izašao
2nd per	Ти си изашао Ti si izašao	Ти си био изашао Ti si bio izašao	Ти би изашао Ti bi izašao
3rd per (M)	Он је изашао On je izašao	Он је био изашао On je bio izašao	Он би изашао On bi izašao
3rd per (F)	Она је изашла Ona je izašla	Она је била изашла Ona je bila izašla	Она би изашла Ona bi izašla
3rd per (N)	Оно је изашло Ono je izašlo	Оно је било изашло Ono je bilo izašlo	Оно би изашло Ono bi izašlo
1st per pl	Ми смо изашли Mi smo izašli	Ми смо били изашли Mi smo bili izašli	Ми бисмо изашли Mi bismo izašli
2nd per pl	Ви сте изашли Vi ste izašli	Ви сте били изашли Vi ste bili izašli	Ви бисте изашли Vi biste izašli
3rd per pl	Они су изашли Oni su izašli	Они су били изашли Oni su bili izašli	Они би изашли Oni bi izašli

	Imperative (Императив)
2nd per sg	(Ти) изáћи (Ti) izađi
1st per pl	(Ми) изáћимо (Mi) izađimo

2nd per pl	(Ви) изáђите
	(Vi) izađite

Non-finite Forms

Infinitive (Инфинитив)	изáћи
	izaći
Present Adverbial Participle (Глаголски прилог садашњи)	--
Past Adverbial Participle (Глаголски прилог прошли)	изáшавши
	izašavši

	Active Adjectival Participle (Глаголски придев радни)		Passive Adjectival Participle (Глаголски придев трпни)	
Gender	Singular	Plural	Singular	Plural
Feminine	изашла	изашле	--	--
	izašla	izašle		
Masculine	изашао	изашли	--	--
	izašao	izašli		
Neuter	изашло	изашла	--	--
	izašlo	izašla		

To Explain - објáснити - objasniti

	Present (Презент)	Future I (Футур први)	Future II (Футур други)
1st per	Ja òбјасним Ja **ob**jasnim	Ja ћу објáснити/Објáснићу Ja ću objasniti/Objasniću	Ja будем објáснио/објáснила Ja budem objasnio/objasnila
2nd per	Ти òбјасниш Ti **ob**jasniš	Ти ћеш објáснити/Објáснићеш Ti ćeš objasniti/Objasnićeš	Ти будеш објáснио/објáснила Ti budeš objasnio/objasnila
3rd per (M)	Он òбјасни On **ob**jasni	Он ће објáснити/Објáсниће On će objasniti/Objasniće	Он буде објáснио On bude objasnio
3rd per (F)	Она òбјасни Ona **ob**jasni	Она ће објáснити/Објáсниће Ona će objasniti/Objasniće	Она буде објáснила Ona bude objasnila
3rd per (N)	Оно òбјасни Ono **ob**jasni	Оно ће објáснити/Објáсниће Ono će objasniti/Objasniće	Оно буде објáснило Ono bude objasnilo
1st per pl	Ми òбјаснимо Mi **ob**jasnimo	Ми ћемо објáснити/Објáснићемо Mi ćemo objasniti/Objasnićemo	Ми будемо објáснили/објáсниле Mi budemo objasnili/objasnile
2nd per pl	Ви òбјасните Vi **ob**jasnite	Ви ћете објáснити/Објáснићете Vi ćete objasniti/Objasnićete	Ви будете објáснили/објáсниле Vi budete objasnili/objasnile
3rd per pl	Они/Оне òбјасне Oni/One **ob**jasne	Они/Оне ће објáснити/Објáсниће Oni/One će objasniti/Objasniće	Они/Оне буду објáснили/објáсниле Oni/One budu objasnili/objasnile

	Past Tense (Перфект)	Pluperfect (Плусквамперфект)	Conditional (Потенцијал)
1st per	Ja сам објáснио Ja sam objasnio	Ja сам био објáснио Ja sam bio objasnio	Ja бих објáснио Ja bih objasnio
2nd per	Ти си објáснио Ti si objasnio	Ти си био објáснио Ti si bio objasnio	Ти би објáснио Ti bi objasnio
3rd per (M)	Он је објáснио On je objasnio	Он је био објáснио On je bio objasnio	Он би објáснио On bi objasnio
3rd per (F)	Она је објáснила Ona je objasnila	Она је била објáснила Ona je bila objasnila	Она би објáснила Ona bi objasnila
3rd per (N)	Оно је објáснило Ono je objasnilo	Оно је било објáснило Ono je bilo objasnilo	Оно би објáснило Ono bi objasnilo
1st per pl	Ми смо објáснили Mi smo objasnili	Ми смо били објáснили Mi smo bili objasnili	Ми бисмо објáснили Mi bismo objasnili
2nd per pl	Ви сте објáснили Vi ste objasnili	Ви сте били објáснили Vi ste bili objasnili	Ви бисте објáснили Vi biste objasnili
3rd per pl	Они су објáснили Oni su objasnili	Они су били објáснили Oni su bili objasnili	Они би објáснили Oni bi objasnili

	Imperative (Императив)
2nd per sg	(Ти) објáсни (Ti) objasni
1st per pl	(Ми) објáснимо (Mi) objasnimo

2nd per pl	(Ви) објáсните
	(Vi) ob**ja**snite

Non-finite Forms

Infinitive (Инфинитив)	објáснити
	ob**ja**sniti
Present Adverbial Participle (Глаголски прилог садашњи)	--
Past Adverbial Participle (Глаголски прилог прошли)	објáснивши
	ob**ja**snivši

	Active Adjectival Participle (Глаголски придев радни)		Passive Adjectival Participle (Глаголски придев трпни)	
Gender	Singular	Plural	Singular	Plural
Feminine	објáснила	објáсниле	о̀бјашњена	о̀бјашњене
	ob**ja**snila	ob**ja**snile	**ob**jašnjena	**ob**jašnjene
Masculine	објáснио	објáснили	о̀бјашњен	о̀бјашњени
	ob**ja**snio	ob**ja**snili	**ob**jašnjen	**ob**jašnjeni
Neuter	објáснило	објáснила	о̀бјашњено	о̀бјашњена
	ob**ja**snilo	ob**ja**snila	**ob**jašnjeno	**ob**jašnjena

To Fall - па̏сти - pasti

	Present (Презент)	Future I (Футур први)	Future II (Футур други)
1st per	Ja па̏днем Ja **pad**nem	Ja ћу па̏сти/Па̏шћу Ja ću **pa**sti/**Pa**šću	Ja будем па̏о/па̏ла Ja budem **pa**o/**pa**la
2nd per	Ти па̏днеш Ti **pad**neš	Ти ћеш па̏сти/Па̏шћеш Ti ćeš **pa**sti/**Pa**šćeš	Ти будеш па̏о/па̏ла Ti budeš **pa**o/**pa**la
3rd per (M)	Он па̏дне On **pad**ne	Он ће па̏сти/Па̏шће On će **pa**sti/**Pa**šće	Он буде па̏о On bude **pa**o
3rd per (F)	Она па̏дне Ona **pad**ne	Она ће па̏сти/Па̏шће Ona će **pa**sti/**Pa**šće	Она буде па̏ла Ona bude **pa**la
3rd per (N)	Оно па̏дне Ono **pad**ne	Оно ће па̏сти/Па̏шће Ono će **pa**sti/**Pa**šće	Оно буде па̏ло Ono bude **pa**lo
1st per pl	Ми па̏днемо Mi **pad**nemo	Ми ћемо па̏сти/Па̏шћемо Mi ćemo **pa**sti/**Pa**šćemo	Ми будемо па̏ли/па̏ле Mi budemo **pa**li/**pa**le
2nd per pl	Ви па̏днете Vi **pad**nete	Ви ћете па̏сти/Па̏шћете Vi ćete **pa**sti/**Pa**šćete	Ви будете па̏ли/па̏ле Vi budete **pa**li/**pa**le
3rd per pl	Они/Оне па̏дну Oni/One **pad**nu	Они/Оне ће па̏сти/Па̏шће Oni/One će **pa**sti/**Pa**šće	Они/Оне буду па̏ли/па̏ле Oni/One budu **pa**li/**pa**le

	Past Tense (Перфект)	Pluperfect (Плусквамперфект)	Conditional (Потенцијал)
1st per	Ja сам па̏о Ja sam **pa**o	Ja сам био па̏о Ja sam bio **pa**o	Ja бих па̏о Ja bih **pa**o
2nd per	Ти си па̏о Ti si **pa**o	Ти си био па̏о Ti si bio **pa**o	Ти би па̏о Ti bi **pa**o
3rd per (M)	Он је па̏о On je **pa**o	Он је био па̏о On je bio **pa**o	Он би па̏о On bi **pa**o
3rd per (F)	Она је па̏ла Ona je **pa**la	Она је била па̏ла Ona je bila **pa**la	Она би па̏ла Ona bi **pa**la
3rd per (N)	Оно је па̏ло Ono je **pa**lo	Оно је било па̏ло Ono je bilo **pa**lo	Оно би па̏ло Ono bi **pa**lo
1st per pl	Ми смо па̏ли Mi smo **pa**li	Ми смо били па̏ли Mi smo bili **pa**li	Ми бисмо па̏ли Mi bismo **pa**li
2nd per pl	Ви сте па̏ли Vi ste **pa**li	Ви сте били па̏ли Vi ste bili **pa**li	Ви бисте па̏ли Vi biste **pa**li
3rd per pl	Они су па̏ли Oni su **pa**li	Они су били па̏ли Oni su bili **pa**li	Они би па̏ли Oni bi **pa**li

	Imperative (Императив)
2nd per sg	(Ти) па̏дни (Ti) **pad**ni
1st per pl	(Ми) па̏днимо (Mi) **pad**nimo

69

2ⁿᵈ per pl	(Ви) пȁдните
	(Vi) **pa**dnite

Non-finite Forms

Infinitive (Инфинитив)	пȁсти
	pasti
Present Adverbial Participle (Глаголски прилог садашњи)	--
Past Adverbial Participle (Глаголски прилог прошли)	пȁднувши
	padnuvši

	Active Adjectival Participle (Глаголски придев радни)		Passive Adjectival Participle (Глаголски придев трпни)	
Gender	Singular	Plural	Singular	Plural
Feminine	пȁла	пȁле	--	--
	pala	**pa**le		
Masculine	пȁо	пȁли	--	--
	pao	**pa**li		
Neuter	пȁло	пȁла	--	--
	palo	**pa**la		

To Feel – òсећати - osećati

	Present (Презент)	Future I (Футур први)	Future II (Футур други)
1st per	Ja òсећам / Ja osećam	Ja ћу òсећати/Òсећаћу / Ja ћu osećati/Osećaћu	Ja будем òсећао/òсећала / Ja budem osećao/osećala
2nd per	Ти òсећаш / Ti osećaš	Ти ћеш òсећати/Òсећаћеш / Ti ћeš osećati/Osećaћeš	Ти будеш òсећао/òсећала / Ti budeš osećao/osećala
3rd per (M)	Он òсећа / On oseća	Он ће òсећати/Òсећаће / On ће osećati/Osećaće	Он буде òсећао / On bude osećao
3rd per (F)	Она òсећа / Ona oseća	Она ће òсећати/Òсећаће / Ona ће osećati/Osećaće	Она буде òсећала / Ona bude osećala
3rd per (N)	Оно òсећа / Ono oseća	Оно ће òсећати/Òсећаће / Ono ће osećati/Osećaће	Оно буде òсећало / Ono bude osećalo
1st per pl	Ми òсећамо / Mi osećamo	Ми ћемо òсећати/Òсећаћемо / Mi ћemo osećati/Osećaћemo	Ми будемо òсећали/òсећале / Mi budemo osećali/osećale
2nd per pl	Ви òсећате / Vi osećate	Ви ћете òсећати/Òсећаћете / Vi ћete osećati/Osećaћete	Ви будете òсећали/òсећале / Vi budete osećali/osećale
3rd per pl	Они/Оне òсећају / Oni/One osećaju	Они/Оне ће òсећати/Òсећаће / Oni/One ће osećati/Osećaће	Они/Оне буду òсећали/òсећале / Oni/One budu osećali/osećale

	Past Tense (Перфект)	Pluperfect (Плусквамперфект)	Conditional (Потенцијал)
1st per	Ja сам òсећао / Ja sam osećao	Ja сам био òсећао / Ja sam bio osećao	Ja бих òсећао / Ja bih osećao
2nd per	Ти си òсећао / Ti si osećao	Ти си био òсећао / Ti si bio osećao	Ти би òсећао / Ti bi osećao
3rd per (M)	Он је òсећао / On je osećao	Он је био òсећао / On je bio osećao	Он би òсећао / On bi osećao
3rd per (F)	Она је òсећала / Ona je osećala	Она је била òсећала / Ona je bila osećala	Она би òсећала / Ona bi osećala
3rd per (N)	Оно је òсећало / Ono je osećalo	Оно је било òсећало / Ono je bilo osećalo	Оно би òсећало / Ono bi osećalo
1st per pl	Ми смо òсећали / Mi smo osećali	Ми смо били òсећали / Mi smo bili osećali	Ми бисмо òсећали / Mi bismo osećali
2nd per pl	Ви сте òсећали / Vi ste osećali	Ви сте били òсећали / Vi ste bili osećali	Ви бисте òсећали / Vi biste osećali
3rd per pl	Они су òсећали / Oni su osećali	Они су били òсећали / Oni su bili osećali	Они би òсећали / Oni bi osećali

	Imperative (Императив)
2nd per sg	(Ти) òсећај / (Ti) osećaj
1st per pl	(Ми) òсећајмо / (Mi) osećajmo

| 2nd per pl | (Ви) òсећајте |
| | (Vi) osećajte |

Non-finite Forms

Infinitive (Инфинитив)	òсећати
	osećati
Present Adverbial Participle (Глаголски прилог садашњи)	òсећајући
	osećajući
Past Adverbial Participle (Глаголски прилог прошли)	òсећавши
	osećavši

	Active Adjectival Participle (Глаголски придев радни)		Passive Adjectival Participle (Глаголски придев трпни)	
Gender	Singular	Plural	Singular	Plural
Feminine	òсећала	òсећале	--	--
	osećala	osećale		
Masculine	òсећао	òсећали	--	--
	osećao	osećali		
Neuter	òсећало	òсећала	--	--
	osećalo	osećala		

To Fight – бȍрити се – boriti se

	Present (Презент)	Future I (Футур први)	Future II (Футур други)
1st per	Ja се бȍрим Ja se **bo**rim	Ja ћу се бȍрити/Бȍрићу се Ja ću se **bo**riti/**Bo**riću se	Ja се будем бȍрио/бȍрила Ja se budem **bo**rio/**bo**rila
2nd per	Ти се бȍриш Ti se **bo**riš	Ти ћеш се бȍрити/Бȍрићеш се Ti ćeš se **bo**riti/**Bo**rićeš se	Ти се будеш бȍрио/бȍрила Ti se budeš **bo**rio/**bo**rila
3rd per (M)	Он се бȍри On se **bo**ri	Он ће се бȍрити/Бȍриће се On će se **bo**riti/**Bo**riće se	Он се буде бȍрио On se bude **bo**rio
3rd per (F)	Она се бȍри Ona se **bo**ri	Она ће се бȍрити/Бȍриће се Ona će se **bo**riti/**Bo**riće se	Она се буде бȍрила Ona se bude **bo**rila
3rd per (N)	Оно се бȍри Ono se **bo**ri	Оно ће се бȍрити/Бȍриће се Ono će se **bo**riti/**Bo**riće se	Оно се буде бȍрило Ono se bude **bo**rilo
1st per pl	Ми се бȍримо Mi se **bo**rimo	Ми ћемо се бȍрити/Бȍрићемо се Mi ćemo se **bo**riti/**Bo**rićemo se	Ми се будемо бȍрили/бȍриле Mi se budemo **bo**rili/**bo**rile
2nd per pl	Ви се бȍрите Vi se **bo**rite	Ви ћете се бȍрити/Бȍрићете се Vi ćete se **bo**riti/**Bo**rićete se	Ви се будете бȍрили/бȍриле Vi se budete **bo**rili/**bo**rile
3rd per pl	Они/Оне се бȍре Oni/One se **bo**re	Они/Оне ће се бȍрити/Бȍриће се Oni/One će se **bo**riti/**Bo**riće se	Они/Оне се буду бȍрили/бȍриле Oni/One se budu **bo**rili/**bo**rile

	Past Tense (Перфект)	Pluperfect (Плусквамперфект)	Conditional (Потенцијал)
1st per	Ja сам се бȍрио Ja sam se **bo**rio	Ja сам се био бȍрио Ja sam se bio **bo**rio	Ja бих се бȍрио Ja bih se **bo**rio
2nd per	Ти си се бȍрио Ti si se **bo**rio	Ти си се био бȍрио Ti si se bio **bo**rio	Ти би се бȍрио Ti bi se **bo**rio
3rd per (M)	Он се бȍрио On se **bo**rio	Он се био бȍрио On se bio **bo**rio	Он би се бȍрио On bi se **bo**rio
3rd per (F)	Она се бȍрила Ona se **bo**rila	Она се била бȍрила Ona se bila **bo**rila	Она би се бȍрила Ona bi se **bo**rila
3rd per (N)	Оно се бȍрило Ono se **bo**rilo	Оно се било бȍрило Ono se bilo **bo**rilo	Оно би се бȍрило Ono bi se **bo**rilo
1st per pl	Ми смо се бȍрили Mi smo se **bo**rili	Ми смо се били бȍрили Mi smo se bili **bo**rili	Ми бисмо се бȍрили Mi bismo se **bo**rili
2nd per pl	Ви сте се бȍрили Vi ste se **bo**rili	Ви сте се били бȍрили Vi ste se bili **bo**rili	Ви бисте се бȍрили Vi biste se **bo**rili
3rd per pl	Они су се бȍрили Oni su se **bo**rili	Они су се били бȍрили Oni su se bili **bo**rili	Они би се бȍрили Oni bi se **bo**rili

	Imperative (Императив)
2nd per sg	(Ти) бȍри се (Ti) **bo**ri se
1st per pl	(Ми) бȍримо се (Mi) **bo**rimo se

2nd per pl	(Ви) бо̀рите се (Vi) **bo**rite se

Non-finite Forms

Infinitive (Инфинитив)	бо̀рити се **bo**riti se
Present Adverbial Participle (Глаголски прилог садашњи)	бо̀рећи се **bo**reći se
Past Adverbial Participle (Глаголски прилог прошли)	--

	Active Adjectival Participle (Глаголски придев радни)		Passive Adjectival Participle (Глаголски придев трпни)	
Gender	Singular	Plural	Singular	Plural
Feminine	бо̀рила **bo**rila	бо̀риле **bo**rile	--	--
Masculine	бо̀рио **bo**rio	бо̀рили **bo**rili	--	--
Neuter	бо̀рило **bo**rilo	бо̀рила **bo**rila	--	--

To Find - на̀ћи - naći

	Present (Презент)	Future I (Футур први)	Future II (Футур други)
1st per	Ja на̂ђем / Ja naђem	Ja ћу на̀ћи/На̀ћи ћу / Ja ћу naći/Naći ћu	Ja будем на̀шао/на̀шла / Ja budem našao/našla
2nd per	Ти на̂ђеш / Ti naђeš	Ти ћеш на̀ћи/На̀ћи ћеш / Ti ćeš naći/Naći ćeš	Ти будеш на̀шао/на̀шла / Ti budeš našao/našla
3rd per (M)	Он на̂ђе / On naђe	Он ће на̀ћи/На̀ћи ће / On će naći/Naći će	Он буде на̀шао / On bude našao
3rd per (F)	Она на̂ђе / Ona naђe	Она ће на̀ћи/На̀ћи ће / Ona će naći/Naći će	Она буде на̀шла / Ona bude našla
3rd per (N)	Оно на̂ђе / Ono naђe	Оно ће на̀ћи/На̀ћи ће / Ono će naći/Naći će	Оно буде на̀шло / Ono bude našlo
1st per pl	Ми на̂ђемо / Mi naђemo	Ми ћемо на̀ћи/На̀ћи ћемо / Mi ćemo naći/Naći ćemo	Ми будемо на̀шли/на̀шле / Mi budemo našli/našle
2nd per pl	Ви на̂ђете / Vi naђete	Ви ћете на̀ћи/На̀ћи ћете / Vi ćete naći/Naći ćete	Ви будете на̀шли/на̀шле / Vi budete našli/našle
3rd per pl	Они/Оне на̂ђу / Oni/One naђu	Они/Оне ће на̀ћи/На̀ћи ће / Oni/One će naći/Naći će	Они/Оне буду на̀шли/на̀шле / Oni/One budu našli/našle

	Past Tense (Перфект)	Pluperfect (Плусквамперфект)	Conditional (Потенцијал)
1st per	Ja сам на̀шао / Ja sam našao	Ja сам био на̀шао / Ja sam bio našao	Ja бих на̀шао / Ja bih našao
2nd per	Ти си на̀шао / Ti si našao	Ти си био на̀шао / Ti si bio našao	Ти би на̀шао / Ti bi našao
3rd per (M)	Он је на̀шао / On je našao	Он је био на̀шао / On je bio našao	Он би на̀шао / On bi našao
3rd per (F)	Она је на̀шла / Ona je našla	Она је била на̀шла / Ona je bila našla	Она би на̀шла / Ona bi našla
3rd per (N)	Оно је на̀шло / Ono je našlo	Оно је било на̀шло / Ono je bilo našlo	Оно би на̀шло / Ono bi našlo
1st per pl	Ми смо на̀шли / Mi smo našli	Ми смо били на̀шли / Mi smo bili našli	Ми бисмо на̀шли / Mi bismo našli
2nd per pl	Ви сте на̀шли / Vi ste našli	Ви сте били на̀шли / Vi ste bili našli	Ви бисте на̀шли / Vi biste našli
3rd per pl	Они су на̀шли / Oni su našli	Они су били на̀шли / Oni su bili našli	Они би на̀шли / Oni bi našli

	Imperative (Императив)
2nd per sg	(Ти) на̂ђи / (Ti) naђi
1st per pl	(Ми) на̂ђимо / (Mi) naђimo
2nd per pl	(Ви) на̂ђите / (Mi) naђite

Non-finite Forms

Infinitive (Инфинитив)	на̏ћи **na**ći
Present Adverbial Participle (Глаголски прилог садашњи)	--
Past Adverbial Participle (Глаголски прилог прошли)	на̏шавши **na**šavši

	Active Adjectival Participle (Глаголски придев радни)		Passive Adjectival Participle (Глаголски придев трпни)	
Gender	Singular	Plural	Singular	Plural
Feminine	на̏шла **na**šla	на̏шле **na**šle	на̏ђена **na**đena	на̏ђене **na**đene
Masculine	на̏шао **na**šao	на̏шли **na**šli	на̏ђен **na**đen	на̏ђени **na**đeni
Neuter	на̏шло **na**šlo	на̏шла **na**šla	на̏ђено **na**đeno	на̏ђена **na**đena

To Finish – завршити - završiti

	Present (Презент)	Future I (Футур први)	Future II (Футур други)
1st per	Ja завршим Ja završim	Ja ћу завршити/Завршићу Ja ću završiti/Završiću	Ja будем завршио/завршила Ja budem završio/završila
2nd per	Ти завршиш Ti završiš	Ти ћеш завршити/Завршићеш Ti ćeš završiti/Završićeš	Ти будеш завршио/завршила Ti budeš završio/završila
3rd per (M)	Он заврши On završi	Он ће завршити/Завршиће On će završiti/Završiće	Он буде завршио On bude završio
3rd per (F)	Она заврши Ona završi	Она ће завршити/Завршиће Ona će završiti/Završiće	Она буде завршила Ona bude završila
3rd per (N)	Оно заврши Ono završi	Оно ће завршити/Завршиће Ono će završiti/Završiće	Оно буде завршило Ono bude završilo
1st per pl	Ми завршимо Mi završimo	Ми ћемо завршити/Завршићемо Mi ćemo završiti/Završićemo	Ми будемо завршили/завршиле Mi budemo završili/završile
2nd per pl	Ви завршите Vi završite	Ви ћете завршити/Завршићете Vi ćete završiti/Završićete	Ви будете завршили/завршиле Vi budete završili/završile
3rd per pl	Они/Оне заврше Oni/One završe	Они/Оне ће завршити/Завршиће Oni/One će završiti/Završiće	Они/Оне буду завршили/завршиле Oni/One budu završili/završile

	Past Tense (Перфект)	Pluperfect (Плусквамперфект)	Conditional (Потенцијал)
1st per	Ja сам завршио Ja sam završio	Ja сам био завршио Ja sam bio završio	Ja бих завршио Ja bih završio
2nd per	Ти си завршио Ti si završio	Ти си био завршио Ti si bio završio	Ти би завршио Ti bi završio
3rd per (M)	Он је завршио On je završio	Он је био завршио On je bio završio	Он би завршио On bi završio
3rd per (F)	Она је завршила Ona je završila	Она је била завршила Ona je bila završila	Она би завршила Ona bi završila
3rd per (N)	Оно је завршило Ono je završilo	Оно је било завршило Ono je bilo završilo	Оно би завршило Ono bi završilo
1st per pl	Ми смо завршили Mi smo završili	Ми смо били завршили Mi smo bili završili	Ми бисмо завршили Mi bismo završili
2nd per pl	Ви сте завршили Vi ste završili	Ви сте били завршили Vi ste bili završili	Ви бисте завршили Vi biste završili
3rd per pl	Они су завршили Oni su završili	Они су били завршили Oni su bili završili	Они би завршили Oni bi završili

	Imperative (Императив)
2nd per sg	(Ти) заврши (Ti) završi
1st per pl	(Ми) завршимо (Mi) završimo
2nd per pl	(Ви) завршите (Vi) završite

Non-finite Forms

Infinitive (Инфинитив)	завр̀шити završiti
Present Adverbial Participle (Глаголски прилог садашњи)	--
Past Adverbial Participle (Глаголски прилог прошли)	завр̀шивши završivši

	Active Adjectival Participle (Глаголски придев радни)		Passive Adjectival Participle (Глаголски придев трпни)	
Gender	Singular	Plural	Singular	Plural
Feminine	завр̀шила završila	завр̀шиле završile	завр̀шена završena	завр̀шене završene
Masculine	завр̀шио završio	завр̀шили završili	завр̀шен završen	завр̀шени završeni
Neuter	завр̀шило završilo	завр̀шила završila	завр̀шено završeno	завр̀шена završeni

To Fly – лѐтети - leteti

	Present (Презент)	Future I (Футур први)	Future II (Футур други)
1st per	Ja лѐтим / Ja letim	Ja ћу лѐтети/Лѐтећу / Ja ću leteti/Letећу	Ja будем лѐтео/лѐтела / Ja budem leteo/letela
2nd per	Ти лѐтиш / Ti letiš	Ти ћеш лѐтети/Лѐтећеш / Ti ćeš leteti/Letećeš	Ти будеш лѐтео/лѐтела / Ti budeš leteo/letela
3rd per (M)	Он лѐти / On leti	Он ће лѐтети/Лѐтеће / On će leteti/Leteće	Он буде лѐтео / On bude leteo
3rd per (F)	Она лѐти / Ona leti	Она ће лѐтети/Лѐтеће / Ona će leteti/Leteće	Она буде лѐтела / Ona bude letela
3rd per (N)	Оно лѐти / Ono leti	Оно ће лѐтети/Лѐтеће / Ono će leteti/Leteće	Оно буде лѐтело / Ono bude letelo
1st per pl	Ми лѐтимо / Mi letimo	Ми ћемо лѐтети/Лѐтећемо / Mi ćemo leteti/Letećemo	Ми будемо лѐтели/лѐтеле / Mi budemo leteli/letele
2nd per pl	Ви лѐтите / Vi letite	Ви ћете лѐтети/Лѐтећете / Vi ćete leteti/Letećete	Ви будете лѐтели/лѐтеле / Vi budete leteli/letele
3rd per pl	Они/Оне лѐте / Oni/One lete	Они/Оне ће лѐтети/Лѐтеће / Oni/One će leteti/Leteće	Они/Оне буду лѐтели/лѐтеле / Oni/One budu leteli/letele

	Past Tense (Перфект)	Pluperfect (Плусквамперфект)	Conditional (Потенцијал)
1st per	Ja сам лѐтео / Ja sam leteo	Ja сам био лѐтео / Ja sam bio leteo	Ja бих лѐтео / Ja bih leteo
2nd per	Ти си лѐтео / Ti si leteo	Ти си био лѐтео / Ti si bio leteo	Ти би лѐтео / Ti bi leteo
3rd per (M)	Он је лѐтео / On je leteo	Он је био лѐтео / On je bio leteo	Он би лѐтео / On bi leteo
3rd per (F)	Она је лѐтела / Ona je letela	Она је била лѐтела / Ona je bila letela	Она би лѐтела / Ona bi letela
3rd per (N)	Оно је лѐтело / Ono je letelo	Оно је било лѐтело / Ono je bilo letelo	Оно би лѐтело / Ono bi letelo
1st per pl	Ми смо лѐтели / Mi smo leteli	Ми смо били лѐтели / Mi smo bili leteli	Ми бисмо лѐтели / Mi bismo leteli
2nd per pl	Ви сте лѐтели / Vi ste leteli	Ви сте били лѐтели / Vi ste bili leteli	Ви бисте лѐтели / Vi biste leteli
3rd per pl	Они су лѐтели / Oni su leteli	Они су били лѐтели / Oni su bili leteli	Они би лѐтели / Oni bi leteli

	Imperative (Императив)
2nd per sg	(Ти) лѐти / (Ti) leti
1st per pl	(Ми) лѐтимо / (Mi) letimo
2nd per pl	(Ви) лѐтите / (Vi) letite

Non-finite Forms

Infinitive (Инфинитив)	лѐтети **le**teti
Present Adverbial Participle (Глаголски прилог садашњи)	лѐтећи **le**teći
Past Adverbial Participle (Глаголски прилог прошли)	--

	Active Adjectival Participle (Глаголски придев радни)		Passive Adjectival Participle (Глаголски придев трпни)	
Gender	Singular	Plural	Singular	Plural
Feminine	лѐтела **le**tela	лѐтеле **le**tele	--	--
Masculine	лѐтео **le**teo	лѐтели **le**teli	--	--
Neuter	лѐтело **le**telo	лѐтела **le**tela	--	--

To Forget – забо̀равити - zaboraviti

	Present (Презент)	Future I (Футур први)	Future II (Футур други)
1st per	Ja забо̀равим / Ja zaboravim	Ja ћу забо̀равити/Забо̀равићу / Ja ću zaboraviti/Zaboraviću	Ja будем забо̀равио/забо̀равила / Ja budem zaboravio/zaboravila
2nd per	Ти забо̀равиш / Ti zaboraviš	Ти ћеш забо̀равити/Забо̀равиће / Ti ćeš zaboraviti/Zaboravićeš	Ти будеш забо̀равио/забо̀равила / Ti budeš zaboravio/zaboravila
3rd per (M)	Он забо̀рави / On zaboravi	Он ће забо̀равити/Забо̀равиће / On će zaboraviti/Zaboraviće	Он буде забо̀равио / On bude zaboravio
3rd per (F)	Она забо̀рави / Ona zaboravi	Она ће забо̀равити/Забо̀равиће / Ona će zaboraviti/Zaboraviće	Она буде забо̀равила / Ona bude zaboravila
3rd per (N)	Оно забо̀рави / Ono zaboravi	Оно ће забо̀равити/Забо̀равиће / Ono će zaboraviti/Zaboraviće	Оно буде забо̀равило / Ono bude zaboravilo
1st per pl	Ми забо̀равимо / Mi zaboravimo	Ми ћемо забо̀равити/Забо̀равићемо / Mi ćemo zaboraviti/Zaboravićemo	Ми будемо забо̀равили/забо̀равиле / Mi budemo zaboravili/zaboravile
2nd per pl	Ви забо̀равите / Vi zaboravite	Ви ћете забо̀равити/Забо̀равићете / Vi ćete zaboraviti/Zaboravićete	Ви будете забо̀равили/забо̀равиле / Vi budete zaboravili/zaboravile
3rd per pl	Они/Оне забо̀раве / Oni/One zaborave	Они/Оне ће забо̀равити/Забо̀равиће / Oni/One će zaboraviti/Zaboraviće	Они/Оне буду забо̀равили/забо̀равиле / Oni/One budu zaboravili/zaboravile

	Past Tense (Перфект)	Pluperfect (Плусквамперфект)	Conditional (Потенцијал)
1st per	Ja сам забо̀равио / Ja sam zaboravio	Ja сам био забо̀равио / Ja sam bio zaboravio	Ja бих забо̀равио / Ja bih zaboravio
2nd per	Ти си забо̀равио / Ti si zaboravio	Ти си био забо̀равио / Ti si bio zaboravio	Ти би забо̀равио / Ti bi zaboravio
3rd per (M)	Он је забо̀равио / On je zaboravio	Он је био забо̀равио / On je bio zaboravio	Он би забо̀равио / On bi zaboravio
3rd per (F)	Она је забо̀равила / Ona je zaboravila	Она је била забо̀равила / Ona je bila zaboravila	Она би забо̀равила / Ona bi zaboravila
3rd per (N)	Оно је забо̀равило / Ono je zaboravilo	Оно је било забо̀равило / Ono je bilo zaboravilo	Оно би забо̀равило / Ono bi zaboravilo
1st per pl	Ми смо забо̀равили / Mi smo zaboravili	Ми смо били забо̀равили / Mi smo bili zaboravili	Ми бисмо забо̀равили / Mi bismo zaboravili
2nd per pl	Ви сте забо̀равили / Vi ste zaboravili	Ви сте били забо̀равили / Vi ste bili zaboravili	Ви бисте забо̀равили / Vi biste zaboravili
3rd per pl	Они су забо̀равили / Oni su zaboravili	Они су били забо̀равили / Oni su bili zaboravili	Они би забо̀равили / Oni bi zaboravili

	Imperative (Императив)
2nd per sg	(Ти) забо̀рави / (Ti) zaboravi
1st per pl	(Ми) забо̀равимо / (Mi) zaboravimo
2nd per pl	(Ви) забо̀равите / (Vi) zaboravite

Non-finite Forms

Infinitive (Инфинитив)	забòравити zaboraviti
Present Adverbial Participle (Глаголски прилог садашњи)	--
Past Adverbial Participle (Глаголски прилог прошли)	забòравивши zaboravivši

	Active Adjectival Participle (Глаголски придев радни)		Passive Adjectival Participle (Глаголски придев трпни)	
Gender	Singular	Plural	Singular	Plural
Feminine	забòравила zaboravila	забòравиле zaboravile	забòрављена zaboravljena	забòрављене zaboravljene
Masculine	забòравио zaboravio	забòравили zaboravili	забòрављен zaboravljen	забòрављени zaboravljeni
Neuter	забòравило zaboravilo	забòравила zaboravila	забòрављено zaboravljeno	забòрављена zaboravljena

To Get Up – у̀стати - ustati

	Present (Презент)	Future I (Футур први)	Future II (Футур други)
1st per	Ja у̀стаjем Ja ustajem	Ja ħу у̀стати/У̀стаħу Ja ću ustati/Ustaću	Ja будем у̀стао/у̀стала Ja budem ustao/ustala
2nd per	Ти у̀стаjеш Ti ustaješ	Ти ħеш у̀стати/У̀стаħеш Ti ćeš ustati/Ustaćeš	Ти будеш у̀стао/у̀стала Ti budeš ustao/ustala
3rd per (M)	Он у̀стаjе On ustaje	Он ħе у̀стати/У̀стаħе On će ustati/Ustaće	Он буде у̀стао On bude ustao
3rd per (F)	Она у̀стаjе Ona ustaje	Она ħе у̀стати/У̀стаħе Ona će ustati/Ustaće	Она буде у̀стала Ona bude ustala
3rd per (N)	Оно у̀стаjе Ono ustaje	Оно ħе у̀стати/У̀стаħе Ono će ustati/Ustaće	Оно буде у̀стало Ono bude ustalo
1st per pl	Ми у̀стаjемо Mi ustajemo	Ми ħемо у̀стати/У̀стаħемо Mi ćemo ustati/Ustaćemo	Ми будемо у̀стали/у̀стале Mi budemo ustali/ustale
2nd per pl	Ви у̀стаjете Vi ustajete	Ви ħете у̀стати/У̀стаħете Vi ćete ustati/Ustaćete	Ви будете у̀стали/у̀стале Vi budete ustali/ustale
3rd per pl	Они/Оне у̀стаjу Oni/One ustaju	Они/Оне ħе у̀стати/У̀стаħе Oni/One će ustati/Ustaće	Они/Оне буду у̀стали/у̀стале Oni/One budu ustali/ustale

	Past Tense (Перфект)	Pluperfect (Плусквамперфект)	Conditional (Потенциjал)
1st per	Ja сам у̀стао Ja sam ustao	Ja сам био у̀стао Ja sam bio ustao	Ja бих у̀стао Ja bih ustao
2nd per	Ти си у̀стао Ti si ustao	Ти си био у̀стао Ti si bio ustao	Ти би у̀стао Ti bi ustao
3rd per (M)	Он jе у̀стао On je ustao	Он jе био у̀стао On je bio ustao	Он би у̀стао On bi ustao
3rd per (F)	Она jе у̀стала Ona je ustala	Она jе у̀стала Ona je bila ustala	Она би у̀стала Ona bi ustala
3rd per (N)	Оно jе у̀стало Ono je ustalo	Оно jе било у̀стало Ono je bilo ustalo	Оно би у̀стало Ono bi ustalo
1st per pl	Ми смо у̀стали Mi smo ustali	Ми смо били у̀стали Mi smo bili ustali	Ми бисмо у̀стали Mi bismo ustali
2nd per pl	Ви сте у̀стали Vi ste ustali	Ви сте били у̀стали Vi ste bili ustali	Ви бисте у̀стали Vi biste ustali
3rd per pl	Они су у̀стали Oni su ustali	Они су били у̀стали Oni su bili ustali	Они би у̀стали Oni bi ustali

	Imperative (Императив)
2nd per sg	(Ти) у̀стаj/у̀стани (Ti) ustaj/ustani
1st per pl	(Ми) у̀стаjмо/у̀станимо (Mi) ustajmo/ustanimo
2nd per pl	(Ви) у̀стаjте/у̀станите (Vi) ustajte/ustanite

Non-finite Forms

Infinitive (Инфинитив)	у̀стати **us**tati
Present Adverbial Participle (Глаголски прилог садашњи)	--
Past Adverbial Participle (Глаголски прилог прошли)	у̀ставши **us**tavši

	Active Adjectival Participle (Глаголски придев радни)		Passive Adjectival Participle (Глаголски придев трпни)	
Gender	Singular	Plural	Singular	Plural
Feminine	у̀стала **us**tala	у̀стале **us**tale	--	--
Masculine	у̀стао **us**tao	у̀стали **us**tali	--	--
Neuter	у̀стало **us**talo	у̀стала **us**tala	--	--

To Give - да̏ти - dati

	Present (Презент)	Future I (Футур први)	Future II (Футур други)
1st per	Ja да́jем Ja **da**jem	Ja ħy да̏ти/Да̏ħy Ja ću **dati**/**Da**ću	Ja будем да̏о/да́ла Ja budem **dao**/**da**la
2nd per	Ти да́jеш Ti **da**ješ	Ти ħеш да̏ти/Да̏ħеш Ti ćeš **dati**/**Da**ćeš	Ти будеш да̏о/да́ла Ti budeš **dao**/**da**la
3rd per (M)	Он да́jе On **da**je	Он ħе да̏ти/Да̏ħе On će **dati**/**Da**će	Он буде да̏о On bude **dao**
3rd per (F)	Она да́jе Ona **da**je	Она ħе да̏ти/Да̏ħе Ona će **dati**/**Da**će	Она буде да́ла Ona bude **da**la
3rd per (N)	Оно да́jе Ono **da**je	Оно ħе да̏ти/Да̏ħе Ono će **dati**/**Da**će	Оно буде да́ло Ono bude **da**lo
1st per pl	Ми да́jемо Mi **da**jemo	Ми ħемо да̏ти/Да̏ħемо Mi ćemo **dati**/**Da**ćemo	Ми будемо да́ли/да́ле Mi budemo **da**li/**da**le
2nd per pl	Ви да́jете Vi **da**jete	Ви ħете да̏ти/Да̏ħете Vi ćete **dati**/**Da**ćete	Ви будете да́ли/да́ле Vi budete **da**li/**da**le
3rd per pl	Они/Оне да́jy Oni/One **da**ju	Они/Оне ħе да̏ти/Да̏ħе Oni/One će **dati**/**Da**će	Они/Оне буду да́ли/да́ле Oni/One budu **da**li/**da**le

	Past Tense (Перфект)	Pluperfect (Плусквамперфект)	Conditional (Потенцијал)
1st per	Ja сам да̏о Ja sam **dao**	Ja сам био да̏о Ja sam bio **dao**	Ja бих да̏о Ja bih **dao**
2nd per	Ти си да̏о Ti si **dao**	Ти си био да̏о Ti si bio **dao**	Ти би да̏о Ti bi **dao**
3rd per (M)	Он је да̏о On je **dao**	Он је био да̏о On je bio **dao**	Он би да̏о On bi **dao**
3rd per (F)	Она је да́ла Ona je **da**la	Она је била да́ла Ona je bila **da**la	Она би да́ла Ona bi **da**la
3rd per (N)	Оно је да́ло Ono je **da**lo	Оно је било да́ло Ono je bilo **da**lo	Оно би да́ло Ono bi **da**lo
1st per pl	Ми смо да́ли Mi smo **da**li	Ми смо били да́ли Mi smo bili **da**li	Ми бисмо да́ли Mi bismo **da**li
2nd per pl	Ви сте да́ли Vi ste **da**li	Ви сте били да́ли Vi ste bili **da**li	Ви бисте да́ли Vi biste **da**li
3rd per pl	Они су да́ли Oni su **da**li	Они су били да́ли Oni su bili **da**li	Они би да́ли Oni bi **da**li

	Imperative (Императив)
2nd per sg	(Ти) да̂j (Ti) **da**j
1st per pl	(Ми) да̂jмо (Mi) **da**jmo
2nd per pl	(Ви) да̂jте (Vi) **da**jte

Non-finite Forms

Infinitive (Инфинитив)	да̀ти **da**ti
Present Adverbial Participle (Глаголски прилог садашњи)	да́јући **da**jući
Past Adverbial Participle (Глаголски прилог прошли)	--

	Active Adjectival Participle (Глаголски придев радни)		Passive Adjectival Participle (Глаголски придев трпни)	
Gender	Singular	Plural	Singular	Plural
Feminine	да́ла **da**la	да́ле **da**le	да̂та **da**ta	да̂те **da**te
Masculine	да̀о **da**o	да̀ли **da**li	да̂т **da**t	да̂ти **da**ti
Neuter	да́ло **da**lo	да́ла **da**la	да̂то **da**to	да̂та **da**ta

To Go – ѝћи - ići

	Present (Презент)	Future I (Футур први)	Future II (Футур други)
1st per	Ja ѝдем Ja **id**em	Ja ћу ѝћи/Ѝћи ћу Ja ću **ić**i/**Ić**i ću	Ja будем ѝшао/ѝшла Ja budem **iš**ao/**iš**la
2nd per	Ти ѝдеш Ti **id**eš	Ти ћеш ѝћи/Ѝћи ћеш Ti ćeš **ić**i/**Ić**i ćeš	Ти будеш ѝшао/ѝшла Ti budeš **iš**ao/**iš**la
3rd per (M)	Он ѝде On **id**e	Он ће ѝћи/Ѝћи ће On će **ić**i/**Ić**i će	Он буде ѝшао On bude **iš**ao
3rd per (F)	Она ѝде Ona **id**e	Она ће ѝћи/Ѝћи ће Ona će **ić**i/**Ić**i će	Она буде ѝшла Ona bude **iš**la
3rd per (N)	Оно ѝде Ono **id**e	Оно ће ѝћи/Ѝћи ће Ono će **ić**i/**Ić**i će	Оно буде ѝшло Ono bude **iš**lo
1st per pl	Ми ѝдемо Mi **id**emo	Ми ћемо ѝћи/Ѝћи ћемо Mi ćemo **ić**i/**Ić**i ćemo	Ми будемо ѝшли/ѝшле Mi budemo **iš**li/**iš**le
2nd per pl	Ви ѝдете Vi **id**ete	Ви ћете ѝћи/ Ѝћи ћете Vi ćete **ić**i/ **Ić**i ćete	Ви будете ѝшли/ѝшле Vi budete **iš**li/**iš**le
3rd per pl	Они/Оне ѝду Oni/One **id**u	Они/Оне ће ѝћи/Ѝћи ће Oni/One će **ić**i/**Ić**i će	Они/Оне буду ѝшли/ѝшле Oni/One budu **iš**li/**iš**le

	Past Tense (Перфект)	Pluperfect (Плусквамперфект)	Conditional (Потенцијал)
1st per	Ja сам ѝшао Ja sam **iš**ao	Ja сам био ѝшао Ja sam bio **iš**ao	Ja бих ѝшао Ja bih **iš**ao
2nd per	Ти си ѝшао Ti si **iš**ao	Ти си био ѝшао Ti si bio **iš**ao	Ти би ѝшао Ti bi **iš**ao
3rd per (M)	Он је ѝшао On je **iš**ao	Он је био ѝшао On je bio **iš**ao	Он би ѝшао On bi **iš**ao
3rd per (F)	Она је ѝшла Ona je **iš**la	Она је била ѝшла Ona je bila **iš**la	Она би ѝшла Ona bi **iš**la
3rd per (N)	Оно је ѝшло Ono je **iš**lo	Оно је било ѝшло Ono je bilo **iš**lo	Оно би ѝшло Ono bi **iš**lo
1st per pl	Ми смо ѝшли Mi smo **iš**li	Ми смо били ѝшли Mi smo bili **iš**li	Ми бисмо ѝшли Mi bismo **iš**li
2nd per pl	Ви сте ѝшли Vi ste **iš**li	Ви сте били ѝшли Vi ste bili **iš**li	Ви бисте ѝшли Vi biste **iš**li
3rd per pl	Они су ѝшли Oni su **iš**li	Они су били ѝшли Oni su bili **iš**li	Они би ѝшли Oni bi **iš**li

	Imperative (Императив)
2nd per sg	(Ти) ѝди (Ti) **id**i
1st per pl	(Ми) ѝдимо (Mi) **id**imo
2nd per pl	(Ви) ѝдите (Vi) **id**ite

Non-finite Forms

Infinitive (Инфинитив)	ѝћи ići
Present Adverbial Participle (Глаголски прилог садашњи)	ѝдући idući
Past Adverbial Participle (Глаголски прилог прошли)	ѝшавши išavši

	Active Adjectival Participle (Глаголски придев радни)		Passive Adjectival Participle (Глаголски придев трпни)	
Gender	Singular	Plural	Singular	Plural
Feminine	ѝшла išla	ѝшле išle	--	--
Masculine	ѝшао išao	ѝшли išli	--	--
Neuter	ѝшло išlo	ѝшла išla	--	--

To Happen - дѐсити се – desiti se

	Present (Презент)	Future I (Футур први)	Future II (Футур други)
1st per	Ja се дѐсим / Ja se **de**sim	Ja ћу се дѐсити/Дѐсићу се / Ja ću se **de**siti/**De**siću se	Ja се будем дѐсио/дѐсила / Ja se budem **de**sio/**de**sila
2nd per	Ти се дѐсиш / Ti se **de**siš	Ти ћеш се дѐсити/Дѐсићеш се / Ti ćeš se **de**siti/**De**sićeš se	Ти се будеш дѐсио/дѐсила / Ti se budeš **de**sio/**de**sila
3rd per (M)	Он се дѐси / On se **de**si	Он ће се дѐсити/Дѐсиће се / On će se **de**siti/**De**siće se	Он се буде дѐсио / On se bude **de**sio
3rd per (F)	Она се дѐси / Ona se **de**si	Она ће се дѐсити/Дѐсиће се / Ona će se **de**siti/**De**siće se	Она се буде дѐсила / Ona se bude **de**sila
3rd per (N)	Оно се дѐси / Ono se **de**si	Оно ће се дѐсити/Дѐсиће се / Ono će se **de**siti/**De**siće se	Оно се буде дѐсило / Ono se bude **de**silo
1st per pl	Ми се дѐсимо / Mi se **de**simo	Ми ћемо се дѐсити/Дѐсићемо се / Mi ćemo se **de**siti/**De**sićemo se	Ми се будемо дѐсили/дѐсиле / Mi se budemo **de**sili/**de**sile
2nd per pl	Ви се дѐсите / Vi se **de**site	Ви ћете се дѐсити/Дѐсићете се / Vi ćete se **de**siti/**De**sićete se	Ви се будете дѐсили/дѐсиле / Vi se budete **de**sili/**de**sile
3rd per pl	Они/Оне се дѐсе / Oni/One se **de**se	Они/Оне ће се дѐсити/Дѐсиће се / Oni/One će se **de**siti/**De**siće se	Они/Оне се буду дѐсили/дѐсиле / Oni/One se budu **de**sili/**de**sile

	Past Tense (Перфект)	Pluperfect (Плусквамперфект)	Conditional (Потенцијал)
1st per	Ja сам се дѐсио / Ja sam se **de**sio	Ja сам се био дѐсио / Ja sam se bio **de**sio	Ja бих се дѐсио / Ja bih se **de**sio
2nd per	Ти си се дѐсио / Ti si se **de**sio	Ти си се био дѐсио / Ti si se bio **de**sio	Ти би се дѐсио / Ti bi se **de**sio
3rd per (M)	Он се дѐсио / On se **de**sio	Он се био дѐсио / On se bio **de**sio	Он би се дѐсио / On bi se **de**sio
3rd per (F)	Она се дѐсила / Ona se **de**sila	Она се била дѐсила / Ona se bila **de**sila	Она би се дѐсила / Ona bi se **de**sila
3rd per (N)	Оно се дѐсило / Ono se **de**silo	Оно се било дѐсило / Ono se bilo **de**silo	Оно би се дѐсило / Ono bi se **de**silo
1st per pl	Ми смо се дѐсили / Mi smo se **de**sili	Ми смо се били дѐсили / Mi smo se bili **de**sili	Ми бисмо се дѐсили / Mi bismo se **de**sili
2nd per pl	Ви сте се дѐсили / Vi ste se **de**sili	Ви сте се били дѐсили / Vi ste se bili **de**sili	Ви бисте се дѐсили / Vi biste se **de**sili
3rd per pl	Они су се дѐсили / Oni su se **de**sili	Они су се били дѐсили / Oni su se bili **de**sili	Они би се дѐсили / Oni bi se **de**sili

	Imperative (Императив)
2nd per sg	(Ти) дѐси се / (Ti) **de**si se
1st per pl	(Ми) дѐсимо се / (Mi) **de**simo se
2nd per pl	(Ви) дѐсите се / (Vi) **de**site se

Non-finite Forms

Infinitive (Инфинитив)	дѐсити се **de**siti se
Present Adverbial Participle (Глаголски прилог садашњи)	--
Past Adverbial Participle (Глаголски прилог прошли)	дѐсивши се **de**sivši se

	Active Adjectival Participle (Глаголски придев радни)		Passive Adjectival Participle (Глаголски придев трпни)	
Gender	Singular	Plural	Singular	Plural
Feminine	дѐсила **de**sila	дѐсиле **de**sile	--	--
Masculine	дѐсио **de**sio	дѐсили **de**sili	--	--
Neuter	дѐсило **de**silo	дѐсила **de**sila	--	--

To Have – имати - imati

	Present (Презент)	Future I (Футур први)	Future II (Футур други)
1st per	Ja имам / Ja imam	Ja ћу имати/Имаћу / Ja ću imati/Imaću	Ja будем имао/имала / Ja budem imao/imala
2nd per	Ти имаш / Ti imaš	Ти ћеш имати/Имаћеш / Ti ćeš imati/Imaćeš	Ти будеш имао/имала / Ti budeš imao/imala
3rd per (M)	Он има / On ima	Он ће имати/Имаће / On će imati/Imaće	Он буде имао / On bude imao
3rd per (F)	Она има / Ona ima	Она ће имати/Имаће / Ona će imati/Imaće	Она буде имала / Ona bude imala
3rd per (N)	Оно има / Ono ima	Оно ће имати/Имаће / Ono će imati/Imaće	Оно буде имало / Ono bude imalo
1st per pl	Ми имамо / Mi imamo	Ми ћемо имати/Имаћемо / Mi ćemo imati/Imaćemo	Ми будемо имали/имале / Mi budemo imali/imale
2nd per pl	Ви имате / Vi imate	Ви ћете имати/Имаћете / Vi ćete imati/Imaćete	Ви будете имали/имале / Vi budete imali/imale
3rd per pl	Они/Оне имају / Oni/One imaju	Они/Оне ће имати/Имаће / Oni/One će imati/Imaće	Они/Оне буду имали/имале / Oni/One budu imali/imale

	Past Tense (Перфект)	Pluperfect (Плусквамперфект)	Conditional (Потенцијал)
1st per	Ja сам имао / Ja sam imao	Ja сам био имао / Ja sam bio imao	Ja бих имао / Ja bih imao
2nd per	Ти си имао / Ti si imao	Ти си био имао / Ti si bio imao	Ти би имао / Ti bi imao
3rd per (M)	Он је имао / On je imao	Он је био имао / On je bio imao	Он би имао / On bi imao
3rd per (F)	Она је имала / Ona je imala	Она је била имала / Ona je bila imala	Она би имала / Ona bi imala
3rd per (N)	Оно је имало / Ono je imalo	Оно је било имало / Ono je bilo imalo	Оно би имало / Ono bi imalo
1st per pl	Ми смо имали / Mi smo imali	Ми смо били имали / Mi smo bili imali	Ми бисмо имали / Mi bismo imali
2nd per pl	Ви сте имали / Vi ste imali	Ви сте били имали / Vi ste bili imali	Ви бисте имали / Vi biste imali
3rd per pl	Они су имали / Oni su imali	Они су били имали / Oni su bili imali	Они би имали / Oni bi imali

	Imperative (Императив)
2nd per sg	(Ти) имај / (Ti) imaj
1st per pl	(Ми) имајмо / (Mi) imajmo
2nd per pl	(Ви) имајте / (Vi) imajte

Non-finite Forms

Infinitive (Инфинитив)	ѝмати ìmati
Present Adverbial Participle (Глаголски прилог садашњи)	ѝмајући ìmajući
Past Adverbial Participle (Глаголски прилог прошли)	--

	Active Adjectival Participle (Глаголски придев радни)		Passive Adjectival Participle (Глаголски придев трпни)	
Gender	Singular	Plural	Singular	Plural
Feminine	ѝмала ìmala	ѝмале ìmale	--	--
Masculine	ѝмао ìmao	ѝмали ìmali	--	--
Neuter	ѝмало ìmalo	ѝмала ìmala	--	--

To Hear - чу̏ти - čuti

	Present (Презент)	Future I (Футур први)	Future II (Футур други)
1st per	Ja чу̏јем / Ja čujem	Ja ћу чу̏ти/Чу̏ћу / Ja ću čuti/Ćuću	Ja будем чу̏о/чу̏ла / Ja budem čuo/čula
2nd per	Ти чу̏јеш / Ti čuješ	Ти ћеш чу̏ти/Чу̏ћеш / Ti ćeš čuti/Ćućeš	Ти будеш чу̏о/чу̏ла / Ti budeš čuo/čula
3rd per (M)	Он чу̏је / On čuje	Он ће чу̏ти/Чу̏ће / On će čuti/Ćuće	Он буде чу̏о / On bude čuo
3rd per (F)	Она чу̏је / Ona čuje	Она ће чу̏ти/Чу̏ће / Ona će čuti/Ćuće	Она буде чу̏ла / Ona bude čula
3rd per (N)	Оно чу̏је / Ono čuje	Оно ће чу̏ти/Чу̏ће / Ono će čuti/Ćuće	Оно буде чу̏ло / Ono bude čulo
1st per pl	Ми чу̏јемо / Mi čujemo	Ми ћемо чу̏ти/Чу̏ћемо / Mi ćemo čuti/Ćućemo	Ми будемо чу̏ли/чу̏ле / Mi budemo čuli/čule
2nd per pl	Ви чу̏јете / Vi čujete	Ви ћете чу̏ти/Чу̏ћете / Vi ćete čuti/Ćućete	Ви будете чу̏ли/чу̏ле / Vi budete čuli/čule
3rd per pl	Они/Оне чу̏ју / Oni/One čuju	Они/Оне ће чу̏ти/Чу̏ће / Oni/One će čuti/Ćuće	Они/Оне буду чу̏ли/чу̏ле / Oni/One budu čuli/čule

	Past Tense (Перфект)	Pluperfect (Плусквамперфект)	Conditional (Потенцијал)
1st per	Ja сам чу̏о / Ja sam čuo	Ja сам био чу̏о / Ja sam bio čuo	Ja бих чу̏о / Ja bih čuo
2nd per	Ти си чу̏о / Ti si čuo	Ти си био чу̏о / Ti si bio čuo	Ти би чу̏о / Ti bi čuo
3rd per (M)	Он је чу̏о / On je čuo	Он је био чу̏о / On je bio čuo	Он би чу̏о / On bi čuo
3rd per (F)	Она је чу̏ла / Ona je čula	Она је била чу̏ла / Ona je bila čula	Она би чу̏ла / Ona bi čula
3rd per (N)	Оно је чу̏ло / Ono je čulo	Оно је било чу̏ло / Ono je bilo čulo	Оно би чу̏ло / Ono bi čulo
1st per pl	Ми смо чу̏ли / Mi smo čuli	Ми смо били чу̏ли / Mi smo bili čuli	Ми бисмо чу̏ли / Mi bismo čuli
2nd per pl	Ви сте чу̏ли / Vi ste čuli	Ви сте били чу̏ли / Vi ste bili čuli	Ви бисте чу̏ли / Vi biste čuli
3rd per pl	Они су чу̏ли / Oni su čuli	Они су били чу̏ли / Oni su bili čuli	Они би чу̏ли / Oni bi čuli

	Imperative (Императив)
2nd per sg	(Ти) чу̏ј / (Ti) čuj
1st per pl	(Ми) чу̏јмо / (Mi) čujmo
2nd per pl	(Ви) чу̏јте / (Vi) čujte

Non-finite Forms

Infinitive (Инфинитив)	чу̏ти **ču**ti
Present Adverbial Participle (Глаголски прилог садашњи)	--
Past Adverbial Participle (Глаголски прилог прошли)	чу̑вши **ču**vši

	Active Adjectival Participle (Глаголски придев радни)		Passive Adjectival Participle (Глаголски придев трпни)	
Gender	Singular	Plural	Singular	Plural
Feminine	чу̏ла **ču**la	чу̏ле **ču**le	--	--
Masculine	чу̏о **ču**o	чу̏ли **ču**li	--	--
Neuter	чу̏ло **ču**lo	чу̏ла **ču**la	--	--

To Help – помòћи - pomoći

	Present (Презент)	Future I (Футур први)	Future II (Футур други)
1st per	Ja пòмогнем Ja **po**mognem	Ja ћу помòћи/Помòћи ћу Ja ću po**mo**ći/Po**mo**ći ću	Ja будем пòмогао/пòмогла Ja budem **po**mogao/**po**mogla
2nd per	Ти пòмогнеш Ti **po**mogneš	Ти ћеш помòћи/Помòћи ћеш Ti ćeš po**mo**ći/Po**mo**ći ćeš	Ти будеш пòмогао/пòмогла Ti budeš **po**mogao/**po**mogla
3rd per (M)	Он пòмогне On **po**mogne	Он ће помòћи/Помòћи ће On će po**mo**ći/Po**mo**ći će	Он буде пòмогао On bude **po**mogao
3rd per (F)	Она пòмогне Ona **po**mogne	Она ће помòћи/Помòћи ће Ona će po**mo**ći/Po**mo**ći će	Она буде пòмогла Ona bude **po**mogla
3rd per (N)	Оно пòмогне Ono **po**mogne	Оно ће помòћи/Помòћи ће Ono će po**mo**ći/Po**mo**ći će	Оно буде пòмогло Ono bude **po**moglo
1st per pl	Ми пòмогнемо Mi **po**mognemo	Ми ћемо помòћи/Помòћи ћемо Mi ćemo po**mo**ći/Po**mo**ći ćemo	Ми будемо пòмогли/пòмогле Mi budemo **po**mogli/**po**mogle
2nd per pl	Ви пòмогнете Vi **po**mognete	Ви ћете помòћи/Помòћи ћете Vi ćete po**mo**ći/Po**mo**ći ćete	Ви будете пòмогли/пòмогле Vi budete **po**mogli/**po**mogle
3rd per pl	Они/Оне пòмогну Oni/One **po**mognu	Они/Оне ће помòћи/Помòћи ће Oni/One će po**mo**ći/Po**mo**ći će	Они/Оне буду пòмогли/пòмогле Oni/One budu **po**mogli/**po**mogle

	Past Tense (Перфект)	Pluperfect (Плусквамперфект)	Conditional (Потенцијал)
1st per	Ja сам пòмогао Ja sam **po**mogao	Ja сам био пòмогао Ja sam bio **po**mogao	Ja бих пòмогао Ja bih **po**mogao
2nd per	Ти си пòмогао Ti si **po**mogao	Ти си био пòмогао Ti si bio **po**mogao	Ти би пòмогао Ti bi **po**mogao
3rd per (M)	Он је пòмогао On je **po**mogao	Он је био пòмогао On je bio **po**mogao	Он би пòмогао On bi **po**mogao
3rd per (F)	Она је пòмогла Ona je **po**mogla	Она је била пòмогла Ona je bila **po**mogla	Она би пòмогла Ona bi **po**mogla
3rd per (N)	Оно је пòмогло Ono je **po**moglo	Оно је било пòмогло Ono je bilo **po**moglo	Оно би пòмогло Ono bi **po**moglo
1st per pl	Ми смо пòмогли Mi smo **po**mogli	Ми смо били пòмогли Mi smo bili **po**mogli	Ми бисмо пòмогли Mi bismo **po**mogli
2nd per pl	Ви сте пòмогли Vi ste **po**mogli	Ви сте били пòмогли Vi ste bili **po**mogli	Ви бисте пòмогли Vi biste **po**mogli
3rd per pl	Они су пòмогли Oni su **po**mogli	Они су били пòмогли Oni su bili **po**mogli	Они би пòмогли Oni bi **po**mogli

	Imperative (Императив)
2nd per sg	(Ти) помòзи (Ti) po**mo**zi
1st per pl	(Ми) помòзимо (Mi) po**mo**zimo
2nd per pl	(Ви) помòзите (Vi) po**mo**zite

Non-finite Forms

Infinitive (Инфинитив)	помо̀ћи pomòći
Present Adverbial Participle (Глаголски прилог садашњи)	--
Past Adverbial Participle (Глаголски прилог прошли)	помо̀гавши pomògavši

	Active Adjectival Participle (Глаголски придев радни)		Passive Adjectival Participle (Глаголски придев трпни)	
Gender	Singular	Plural	Singular	Plural
Feminine	по̀могла pomogla	по̀могле pomogle	--	--
Masculine	по̀могао pomogao	по̀могли pomogli	--	--
Neuter	по̀могло pomoglo	по̀могла pomogla	--	--

To Hold – др̏жати - držati

	Present (Презент)	Future I (Футур први)	Future II (Футур други)
1st per	Ja др̏жим Ja **drž**im	Ja ћу др̏жати/Др̏жаћу Ja ću **drž**ati/**Drž**aću	Ja будем др̏жао/др̏жала Ja budem **drž**ao/**drž**ala
2nd per	Ти др̏жиш Ti **drž**iš	Ти ћеш др̏жати/Др̏жаћеш Ti ćeš **drž**ati/**Drž**aćeš	Ти будеш др̏жао/др̏жала Ti budeš **drž**ao/**drž**ala
3rd per (M)	Он др̏жи On **drž**i	Он ће др̏жати/Др̏жаће On će **drž**ati/**Drž**aće	Он буде др̏жао On bude **drž**ao
3rd per (F)	Она др̏жи Ona **drž**i	Она ће др̏жати/Др̏жаће Ona će **drž**ati/**Drž**aće	Она буде др̏жала Ona bude **drž**ala
3rd per (N)	Оно др̏жи Ono **drž**i	Оно ће др̏жати/Др̏жаће Ono će **drž**ati/**Drž**aće	Оно буде др̏жало Ono bude **drž**alo
1st per pl	Ми др̏жимо Mi **drž**imo	Ми ћемо др̏жати/Др̏жаћемо Mi ćemo **drž**ati/**Drž**aćemo	Ми будемо др̏жали/др̏жале Mi budemo **drž**ali/**drž**ale
2nd per pl	Ви др̏жите Vi **drž**ite	Ви ћете др̏жати/Др̏жаћете Vi ćete **drž**ati/**Drž**aćete	Ви будете др̏жали/др̏жале Vi budete **drž**ali/**drž**ale
3rd per pl	Они/Оне др̏же Oni/One **drž**e	Они/Оне ће др̏жати/Др̏жаће Oni/One će **drž**ati/**Drž**aće	Они/Оне буду др̏жали/др̏жале Oni/One budu **drž**ali/**drž**ale

	Past Tense (Перфект)	Pluperfect (Плусквамперфект)	Conditional (Потенцијал)
1st per	Ja сам др̏жао Ja sam **drž**ao	Ja сам био др̏жао Ja sam bio **drž**ao	Ja бих др̏жао Ja bih **drž**ao
2nd per	Ти си др̏жао Ti si **drž**ao	Ти си био др̏жао Ti si bio **drž**ao	Ти би др̏жао Ti bi **drž**ao
3rd per (M)	Он је др̏жао On je **drž**ao	Он је био др̏жао On je bio **drž**ao	Он би др̏жао On bi **drž**ao
3rd per (F)	Она је др̏жала Ona je **drž**ala	Она је била др̏жала Ona je bila **drž**ala	Она би др̏жала Ona bi **drž**ala
3rd per (N)	Оно је др̏жало Ono je **drž**alo	Оно је било др̏жало Ono je bilo **drž**alo	Оно би др̏жало Ono bi **drž**alo
1st per pl	Ми смо др̏жали Mi smo **drž**ali	Ми смо били др̏жали Mi smo bili **drž**ali	Ми бисмо др̏жали Mi bismo **drž**ali
2nd per pl	Ви сте др̏жали Vi ste **drž**ali	Ви сте били др̏жали Vi ste bili **drž**ali	Ви бисте др̏жали Vi biste **drž**ali
3rd per pl	Они су др̏жали Oni su **drž**ali	Они су били др̏жали Oni su bili **drž**ali	Они би др̏жали Oni bi **drž**ali

	Imperative (Императив)
2nd per sg	(Ти) др̏жи (Ti) **drž**i
1st per pl	(Ми) др̏жимо (Mi) **drž**imo

2nd per pl	(Ви) др̀жите
	(Vi) **dr**žite

Non-finite Forms

Infinitive (Инфинитив)	др̀жати
	držati
Present Adverbial Participle (Глаголски прилог садашњи)	др̀жећи
	držeći
Past Adverbial Participle (Глаголски прилог прошли)	--

	Active Adjectival Participle (Глаголски придев радни)		Passive Adjectival Participle (Глаголски придев трпни)	
Gender	Singular	Plural	Singular	Plural
Feminine	др̀жала	др̀жале	др̀жана	др̀жане
	držala	**dr**žale	**dr**žana	**dr**žane
Masculine	др̀жао	др̀жали	др̀жан	др̀жани
	držao	**dr**žali	**dr**žan	**dr**žani
Neuter	др̀жало	др̀жала	др̀жано	др̀жана
	držalo	**dr**žala	**dr**žano	**dr**žana

To Increase – повѐћати - povećati

	Present (Презент)	Future I (Футур први)	Future II (Футур други)
1st per	Ja повѐћам Ja povećam	Ja ћу повѐћати/Повѐћаћу Ja ću povećati/Povećaću	Ja будем пȍвећао/пȍвећала Ja budem povećao/povećala
2nd per	Ти повѐћаш Ti povećaš	Ти ћеш повѐћати/Повѐћаћеш Ti ćeš povećati/Povećaćeš	Ти будеш пȍвећао/пȍвећала Ti budeš povećao/povećala
3rd per (M)	Он повѐћа On poveća	Он ће повѐћати/Повѐћаће On će povećati/Povećaće	Он буде пȍвећао On bude povećao
3rd per (F)	Она повѐћа Ona poveća	Она ће повѐћати/Повѐћаће Ona će povećati/Povećaće	Она буде пȍвећала Ona bude povećala
3rd per (N)	Оно повѐћа Ono poveća	Оно ће повѐћати/Повѐћаће Ono će povećati/Povećaće	Оно буде пȍвећало Ono bude povećalo
1st per pl	Ми повѐћамо Mi povećamo	Ми ћемо повѐћати/Повѐћаћемо Mi ćemo povećati/Povećaćemo	Ми будемо пȍвећали/пȍвећале Mi budemo povećali/povećale
2nd per pl	Ви повѐћате Vi povećate	Ви ћете повѐћати/Повѐћаћете Vi ćete povećati/Povećaćete	Ви будете пȍвећали/пȍвећале Vi budete povećali/povećale
3rd per pl	Они/Оне повѐћају Oni/One povećaju	Они/Оне ће повѐћати/Повѐћаће Oni/One će povećati/Povećaće	Они/Оне буду пȍвећали/пȍвећале Oni/One budu povećali/povećale

	Past Tense (Перфект)	Pluperfect (Плусквамперфект)	Conditional (Потенцијал)
1st per	Ja сам пȍвећао Ja sam povećao	Ja сам био пȍвећао Ja sam bio povećao	Ja бих пȍвећао Ja bih povećao
2nd per	Ти си пȍвећао Ti si povećao	Ти си био пȍвећао Ti si bio povećao	Ти би пȍвећао Ti bi povećao
3rd per (M)	Он је пȍвећао On je povećao	Он је био пȍвећао On je bio povećao	Он би пȍвећао On bi povećao
3rd per (F)	Она је пȍвећала Ona je povećala	Она је била пȍвећала Ona je bila povećala	Она би пȍвећала Ona bi povećala
3rd per (N)	Оно је пȍвећало Ono je povećalo	Оно је било пȍвећало Ono je bilo povećalo	Оно би пȍвећало Ono bi povećalo
1st per pl	Ми смо пȍвећали Mi smo povećali	Ми смо били пȍвећали Mi smo bili povećali	Ми бисмо пȍвећали Mi bismo povećali
2nd per pl	Ви сте пȍвећали Vi ste povećali	Ви сте били пȍвећали Vi ste bili povećali	Ви бисте пȍвећали Vi biste povećali
3rd per pl	Они су пȍвећали Oni su povećali	Они су били пȍвећали Oni su bili povećali	Они би пȍвећали Oni bi povećali

	Imperative (Императив)
2nd per sg	(Ти) повѐћај (Ti) povećaj
1st per pl	(Ми) повѐћајмо (Mi) povećajmo

2nd per pl	(Ви) повѐћајте
	(Vi) po**ve**ćajte

Non-finite Forms

Infinitive (Инфинитив)	повѐћати
	po**ve**ćati
Present Adverbial Participle (Глаголски прилог садашњи)	--
Past Adverbial Participle (Глаголски прилог прошли)	повѐћавши
	po**ve**ćavši

Gender	Active Adjectival Participle (Глаголски придев радни)		Passive Adjectival Participle (Глаголски придев трпни)	
	Singular	Plural	Singular	Plural
Feminine	повѐћала	повѐћале	повѐћана	повѐћане
	po**ve**ćala	po**ve**ćale	po**ve**ćana	po**ve**ćane
Masculine	повѐћао	повѐћали	повѐћан	повѐћани
	po**ve**ćao	po**ve**ćali	po**ve**ćan	po**ve**ćani
Neuter	повѐћало	повѐћала	повѐћано	повѐћана
	po**ve**ćalo	po**ve**ćala	po**ve**ćano	po**ve**ćana

To Introduce – прѐдставити - pradstaviti

	Present (Презент)	Future I (Футур први)	Future II (Футур други)
1st per	Ја прѐдставим Ja **pre**dstavim	Ја ћу прѐдставити/Прѐдставићу Ja ću **pre**dstaviti/**Pre**dstaviću	Ја будем прѐдставио/прѐдставила Ja budem **pre**dstavio/**pre**dstavila
2nd per	Ти прѐдставиш Ti **pre**dstaviš	Ти ћеш прѐдставити/Прѐдставиће Ti ćeš **pre**dstaviti/**Pre**dstavićeš	Ти будеш прѐдставио/прѐдставила Ti budeš **pre**dstavio/**pre**dstavila
3rd per (M)	Он прѐдстави On **pre**dstavi	Он ће прѐдставити/Прѐдставиће On će **pre**dstaviti/**Pre**dstaviće	Он буде прѐдставио On bude **pre**dstavio
3rd per (F)	Она прѐдстави Ona **pre**dstavi	Она ће прѐдставити/Прѐдставиће Ona će **pre**dstaviti/**Pre**dstaviće	Она буде прѐдставила Ona bude **pre**dstavila
3rd per (N)	Оно прѐдстави Ono **pre**dstavi	Оно ће прѐдставити/Прѐдставиће Ono će **pre**dstaviti/**Pre**dstaviće	Оно буде прѐдставило Ono bude **pre**dstavilo
1st per pl	Ми прѐдставимо Mi **pre**dstavimo	Ми ћемо прѐдставити/Прѐдставићемо Mi ćemo **pre**dstaviti/**Pre**dstavićemo	Ми будемо прѐдставили/ прѐдставиле Mi budemo **pre**dstavili/ **pre**dstavile
2nd per pl	Ви прѐдставите Vi **pre**dstavite	Ви ћете прѐдставити/Прѐдставићете Vi ćete **pre**dstaviti/**Pre**dstavićete	Ви будете прѐдставили/прѐдставиле Vi budete **pre**dstavili/**pre**dstavile
3rd per pl	Они/Оне прѐдставе Oni/One **pre**dstave	Они/Оне ће прѐдставити/Прѐдставиће Oni/One će **pre**dstaviti/**Pre**dstaviće	Они/Оне буду прѐдставили/прѐдставиле Oni/One budu **pre**dstavili/**pre**dstavile

	Past Tense (Перфект)	Pluperfect (Плусквамперфект)	Conditional (Потенцијал)
1st per	Ја сам прѐдставио Ja sam **pre**dstavio	Ја сам био прѐдставио Ja sam bio **pre**dstavio	Ја бих прѐдставио Ja bih **pre**dstavio
2nd per	Ти си прѐдставио Ti si **pre**dstavio	Ти си био прѐдставио Ti si bio **pre**dstavio	Ти би прѐдставио Ti bi **pre**dstavio
3rd per (M)	Он је прѐдставио On je **pre**dstavio	Он је био прѐдставио On je bio **pre**dstavio	Он би прѐдставио On bi **pre**dstavio
3rd per (F)	Она је прѐдставила Ona je **pre**dstavila	Она је била прѐдставила Ona je bila **pre**dstavila	Она би прѐдставила Ona bi **pre**dstavila
3rd per (N)	Оно је прѐдставило Ono je **pre**dstavilo	Оно је било прѐдставило Ono je bilo **pre**dstavilo	Оно би прѐдставило Ono bi **pre**dstavilo
1st per pl	Ми смо прѐдставили Mi smo **pre**dstavili	Ми смо били прѐдставили Mi smo bili **pre**dstavili	Ми бисмо прѐдставили Mi bismo **pre**dstavili
2nd per pl	Ви сте прѐдставили Vi ste **pre**dstavili	Ви сте били прѐдставили Vi ste bili **pre**dstavili	Ви бисте прѐдставили Vi biste **pre**dstavili
3rd per pl	Они су прѐдставили Oni su **pre**dstavili	Они су били прѐдставили Oni su bili **pre**dstavili	Они би прѐдставили Oni bi **pre**dstavili

	Imperative (Императив)
2nd per sg	(Ти) прѐдстави (Ti) **pre**dstavi
1st per pl	(Ми) прѐдставимо (Mi) **pre**dstavimo
2nd per pl	(Ви) прѐдставите (Vi) **pre**dstavite

Non-finite Forms

Infinitive (Инфинитив)	прѐдставити **pre**dstaviti
Present Adverbial Participle (Глаголски прилог садашњи)	--
Past Adverbial Participle (Глаголски прилог прошли)	прѐдставивши **pre**dstavivši

	Active Adjectival Participle (Глаголски придев радни)		Passive Adjectival Participle (Глаголски придев трпни)	
Gender	Singular	Plural	Singular	Plural
Feminine	прѐдставила **pre**dstavila	прѐдставиле **pre**dstavile	прѐдстављена **pre**dstavljena	прѐдстављене **pre**dstavljene
Masculine	прѐдставио **pre**dstavio	прѐдставили **pre**dstavili	прѐдстављен **pre**dstavljen	прѐдстављени **pre**dstavljeni
Neuter	прѐдставило **pre**dstavilo	прѐдставила **pre**dstavila	прѐдстављено **pre**dstavljeno	прѐдстављена **pre**dstavljena

To Invite – пòзвати - pozvati

	Present (Презент)	Future I (Футур први)	Future II (Футур други)
1st per	Ja пòзовем	Ja ћу пòзвати/Пòзваћу	Ja будем пòзвао/пòзвала
	Ja pozovem	Ja ću pozvati/Pozvaću	Ja budem pozvao/pozvala
2nd per	Ти пòзовеш	Ти ћеш пòзвати/Пòзваћеш	Ти будеш пòзвао/пòзвала
	Ti pozoveš	Ti ćeš pozvati/Pozvaćeš	Ti budeš pozvao/pozvala
3rd per (M)	Он пòзове	Он ће пòзвати/Пòзваће	Он буде пòзвао
	On pozove	On će pozvati/Pozvaće	On bude pozvao
3rd per (F)	Она пòзове	Она ће пòзвати/Пòзваће	Она буде пòзвала
	Ona pozove	Ona će pozvati/Pozvaće	Ona bude pozvala
3rd per (N)	Оно пòзове	Оно ће пòзвати/Пòзваће	Оно буде пòзвало
	Ono pozove	Ono će pozvati/Pozvaće	Ono bude pozvalo
1st per pl	Ми пòзовемо	Ми ћемо пòзвати/Пòзваћемо	Ми будемо пòзвали/пòзвале
	Mi pozovemo	Mi ćemo pozvati/Pozvaćemo	Mi budemo pozvali/pozvale
2nd per pl	Ви пòзовете	Ви ћете пòзвати/Пòзваћете	Ви будете пòзвали/пòзвале
	Vi pozovete	Vi ćete pozvati/Pozvaćete	Vi budete pozvali/pozvale
3rd per pl	Они/Оне пòзову	Они/Оне ће пòзвати/Пòзваће	Они/Оне буду пòзвали/пòзвале
	Oni/One pozovu	Oni/One će pozvati/Pozvaće	Oni/One budu pozvali/pozvale

	Past Tense (Перфект)	Pluperfect (Плусквамперфект)	Conditional (Потенцијал)
1st per	Ja сам пòзвао	Ja сам био пòзвао	Ja бих пòзвао
	Ja sam pozvao	Ja sam bio pozvao	Ja bih pozvao
2nd per	Ти си пòзвао	Ти си био пòзвао	Ти би пòзвао
	Ti si pozvao	Ti si bio pozvao	Ti bi pozvao
3rd per (M)	Он је пòзвао	Он је био пòзвао	Он би пòзвао
	On je pozvao	On je bio pozvao	On bi pozvao
3rd per (F)	Она је пòзвала	Она је била пòзвала	Она би пòзвала
	Ona je pozvala	Ona je bila pozvala	Ona bi pozvala
3rd per (N)	Оно је пòзвало	Оно је било пòзвало	Оно би пòзвало
	Ono je pozvalo	Ono je bilo pozvalo	Ono bi pozvalo
1st per pl	Ми смо пòзвали	Ми смо били пòзвали	Ми бисмо пòзвали
	Mi smo pozvali	Mi smo bili pozvali	Mi bismo pozvali
2nd per pl	Ви сте пòзвали	Ви сте били пòзвали	Ви бисте пòзвали
	Vi ste pozvali	Vi ste bili pozvali	Vi biste pozvali
3rd per pl	Они су пòзвали	Они су били пòзвали	Они би пòзвали
	Oni su pozvali	Oni su bili pozvali	Oni bi pozvali

	Imperative (Императив)
2nd per sg	(Ти) позòви
	(Ti) pozovi
1st per pl	(Ми) позòвимо
	(Mi) pozovimo

2nd per pl	(Ви) позо̀вите
	(Vi) po**zo**vite

Non-finite Forms

Infinitive (Инфинитив)	по̀звати
	pozvati
Present Adverbial Participle (Глаголски прилог садашњи)	--
Past Adverbial Participle (Глаголски прилог прошли)	по̀звавши
	pozvavši

Gender	Active Adjectival Participle (Глаголски придев радни)		Passive Adjectival Participle (Глаголски придев трпни)	
	Singular	Plural	Singular	Plural
Feminine	по̀звала	по̀звале	по̀звана	по̀зване
	pozvala	**po**zvale	**po**zvana	**po**zvane
Masculine	по̀звао	по̀звали	по̀зван	по̀звани
	pozvao	**po**zvali	**po**zvan	**po**zvani
Neuter	по̀звало	по̀звала	по̀звано	по̀звана
	pozvalo	**po**zvala	**po**zvano	**po**zvana

To Kill – ỳбити - ubiti

	Present (Презент)	Future I (Футур први)	Future II (Футур други)
1st per	Ja ỳбијем / Ja ubijem	Ja ћу ỳбити/Ỳбићу / Ja ću ubiti/Ubiću	Ja будем ỳбио/ỳбила / Ja budem ubio/ubila
2nd per	Ти ỳбијеш / Ti ubiješ	Ти ћеш ỳбити/Ỳбићеш / Ti ćeš ubiti/Ubićeš	Ти будеш ỳбио/ỳбила / Ti budeš ubio/ubila
3rd per (M)	Он ỳбије / On ubije	Он ће ỳбити/Ỳбиће / On će ubiti/Ubiće	Он буде ỳбио / On bude ubio
3rd per (F)	Она ỳбије / Ona ubije	Она ће ỳбити/Ỳбиће / Ona će ubiti/Ubiće	Она буде ỳбила / Ona bude ubila
3rd per (N)	Оно ỳбије / Ono ubije	Оно ће ỳбити/Ỳбиће / Ono će ubiti/Ubiće	Оно буде ỳбило / Ono bude ubilo
1st per pl	Ми ỳбијемо / Mi ubijemo	Ми ћемо ỳбити/Ỳбићемо / Mi ćemo ubiti/Ubićemo	Ми будемо ỳбили/ỳбиле / Mi budemo ubili/ubile
2nd per pl	Ви ỳбијете / Vi ubijete	Ви ћете ỳбити/Ỳбићете / Vi ćete ubiti/Ubićete	Ви будете ỳбили/ỳбиле / Vi budete ubili/ubile
3rd per pl	Они/Оне ỳбију / Oni/One ubiju	Они/Оне ће ỳбити/Ỳбиће / Oni/One će ubiti/Ubiće	Они/Оне буду ỳбили/ỳбиле / Oni/One budu ubili/ubile

	Past Tense (Перфект)	Pluperfect (Плусквамперфект)	Conditional (Потенцијал)
1st per	Ja сам ỳбио / Ja sam ubio	Ja сам био ỳбио / Ja sam bio ubio	Ja бих ỳбио / Ja bih ubio
2nd per	Ти си ỳбио / Ti si ubio	Ти си био ỳбио / Ti si bio ubio	Ти би ỳбио / Ti bi ubio
3rd per (M)	Он је ỳбио / On je ubio	Он је био ỳбио / On je bio ubio	Он би ỳбио / On bi ubio
3rd per (F)	Она је ỳбила / Ona je ubila	Она је била ỳбила / Ona je bila ubila	Она би ỳбила / Ona bi ubila
3rd per (N)	Оно је ỳбило / Ono je ubilo	Оно је било ỳбило / Ono je bilo ubilo	Оно би ỳбило / Ono bi ubilo
1st per pl	Ми смо ỳбили / Mi smo ubili	Ми смо били ỳбили / Mi smo bili ubili	Ми бисмо ỳбили / Mi bismo ubili
2nd per pl	Ви сте ỳбили / Vi ste ubili	Ви сте били ỳбили / Vi ste bili ubili	Ви бисте ỳбили / Vi biste ubili
3rd per pl	Они су ỳбили / Oni su ubili	Они су били ỳбили / Oni su bili ubili	Они би ỳбили / Oni bi ubili

	Imperative (Императив)
2nd per sg	(Ти) ỳбиј / (Ti) ubij
1st per pl	(Ми) ỳбијмо / (Mi) ubijmo

2nd per pl	(Ви) у̀бијте
	(Vi) **u**bijte

Non-finite Forms

Infinitive (Инфинитив)	у̀бити
	ubiti
Present Adverbial Participle (Глаголски прилог садашњи)	--
Past Adverbial Participle (Глаголски прилог прошли)	у̀бивши
	ubivši

	Active Adjectival Participle (Глаголски придев радни)		Passive Adjectival Participle (Глаголски придев трпни)	
Gender	Singular	Plural	Singular	Plural
Feminine	у̀била	у̀биле	убѝјена	убѝјене
	ubila	**u**bile	**u**bijena	**u**bijene
Masculine	у̀био	у̀били	убѝјен	убѝјени
	ubio	**u**bili	**u**bijen	**u**bijeni
Neuter	у̀било	у̀била	убѝјено	убѝјена
	ubilo	**u**bila	**u**bijeno	**u**bijena

To Kiss - пољу́бити - poljubiti

	Present (Презент)	Future I (Футур први)	Future II (Футур други)
1st per	Ja пољу́бим Ja poljubim	Ja ћу пољу́бити/Пољу́бићу Ja ću poljubiti/Poljubiću	Ja будем пољу́био/пољу́била Ja budem poljubio/poljubila
2nd per	Ти пољу́биш Ti poljubiš	Ти ћеш пољу́бити/Пољу́бићеш Ti ćeš poljubiti/Poljubićeš	Ти будеш пољу́био/пољу́била Ti budeš poljubio/poljubila
3rd per (M)	Он пољу́би On poljubi	Он ће пољу́бити/Пољу́биће On će poljubiti/Poljubiće	Он буде пољу́био On bude poljubio
3rd per (F)	Она пољу́би Ona poljubi	Она ће пољу́бити/Пољу́биће Ona će poljubiti/Poljubiće	Она буде пољу́била Ona bude poljubila
3rd per (N)	Оно пољу́би Ono poljubi	Оно ће пољу́бити/Пољу́биће Ono će poljubiti/Poljubiće	Оно буде пољу́било Ono bude poljubilo
1st per pl	Ми пољу́бимо Mi poljubimo	Ми ћемо пољу́бити/Пољу́бићемо Mi ćemo poljubiti/Poljubićemo	Ми будемо пољу́били/пољу́биле Mi budemo poljubili/poljubile
2nd per pl	Ви пољу́бите Vi poljubite	Ви ћете пољу́бити/Пољу́бићете Vi ćete poljubiti/Poljubićete	Ви будете пољу́били/пољу́биле Vi budete poljubili/poljubile
3rd per pl	Они/Оне пољу́бе Oni/One poljube	Они/Оне ће пољу́бити/Пољу́биће Oni/One će poljubiti/Poljubiće	Они/Оне буду пољу́били/пољу́биле Oni/One budu poljubili/poljubile

	Past Tense (Перфект)	Pluperfect (Плусквамперфект)	Conditional (Потенцијал)
1st per	Ja сам пољу́био Ja sam poljubio	Ja сам био пољу́био Ja sam bio poljubio	Ja бих пољу́био Ja bih poljubio
2nd per	Ти си пољу́био Ti si poljubio	Ти си био пољу́био Ti si bio poljubio	Ти би пољу́био Ti bi poljubio
3rd per (M)	Он је пољу́био On je poljubio	Он је био пољу́био On je bio poljubio	Он би пољу́био On bi poljubio
3rd per (F)	Она је пољу́била Ona je poljubila	Она је била пољу́била Ona je bila poljubila	Она би пољу́била Ona bi poljubila
3rd per (N)	Оно је пољу́било Ono je poljubilo	Оно је било пољу́било Ono je bilo poljubilo	Оно би пољу́било Ono bi poljubilo
1st per pl	Ми смо пољу́били Mi smo poljubili	Ми смо били пољу́били Mi smo bili poljubili	Ми бисмо пољу́били Mi bismo poljubili
2nd per pl	Ви сте пољу́били Vi ste poljubili	Ви сте били пољу́били Vi ste bili poljubili	Ви бисте пољу́били Vi biste poljubili
3rd per pl	Они су пољу́били Oni su poljubili	Они су били пољу́били Oni su bili poljubili	Они би пољу́били Oni bi poljubili

	Imperative (Императив)
2nd per sg	(Ти) пољу́би (Ti) poljubi
1st per pl	(Ми) пољу́бимо (Mi) poljubimo

2nd per pl	(Ви) пољу́бите
	(Vi) poljubite

Non-finite Forms

Infinitive (Инфинитив)	пољу́бити
	poljubiti
Present Adverbial Participle (Глаголски прилог садашњи)	--
Past Adverbial Participle (Глаголски прилог прошли)	пољу́бивши
	poljubivši

Gender	Active Adjectival Participle (Глаголски придев радни)		Passive Adjectival Participle (Глаголски придев трпни)	
	Singular	Plural	Singular	Plural
Feminine	пољу́била	пољу́биле	по̀љубљена	по̀љубљене
	poljubila	poljubile	poljubljena	poljubljene
Masculine	пољу́био	пољу́били	по̀љубљен	по̀љубљени
	poljubio	poljubili	poljubljen	poljubljeni
Neuter	пољу́било	пољу́била	по̀љубљено	по̀љубљена
	poljubilo	poljubila	poljubljeno	poljubljena

To Know - зна̀ти - znati

	Present (Презент)	Future I (Футур први)	Future II (Футур други)
1st per	Ja зна̑м / Ja znam	Ja ħy зна̀ти/Зна̀ħy / Ja ću znati/Znaću	Ja будем зна̏о/зна̏ла / Ja budem znao/znala
2nd per	Ти зна̑ш / Ti znaš	Ти ħеш зна̀ти/Зна̀ħеш / Ti ćeš znati/Znaćeš	Ти будеш зна̏о/зна̏ла / Ti budeš znao/znala
3rd per (M)	Он зна̑ / On zna	Он ħе зна̀ти/Зна̀ħе / On će znati/Znaće	Он буде зна̏о / On bude znao
3rd per (F)	Она зна̑ / Ona zna	Она ħе зна̀ти/Зна̀ħе / Ona će znati/Znaće	Она буде зна̏ла / Ona bude znala
3rd per (N)	Оно зна̑ / Ono zna	Оно ħе зна̀ти/Зна̀ħе / Ono će znati/Znaće	Оно буде зна̏ло / Ono bude znalo
1st per pl	Ми зна́мо / Mi znamo	Ми ħемо зна̀ти/Зна̀ħемо / Mi ćemo znati/Znaćemo	Ми будемо зна̏ли/зна̏ле / Mi budemo znali/znale
2nd per pl	Ви зна́те / Vi znate	Ви ħете зна̀ти/Зна̀ħете / Vi ćete znati/Znaćete	Ви будете зна̏ли/зна̏ле / Vi budete znali/znale
3rd per pl	Они/Оне зна̀jy / Oni/One znaju	Они/Оне ħе зна̀ти/Зна̀ħе / Oni/One će znati/Znaće	Они/Оне буду зна̏ли/зна̏ле / Oni/One budu znali/znale

	Past Tense (Перфект)	Pluperfect (Плусквамперфект)	Conditional (Потенцијал)
1st per	Ja сам зна̏о / Ja sam znao	Ja сам био зна̏о / Ja sam bio znao	Ja бих зна̏о / Ja bih znao
2nd per	Ти си зна̏о / Ti si znao	Ти си био зна̏о / Ti si bio znao	Ти би зна̏о / Ti bi znao
3rd per (M)	Он је зна̏о / On je znao	Он је био зна̏о / On je bio znao	Он би зна̏о / On bi znao
3rd per (F)	Она је зна̏ла / Ona je znala	Она је била зна̏ла / Ona je bila znala	Она би зна̏ла / Ona bi znala
3rd per (N)	Оно је зна̏ло / Ono je znalo	Оно је било зна̏ло / Ono je bilo znalo	Оно би зна̏ло / Ono bi znalo
1st per pl	Ми смо зна̏ли / Mi smo znali	Ми смо били зна̏ли / Mi smo bili znali	Ми бисмо зна̏ли / Mi bismo znali
2nd per pl	Ви сте зна̏ли / Vi ste znali	Ви сте били зна̏ли / Vi ste bili znali	Ви бисте зна̏ли / Vi biste znali
3rd per pl	Они су зна̏ли / Oni su znali	Они су били зна̏ли / Oni su bili znali	Они би зна̏ли / Oni bi znali

	Imperative (Императив)
2nd per sg	(Ти) зна̑j / (Ti) znaj
1st per pl	(Ми) зна̑jмо / (Mi) znajmo

2nd per pl	(Ви) зна̂јте (Vi) **zna**jte

Non-finite Forms

Infinitive (Инфинитив)	зна̏ти **zna**ti
Present Adverbial Participle (Глаголски прилог садашњи)	зна̏јући **zna**jući
Past Adverbial Participle (Глаголски прилог прошли)	--

	Active Adjectival Participle (Глаголски придев радни)		Passive Adjectival Participle (Глаголски придев трпни)	
Gender	Singular	Plural	Singular	Plural
Feminine	зна̏ла **zna**la	зна̏ле **zna**le	зна̂на **zna**na	зна̂не **zna**ne
Masculine	зна̏о **zna**o	зна̏ли **zna**li	зна̂н **zna**n	зна̂ни **zna**ni
Neuter	зна̏ло **zna**lo	зна̏ла **zna**la	зна̂но **zna**no	зна̂на **zna**na

To Laugh - смѐјати се – smejati se

	Present (Презент)	Future I (Футур први)	Future II (Футур други)
1st per	Ја се смѐјем Ja se **sme**jem	Ја ћу се смѐјати/Смѐјаћу се Ja ću se **sme**jati/**Sme**jaću se	Ја се будем смѐјао/смѐјала Ja se budem **sme**jao/**sme**jala
2nd per	Ти се смѐјеш Ti se **sme**ješ	Ти ћеш се смѐјати/Смѐјаћеш се Ti ćeš se **sme**jati/**Sme**jaćeš se	Ти се будеш смѐјао/смѐјала Ti se budeš **sme**jao/**sme**jala
3rd per (M)	Он се смѐје On se **sme**je	Он ће се смѐјати/Смѐјаће се On će se **sme**jati/**Sme**jaće se	Он се буде смѐјао On se bude **sme**jao
3rd per (F)	Она се смѐје Ona se **sme**je	Она ће се смѐјати/Смѐјаће се Ona će se **sme**jati/**Sme**jaće se	Она се буде смѐјала Ona se bude **sme**jala
3rd per (N)	Оно се смѐје Ono se **sme**je	Оно ће се смѐјати/Смѐјаће се Ono će se **sme**jati/**Sme**jaće se	Оно се буде смѐјало Ono se bude **sme**jalo
1st per pl	Ми се смѐјемо Mi se **sme**jemo	Ми ћемо се смѐјати/Смѐјаћемо се Mi ćemo se **sme**jati/**Sme**jaćemo se	Ми се будемо смѐјали/смѐјале Mi se budemo **sme**jali/**sme**jale
2nd per pl	Ви се смѐјете Vi se **sme**jete	Ви ћете се смѐјати/Смѐјаћете се Vi ćete se **sme**jati/**Sme**jaćete se	Ви се будете смѐјали/смѐјале Vi se budete **sme**jali/**sme**jale
3rd per pl	Они/Оне се смѐју Oni/One se **sme**ju	Они/Оне ће се смѐјати/Смѐјаће се Oni/One će se **sme**jati/**Sme**jaće se	Они/Оне се буду смѐјали/смѐјале Oni/One se budu **sme**jali/**sme**jale

	Past Tense (Перфект)	Pluperfect (Плусквамперфект)	Conditional (Потенцијал)
1st per	Ја сам се смѐјао Ja sam se **sme**jao	Ја сам се био смѐјао Ja sam se bio **sme**jao	Ја бих се смѐјао Ja bih se **sme**jao
2nd per	Ти си се смѐјао Ti si se **sme**jao	Ти си се био смѐјао Ti si se bio **sme**jao	Ти би се смѐјао Ti bi se **sme**jao
3rd per (M)	Он се смѐјао On se **sme**jao	Он се био смѐјао On se bio **sme**jao	Он би се смѐјао On bi se **sme**jao
3rd per (F)	Она се смѐјала Ona se **sme**jala	Она се била смѐјала Ona se bila **sme**jala	Она би се смѐјала Ona bi se **sme**jala
3rd per (N)	Оно се смѐјало Ono se **sme**jalo	Оно се било смѐјало Ono se bilo **sme**jalo	Оно би се смѐјало Ono bi se **sme**jalo
1st per pl	Ми смо се смѐјали Mi smi se **sme**jali	Ми смо се били смѐјали Mi smo se bili **sme**jali	Ми бисмо се смѐјали Mi bismo se **sme**jali
2nd per pl	Ви сте се смѐјали Vi ste se **sme**jali	Ви сте се били смѐјали Vi ste se bili **sme**jali	Ви бисте се смѐјали Vi biste se **sme**jali
3rd per pl	Они су се смѐјали Oni su se **sme**jali	Они су се били смѐјали Oni su se bili **sme**jali	Они би се смѐјали Oni bi se **sme**jali

	Imperative (Императив)
2nd per sg	(Ти) смѐј се (Ti) **sme**j se
1st per pl	(Ми) смѐјмо се (Mi) **sme**jmo se

111

2nd per pl	(Ви) смȇјте се
	(Mi) **sme**jte se

Non-finite Forms

Infinitive (Инфинитив)	смȅјати се
	smejati se
Present Adverbial Participle (Глаголски прилог садашњи)	смȅјући се
	smejući se
Past Adverbial Participle (Глаголски прилог прошли)	--

	Active Adjectival Participle (Глаголски придев радни)		Passive Adjectival Participle (Глаголски придев трпни)	
Gender	Singular	Plural	Singular	Plural
Feminine	смȅјала	смȅјале	--	--
	smejala	**sme**jale		
Masculine	смȅјао	смȅјали	--	--
	smejao	**sme**jali		
Neuter	смȅјало	смȅјала	--	--
	smejalo	**sme**jala		

To Learn – у̀чити - ùčiti

	Present (Презент)	Future I (Футур први)	Future II (Футур други)
1st per	Ja у̀чим / Ja u**č**im	Ja ћу у̀чити/У̀чићу / Ja ću u**č**iti/U**č**ићу	Ja будем у̀чио/у̀чила / Ja budem u**č**io/u**č**ila
2nd per	Ти у̀чиш / Ti u**č**iš	Ти ћеш у̀чити/У̀чићеш / Ti ćeš u**č**iti/U**č**ićeš	Ти будеш у̀чио/у̀чила / Ti budeš u**č**io/u**č**ila
3rd per (M)	Он у̀чи / On u**č**i	Он ће у̀чити/У̀чиће / On će u**č**iti/U**č**iće	Он буде у̀чио / On bude u**č**io
3rd per (F)	Она у̀чи / Ona u**č**i	Она ће у̀чити/У̀чиће / Ona će u**č**iti/U**č**iće	Она буде у̀чила / Ona bude u**č**ila
3rd per (N)	Оно у̀чи / Ono u**č**i	Оно ће у̀чити/У̀чиће / Ono će u**č**iti/U**č**iće	Оно буде у̀чило / Ono bude u**č**ilo
1st per pl	Ми у̀чимо / Mi u**č**imo	Ми ћемо у̀чити/У̀чићемо / Mi ćemo u**č**iti/U**č**ićemo	Ми будемо у̀чили/у̀чиле / Mi budemo u**č**ili/u**č**ile
2nd per pl	Ви у̀чите / Vi u**č**ite	Ви ћете у̀чити/У̀чићете / Vi ćete u**č**iti/U**č**ićete	Ви будете у̀чили/у̀чиле / Vi budete u**č**ili/u**č**ile
3rd per pl	Они/Оне у̀че / Oni/One u**č**e	Они/Оне ће у̀чити/У̀чиће / Oni/One će u**č**iti/U**č**iće	Они/Оне буду у̀чили/у̀чиле / Oni/One budu u**č**ili/u**č**ile

	Past Tense (Перфект)	Pluperfect (Плусквамперфект)	Conditional (Потенцијал)
1st per	Ja сам у̀чио / Ja sam u**č**io	Ja сам био у̀чио / Ja sam bio u**č**io	Ja бих у̀чио / Ja bih u**č**io
2nd per	Ти си у̀чио / Ti si u**č**io	Ти си био у̀чио / Ti si bio u**č**io	Ти би у̀чио / Ti bi u**č**io
3rd per (M)	Он је у̀чио / On je u**č**io	Он је био у̀чио / On je bio u**č**io	Он би у̀чио / On bi u**č**io
3rd per (F)	Она је у̀чила / Ona je u**č**ila	Она је била у̀чила / Ona je bila u**č**ila	Она би у̀чила / Ona bi u**č**ila
3rd per (N)	Оно је у̀чило / Ono je u**č**ilo	Оно је било у̀чило / Ono je bilo u**č**ilo	Оно би у̀чило / Ono bi u**č**ilo
1st per pl	Ми смо у̀чили / Mi smo u**č**ili	Ми смо били у̀чили / Mi smo bili u**č**ili	Ми бисмо у̀чили / Mi bismo u**č**ili
2nd per pl	Ви сте у̀чили / Vi ste u**č**ili	Ви сте били у̀чили / Vi ste bili u**č**ili	Ви бисте у̀чили / Vi biste u**č**ili
3rd per pl	Они су у̀чили / Oni su u**č**ili	Они су били у̀чили / Oni su bili u**č**ili	Они би у̀чили / Oni bi u**č**ili

	Imperative (Императив)
2nd per sg	(Ти) у̀чи / (Ti) u**č**i
1st per pl	(Ми) у̀чимо / (Mi) u**č**imo

SERBIAN LANGUAGE: 101 SERBIAN VERBS

2nd per pl	(Ви) у̀чите (Vi) **u**čite

Non-finite Forms

Infinitive (Инфинитив)	у̀чити **u**čiti
Present Adverbial Participle (Глаголски прилог садашњи)	у̀чећи **u**čeći
Past Adverbial Participle (Глаголски прилог прошли)	--

	Active Adjectival Participle (Глаголски придев радни)		Passive Adjectival Participle (Глаголски придев трпни)	
Gender	Singular	Plural	Singular	Plural
Feminine	у̀чила **u**čila	у̀чиле **u**čile	у̀чена **u**čena	у̀чене **u**čene
Masculine	у̀чио **u**čio	у̀чили **u**čili	у̀чен **u**čen	у̀чени **u**čeni
Neuter	у̀чило **u**čilo	у̀чила **u**čila	у̀чено **u**čeno	у̀чена **u**čena

To Lie Down – лѐћи - leći

	Present (Презент)	Future I (Футур први)	Future II (Футур други)
1st per	Ja лѐгнем Ja **legnem**	Ja ћу лѐћи/Лѐћи ћу Ja ću le**ći**/**Le**ći ću	Ja будем лѐгао/лѐгла Ja budem **legao**/**legla**
2nd per	Ти лѐгнеш Ti **legneš**	Ти ћеш лѐћи/Лѐћи ћеш Ti ćeš le**ći**/**Le**ći ćeš	Ти будеш лѐгао/лѐгла Ti budeš **legao**/**legla**
3rd per (M)	Он лѐгне On **legne**	Он ће лѐћи/Лѐћи ће On će le**ći**/**Le**ći će	Он буде лѐгао On bude **legao**
3rd per (F)	Она лѐгне Ona **legne**	Она ће лѐћи/Лѐћи ће Ona će le**ći**/**Le**ći će	Она буде лѐгла Ona bude **legla**
3rd per (N)	Оно лѐгне Ono **legne**	Оно ће лѐћи/Лѐћи ће Ono će le**ći**/**Le**ći će	Оно буде лѐгло Ono bude **leglo**
1st per pl	Ми лѐгнемо Mi **legnemo**	Ми ћемо лѐћи/Лѐћи ћемо Mi ćemo le**ći**/**Le**ći ćemo	Ми будемо лѐгли/лѐгле Mi budemo **legli**/**legle**
2nd per pl	Ви лѐгнете Vi **legnete**	Ви ћете лѐћи/Лѐћи ћете Vi ćete le**ći**/**Le**ći ćete	Ви будете лѐгли/лѐгле Vi budete **legli**/**legle**
3rd per pl	Они/Оне лѐгну Oni/One **legnu**	Они/Оне ће лѐћи/Лѐћи ће Oni/One će le**ći**/**Le**ći će	Они/Оне буду лѐгли/лѐгле Oni/One budu **legli**/**legle**

	Past Tense (Перфект)	Pluperfect (Плусквамперфект)	Conditional (Потенцијал)
1st per	Ja сам лѐгао Ja sam **legao**	Ja сам био лѐгао Ja sam bio **legao**	Ja бих лѐгао Ja bih **legao**
2nd per	Ти си лѐгао Ti si **legao**	Ти си био лѐгао Ti si bio **legao**	Ти би лѐгао Ti bi **legao**
3rd per (M)	Он је лѐгао On je **legao**	Он је био лѐгао On je bio **legao**	Он би лѐгао On bi **legao**
3rd per (F)	Она је лѐгла Ona je **legla**	Она је била лѐгла Ona je bila **legla**	Она би лѐгла Ona bi **legla**
3rd per (N)	Оно је лѐгло Ono je **leglo**	Оно је било лѐгло Ono je bilo **leglo**	Оно би лѐгло Ono bi **leglo**
1st per pl	Ми смо лѐгли Mi smo **legli**	Ми смо били лѐгли Mi smo bili **legli**	Ми бисмо лѐгли Mi bismo **legli**
2nd per pl	Ви сте лѐгли Vi ste **legli**	Ви сте били лѐгли Vi ste bili **legli**	Ви бисте лѐгли Vi biste **legli**
3rd per pl	Они су лѐгли Oni su **legli**	Они су били лѐгли Oni su bili **legli**	Они би лѐгли Oni bi **legli**

	Imperative (Императив)
2nd per sg	(Ти) лѐзи (Ti) **lezi**
1st per pl	(Ми) лѐзимо (Mi) **lezimo**

2nd per pl	(Ви) лѐзите (Vi) **le**zite

Non-finite Forms

Infinitive (Инфинитив)	лѐћи **le**ći
Present Adverbial Participle (Глаголски прилог садашњи)	--
Past Adverbial Participle (Глаголски прилог прошли)	лѐгнувши **le**gnuvši

Gender	Active Adjectival Participle (Глаголски придев радни)		Passive Adjectival Participle (Глаголски придев трпни)	
	Singular	Plural	Singular	Plural
Feminine	лѐгла **le**gla	лѐгле **le**gle	--	--
Masculine	лѐгао **le**gao	лѐгли **le**gli	--	--
Neuter	лѐгло **le**glo	лѐгла **le**gla	--	--

To Like – во̀лети - voleti

	Present (Презент)	Future I (Футур први)	Future II (Футур други)
1st per	Ja во̀лим Ja volim	Ja ћу во̀лети/Во̀ле́ћу Ja ću voleti/Voléću	Ja будем во̀лео/во̀лела Ja budem voleo/volela
2nd per	Ти во̀лиш Ti voliš	Ти ћеш во̀лети/Во̀ле́ћеш Ti ćeš voleti/Voléćeš	Ти будеш во̀лео/во̀лела Ti budeš voleo/volela
3rd per (M)	Он во̀ли On voli	Он ће во̀лети/Во̀ле́ће On će voleti/Voléće	Он буде во̀лео On bude voleo
3rd per (F)	Она во̀ли Ona voli	Она ће во̀лети/Во̀ле́ће Ona će voleti/Voléće	Она буде во̀лела Ona bude volela
3rd per (N)	Оно во̀ли Ono voli	Оно ће во̀лети/Во̀ле́ће Ono će voleti/Voléće	Оно буде во̀лело Ono bude volelo
1st per pl	Ми во̀лимо Mi volimo	Ми ћемо во̀лети/Во̀ле́ћемо Mi ćemo voleti/Voléćemo	Ми будемо во̀лели/во̀леле Mi budemo voleli/volele
2nd per pl	Ви во̀лите Vi volite	Ви ћете во̀лети/Во̀ле́ћете Vi ćete voleti/Voléćete	Ви будете во̀лели/во̀леле Vi budete voleli/volele
3rd per pl	Они/Оне во̀ле Oni/One vole	Они/Оне ће во̀лети/Во̀ле́ће Oni/One će voleti/Voléće	Они/Оне буду во̀лели/во̀леле Oni/One budu voleli/volele

	Past Tense (Перфект)	Pluperfect (Плусквамперфект)	Conditional (Потенцијал)
1st per	Ja сам во̀лео Ja sam voleo	Ja сам био во̀лео Ja sam bio voleo	Ja бих во̀лео Ja bih voleo
2nd per	Ти си во̀лео Ti si voleo	Ти си био во̀лео Ti si bio voleo	Ти би во̀лео Ti bi voleo
3rd per (M)	Он је во̀лео On je voleo	Он је био во̀лео On je bio voleo	Он би во̀лео On bi voleo
3rd per (F)	Она је во̀лела Ona je volela	Она је била во̀лела Ona je bila volela	Она би во̀лела Ona bi volela
3rd per (N)	Оно је во̀лело Ono je volelo	Оно је било во̀лело Ono je bilo volelo	Оно би во̀лело Ono bi volelo
1st per pl	Ми смо во̀лели Mi smo voleli	Ми смо били во̀лели Mi smo bili voleli	Ми бисмо во̀лели Mi bismo voleli
2nd per pl	Ви сте во̀лели Vi ste voleli	Ви сте били во̀лели Vi ste bili voleli	Ви бисте во̀лели Vi biste voleli
3rd per pl	Они су во̀лели Oni su voleli	Они су били во̀лели Oni su bili voleli	Они би во̀лели Oni bi voleli

	Imperative (Императив)
2nd per sg	(Ти) во̀ли (Ti) voli
1st per pl	(Ми) во̀лимо (Mi) volimo

2nd per pl	(Ви) во̀лите
	(Vi) **vo**lite

Non-finite Forms

Infinitive (Инфинитив)	во̀лети
	voleti
Present Adverbial Participle (Глаголски прилог садашњи)	во̀лећи
	voleći
Past Adverbial Participle (Глаголски прилог прошли)	--

	Active Adjectival Participle (Глаголски придев радни)		Passive Adjectival Participle (Глаголски придев трпни)	
Gender	Singular	Plural	Singular	Plural
Feminine	во̀лела	во̀леле	во̏љена	во̏љене
	volela	**vo**lele	**vo**ljena	**vo**ljene
Masculine	во̀лео	во̀лели	во̏љен	во̏љени
	voleo	**vo**leli	**vo**ljen	**vo**ljeni
Neuter	во̀лело	во̀лела	во̏љено	во̏љена
	volelo	**vo**lela	**vo**ljeno	**vo**ljena

To Listen - слу̏шати - slušati

	Present (Презент)	Future I (Футур први)	Future II (Футур други)
1st per	Ja слу̏шам Ja slušam	Ja ћу слу̏шати/Слу̏ша̎ћу Ja ću slušati/Slušaću	Ja бу̏дем слу̏шао/слу̏шала Ja budem slušao/slušala
2nd per	Ти слу̏шаш Ti slušaš	Ти ћеш слу̏шати/Слу̏ша̎ћеш Ti ćeš slušati/Slušaćeš	Ти бу̏деш слу̏шао/слу̏шала Ti budeš slušao/slušala
3rd per (M)	Он слу̏ша On sluša	Он ће слу̏шати/Слу̏ша̎ће On će slušati/Slušaće	Он бу̏де слу̏шао On bude slušao
3rd per (F)	Она слу̏ша Ona sluša	Она ће слу̏шати/Слу̏ша̎ће Ona će slušati/Slušaće	Она бу̏де слу̏шала Ona bude slušala
3rd per (N)	Оно слу̏ша Ono sluša	Оно ће слу̏шати/Слу̏ша̎ће Ono će slušati/Slušaće	Оно бу̏де слу̏шало Ono bude slušalo
1st per pl	Ми слу̏шамо Mi slušamo	Ми ћемо слу̏шати/Слу̏ша̎ћемо Mi ćemo slušati/Slušaćemo	Ми бу̏демо слу̏шали/слу̏шале Mi budemo slušali/slušale
2nd per pl	Ви слу̏шате Vi slušate	Ви ћете слу̏шати/Слу̏ша̎ћете Vi ćete slušati/Slušaćete	Ви бу̏дете слу̏шали/слу̏шале Vi budete slušali/slušale
3rd per pl	Они/Оне слу̏шају Oni/One slušaju	Они/Оне ће слу̏шати/Слу̏ша̎ће Oni/One će slušati/Slušaće	Они/Оне бу̏ду слу̏шали/слу̏шале Oni/One budu slušali/slušale

	Past Tense (Перфект)	Pluperfect (Плусквамперфект)	Conditional (Потенцијал)
1st per	Ja сам слу̏шао Ja sam slušao	Ja сам био слу̏шао Ja sam bio slušao	Ja бих слу̏шао Ja bih slušao
2nd per	Ти си слу̏шао Ti si slušao	Ти си био слу̏шао Ti si bio slušao	Ти би слу̏шао Ti bi slušao
3rd per (M)	Он је слу̏шао On je slušao	Он је био слу̏шао On je bio slušao	Он би слу̏шао On bi slušao
3rd per (F)	Она је слу̏шала Ona je slušala	Она је била слу̏шала Ona je bila slušala	Она би слу̏шала Ona bi slušala
3rd per (N)	Оно је слу̏шало Ono je slušalo	Оно је било слу̏шало Ono je bilo slušalo	Оно би слу̏шало Ono bi slušalo
1st per pl	Ми смо слу̏шали Mi smo slušali	Ми смо били слу̏шали Mi smo bili slušali	Ми бисмо слу̏шали Mi bismo slušali
2nd per pl	Ви сте слу̏шали Vi ste slušali	Ви сте били слу̏шали Vi ste bili slušali	Ви бисте слу̏шали Vi biste slušali
3rd per pl	Они су слу̏шали Oni su slušali	Они су били слу̏шали Oni su bili slušali	Они би слу̏шали Oni bi slušali

	Imperative (Императив)
2nd per sg	(Ти) слу̏шај (Ti) slušaj
1st per pl	(Ми) слу̏шајмо (Mi) slušajmo

119

2nd per pl	(Ви) слу̏шајте
	(Vi) **slu**šajte

Non-finite Forms

Infinitive (Инфинитив)	слу̏шати
	slušati
Present Adverbial Participle (Глаголски прилог садашњи)	слу̏шајући
	slušajući
Past Adverbial Participle (Глаголски прилог прошли)	слу̏шавши
	slušavši

	Active Adjectival Participle (Глаголски придев радни)		Passive Adjectival Participle (Глаголски придев трпни)	
Gender	Singular	Plural	Singular	Plural
Feminine	слу̏шала	слу̏шале	слу̏шана	слу̏шане
	slušala	**slu**šale	**slu**šana	**slu**šane
Masculine	слу̏шао	слу̏шали	слу̏шан	слу̏шани
	slušao	**slu**šali	**slu**šan	**slu**šani
Neuter	слу̏шало	слу̏шала	слу̏шано	слу̏шана
	slušalo	**slu**šala	**slu**šano	**slu**šana

To Live - жи́вети - živeti

	Present (Презент)	Future I (Футур први)	Future II (Футур други)
1st per	Ja жи́вим / Ja živim	Ja ћу жи́вети/Жи́већу / Ja ću živeti/Živeću	Ja будем жи́вео/жи́вела / Ja budem živeo/živela
2nd per	Ти жи́виш / Ti živiš	Ти ћеш жи́вети/Жи́већеш / Ti ćeš živeti/Živećeš	Ти будеш жи́вео/жи́вела / Ti budeš živeo/živela
3rd per (M)	Он жи́ви / On živi	Он ће жи́вети/Жи́веће / On će živeti/Živeće	Он буде жи́вео / On bude živeo
3rd per (F)	Она жи́ви / Ona živi	Она ће жи́вети/Жи́веће / Ona će živeti/Živeće	Она буде жи́вела / Ona bude živela
3rd per (N)	Оно жи́ви / Ono živi	Оно ће жи́вети/Жи́веће / Ono će živeti/Živeće	Оно буде жи́вело / Ono bude živelo
1st per pl	Ми жи́вимо / Mi živimo	Ми ћемо жи́вети/Жи́већемо / Mi ćemo živeti/Živećemo	Ми будемо жи́вели/жи́веле / Mi budemo živeli/živele
2nd per pl	Ви жи́вите / Vi živite	Ви ћете жи́вети/Жи́већете / Vi ćete živeti/Živećete	Ви будете жи́вели/жи́веле / Vi budete živeli/živele
3rd per pl	Они/Оне жи́ве / Oni/One žive	Они/Оне ће жи́вети/Жи́веће / Oni/One će živeti/Živeće	Они/Оне буду жи́вели/жи́веле / Oni/One budu živeli/živele

	Past Tense (Перфект)	Pluperfect (Плусквамперфект)	Conditional (Потенцијал)
1st per	Ja сам жи́вео / Ja sam živeo	Ja сам био жи́вео / Ja sam bio živeo	Ja бих жи́вео / Ja bih živeo
2nd per	Ти си жи́вео / Ti si živeo	Ти си био жи́вео / Ti si bio živeo	Ти би жи́вео / Ti bi živeo
3rd per (M)	Он је жи́вео / On je živeo	Он је био жи́вео / On je bio živeo	Он би жи́вео / On bi živeo
3rd per (F)	Она је жи́вела / Ona je živela	Она је била жи́вела / Ona je bila živela	Она би жи́вела / Ona bi živela
3rd per (N)	Оно је жи́вело / Ono je živelo	Оно је било жи́вело / Ono je bilo živelo	Оно би жи́вело / Ono bi živelo
1st per pl	Ми смо жи́вели / Mi smo živeli	Ми смо били жи́вели / Mi smo bili živeli	Ми бисмо жи́вели / Mi bismo živeli
2nd per pl	Ви сте жи́вели / Vi ste živeli	Ви сте били жи́вели / Vi ste bili živeli	Ви бисте жи́вели / Vi biste živeli
3rd per pl	Они су жи́вели / Oni su živeli	Они су били жи́вели / Oni su bili živeli	Они би жи́вели / Oni bi živeli

	Imperative (Императив)
2nd per sg	(Ти) жи́ви / (Ti) živi
1st per pl	(Ми) жи́вимо / (Mi) živimo

2nd per pl	(Ви) жи́вите
	(Vi) **živite**

Non-finite Forms

Infinitive (Инфинитив)	жи́вети
	živeti
Present Adverbial Participle (Глаголски прилог садашњи)	жи́већи
	živeći
Past Adverbial Participle (Глаголски прилог прошли)	--

	Active Adjectival Participle (Глаголски придев радни)		Passive Adjectival Participle (Глаголски придев трпни)	
Gender	Singular	Plural	Singular	Plural
Feminine	жи́вела	жи́веле	--	--
	živela	žіvele		
Masculine	жи́вео	жи́вели	--	--
	žіveo	žіveli		
Neuter	жи́вело	жи́вела	--	--
	žіvelo	žіvela		

To Lose – изгу̀бити - izgubiti

	Present (Презент)	Future I (Футур први)	Future II (Футур други)
1st per	Ja ѝзгубим Ja **izgubim**	Ja ħy изгу̀бити/Изгу̀бићу Ja ću **izgubiti/Izgubiću**	Ja будем изгу̀био/изгу̀била Ja budem **izgubio/izgubila**
2nd per	Ти ѝзгубиш Ti **izgubiš**	Ти ħeш изгу̀бити/Изгу̀бићеш Ti ćeš **izgubiti/Izgubićeš**	Ти будеш изгу̀био/изгу̀била Ti budeš **izgubio/izgubila**
3rd per (M)	Он ѝзгуби On **izgubi**	Он ħe изгу̀бити/Изгу̀биће On će **izgubiti/Izgubiće**	Он буде изгу̀био On bude **izgubio**
3rd per (F)	Она ѝзгуби Ona **izgubi**	Она ħe изгу̀бити/Изгу̀биће Ona će **izgubiti/Izgubiće**	Она буде изгу̀била Ona bude **izgubila**
3rd per (N)	Оно ѝзгуби Ono **izgubi**	Оно ħe изгу̀бити/Изгу̀биће Ono će **izgubiti/Izgubiće**	Оно буде изгу̀било Ono bude **izgubilo**
1st per pl	Ми ѝзгубимо Mi **izgubimo**	Ми ħemo изгу̀бити/Изгу̀бићемо Mi ćemo **izgubiti/Izgubićemo**	Ми будемо изгу̀били/изгу̀биле Mi budemo **izgubili/izgubile**
2nd per pl	Ви ѝзгубите Vi **izgubite**	Ви ħete изгу̀бити/ Изгу̀бићете Vi ćete **izgubiti/ Izgubićete**	Ви будете изгу̀били/изгу̀биле Vi budete **izgubili/izgubile**
3rd per pl	Они/Оне ѝзгубе Oni/One **izgube**	Они/Оне ħe изгу̀бити/Изгу̀биће Oni/One će **izgubiti/Izgubiće**	Они/Оне буду изгу̀били/изгу̀биле Oni/One budu **izgubili/izgubile**

	Past Tense (Перфект)	Pluperfect (Плусквамперфект)	Conditional (Потенцијал)
1st per	Ja сам изгу̀био Ja sam **izgubio**	Ja сам био изгу̀био Ja sam bio **izgubio**	Ja бих изгу̀био Ja bih **izgubio**
2nd per	Ти си изгу̀био Ti si **izgubio**	Ти си био изгу̀био Ti si bio **izgubio**	Ти би изгу̀био Ti bi **izgubio**
3rd per (M)	Он је изгу̀био On je **izgubio**	Он је био изгу̀био On je bio **izgubio**	Он би изгу̀био On bi **izgubio**
3rd per (F)	Она је изгу̀била Ona je **izgubila**	Она је била изгу̀била Ona je bila **izgubila**	Она би изгу̀била Ona bi **izgubila**
3rd per (N)	Оно је изгу̀било Ono je **izgubilo**	Оно је било изгу̀било Ono je bilo **izgubilo**	Оно би изгу̀било Ono bi **izgubilo**
1st per pl	Ми смо изгу̀били Mi smo **izgubili**	Ми смо били изгу̀били Mi smo bili **izgubili**	Ми бисмо изгу̀били Mi bismo **izgubili**
2nd per pl	Ви сте изгу̀били Vi ste **izgubili**	Ви сте били изгу̀били Vi ste bili **izgubili**	Ви бисте изгу̀били Vi biste **izgubili**
3rd per pl	Они су изгу̀били Oni su **izgubili**	Они су били изгу̀били Oni su bili **izgubili**	Они би изгу̀били Oni bi **izgubili**

	Imperative (Императив)
2nd per sg	(Ти) изгу̀би (Ti) iz**gubi**
1st per pl	(Ми) изгу̀бимо (Mi) iz**gubimo**

2nd per pl	(Ви) изгу̀бите
	(Vi) iz**gu**bite

Non-finite Forms

Infinitive (Инфинитив)	изгу̀бити
	iz**gu**biti
Present Adverbial Participle (Глаголски прилог садашњи)	--
Past Adverbial Participle (Глаголски прилог прошли)	изгу̀бивши
	iz**gu**bivši

Gender	Active Adjectival Participle (Глаголски придев радни)		Passive Adjectival Participle (Глаголски придев трпни)	
	Singular	Plural	Singular	Plural
Feminine	изгу̀била	изгу̀биле	изгу̏бљена	изгу̏бљене
	iz**gu**bila	iz**gu**bile	iz**gu**bljena	iz**gu**bljene
Masculine	изгу̀био	изгу̀били	изгу̏бљен	изгу̏бљени
	iz**gu**bio	iz**gu**bili	iz**gu**bljen	iz**gu**bljeni
Neuter	изгу̀било	изгу̀била	изгу̏бљено	изгу̏бљена
	iz**gu**bilo	iz**gu**bila	iz**gu**bljeno	iz**gu**bljena

To Love - обожа́вати - obožavati

	Present (Презент)	Future I (Футур први)	Future II (Футур други)
1st per	Ja обожавам Ja obožavam	Ja ћу обожа́вати/Обожа́ваћу Ja ću obožavati/Obožavaću	Ja будем обожа́вао/обожа́вала Ja budem obožavao/obožavala
2nd per	Ти обо̀жаваш Ti obožavaš	Ти ћеш обожа́вати/Обожа́ваћеш Ti ćeš obožavati/Obožavaćeš	Ти будеш обожа́вао/обожа́вала Ti budeš obožavao/obožavala
3rd per (M)	Он обо̀жава On obožava	Он ће обожа́вати/Обожа́ваће On će obožavati/Obožavaće	Он буде обожа́вао On bude obožavao
3rd per (F)	Она обо̀жава Ona obožava	Она ће обожа́вати/Обожа́ваће Ona će obožavati/Obožavaće	Она буде обожа́вала Ona bude obožavala
3rd per (N)	Оно обо̀жава Ono obožava	Оно ће обожа́вати/Обожа́вате Ono će obožavati/Obožavate	Оно буде обожа́вало Ono bude obožavalo
1st per pl	Ми обо̀жавамо Mi obožavamo	Ми ћемо обожа́вати/Обожа́ваћемо Mi ćemo obožavati/Obožavaćemo	Ми будемо обожа́вали/обожа́вале Mi budemo obožavali/obožavale
2nd per pl	Ви обо̀жавате Vi obožavate	Ви ћете обожа́вати/Обожа́ваћете Vi ćete obožavati/Obožavaćete	Ви будете обожа́вали/обожа́вале Vi budete obožavali/obožavale
3rd per pl	Они/Оне обожа́вају Oni/One obožavaju	Они/Оне ће обожа́вати/Обожа́ваће Oni/One će obožavati/Obožavaće	Они/Оне буду обожа́вали/обожа́вале Oni/One budu obožavali/obožavale

	Past Tense (Перфект)	Pluperfect (Плусквамперфект)	Conditional (Потенцијал)
1st per	Ja сам обожа́вао Ja sam obožavao	Ja сам био обожа́вао Ja sam bio obožavao	Ja бих обожа́вао Ja bih obožavao
2nd per	Ти си обожа́вао Ti si obožavao	Ти си био обожа́вао Ti si bio obožavao	Ти би обожа́вао Ti bi obožavao
3rd per (M)	Он је обожа́вао On je obožavao	Он је био обожа́вао On je bio obožavao	Он би обожа́вао On bi obožavao
3rd per (F)	Она је обожа́вала Ona je obožavala	Она је била обожа́вала Ona je bila obožavala	Она би обожа́вала Ona bi obožavala
3rd per (N)	Оно је обожа́вало Ono je obožavalo	Оно је било обожа́вало Ono je bilo obožavalo	Оно би обожа́вало Ono bi obožavalo
1st per pl	Ми смо обожа́вали Mi smo obožavali	Ми смо били обожа́вали Mi smo bili obožavali	Ми бисмо обожа́вали Mi bismo obožavali
2nd per pl	Ви сте обожа́вали Vi ste obožavali	Ви сте били обожа́вали Vi ste bili obožavali	Ви бисте обожа́вали Vi biste obožavali
3rd per pl	Они су обожа́вали Oni su obožavali	Они су били обожа́вали Oni su bili obožavali	Они би обожа́вали Oni bi obožavali

	Imperative (Императив)
2nd per sg	(Ти) обо̀жавај (Ti) obožavaj
1st per pl	(Ми) обо̀жавајмо (Mi) obožavajmo

2ⁿᵈ per pl	(Ви) обо̀жавајте
	(Vi) o**bo**žavajte

Non-finite Forms

Infinitive (Инфинитив)	обожа́вати
	obožavati
Present Adverbial Participle (Глаголски прилог садашњи)	обожа́вајући
	obožavajući
Past Adverbial Participle (Глаголски прилог прошли)	--

	Active Adjectival Participle (Глаголски придев радни)		Passive Adjectival Participle (Глаголски придев трпни)	
Gender	Singular	Plural	Singular	Plural
Feminine	обожа́вала	обожа́вале	обо̀жавана	обо̀жаване
	obožavala	obožavale	o**bo**žavana	o**bo**žavane
Masculine	обожа́вао	обожа́вали	обо̀жаван	обо̀жавани
	obožavao	obožavali	o**bo**žavan	o**bo**žavani
Neuter	обожа́вало	обожа́вала	обо̀жавано	обо̀жавана
	obožavalo	obožavala	o**bo**žavano	o**bo**žavana

To Meet - срѐсти се - sresti se

	Present (Презент)	Future I (Футур први)	Future II (Футур други)
1st per	Ja se срѐћем Ja se **srećem**	Ja ћу се срѐсти/Срѐшћу се Ja ću se sresti/**Sre**šću se	Ja se будем срѐо/срѐла Ja se budem **sreo/srela**
2nd per	Ти се срѐћеш Ti se **srećeš**	Ти ћеш се срѐсти/Срѐшћеш се Ti ćeš se sresti/**Sre**šćeš se	Ти се будеш срѐо/срѐла Ti se budeš **sreo/srela**
3rd per (M)	Он се срѐће On se **sreće**	Он ће се срѐсти/Срѐшће се On će se sresti/**Sre**šće se	Он се буде срѐо On se bude **sreo**
3rd per (F)	Она се срѐће Ona se **sreće**	Она ће се срѐсти/Срѐшће се Ona će se sresti/**Sre**šće se	Она се буде срѐла Ona se bude **srela**
3rd per (N)	Оно се срѐће Ono se **sreće**	Оно ће се срѐсти/Срѐшће се Ono će se sresti/**Sre**šće se	Оно се буде срѐло Ono se bude **srelo**
1st per pl	Ми се срѐћемо Mi se **srećemo**	Ми ћемо се срѐсти/Срѐшћемо се Mi ćemo se sresti/**Sre**šćemo se	Ми се будемо срѐли/срѐле Mi se budemo **sreli/srele**
2nd per pl	Ви се срѐћете Vi se **srećete**	Ви ћете се срѐсти/Срѐшћете се Vi ćete se sresti/**Sre**šćete se	Ви се будете срѐли/срѐле Vi se budete **sreli/srele**
3rd per pl	Они/Оне се срѐћу Oni/One se **sreću**	Они/Оне ће се срѐсти/Срѐшће се Oni/One će se sresti/**Sre**šće se	Они/Оне се буду срѐли/срѐле Oni/One se budu **sreli/srele**

	Past Tense (Перфект)	Pluperfect (Плусквамперфект)	Conditional (Потенцијал)
1st per	Ja сам се срѐо Ja sam se **sreo**	Ja сам се био срѐо Ja sam se bio **sreo**	Ja бих се срѐо Ja bih se **sreo**
2nd per	Ти си се срѐо Ti si se **sreo**	Ти си се био срѐо Ti si se bio **sreo**	Ти би се срѐо Ti bi se **sreo**
3rd per (M)	Он се срѐо On se **sreo**	Он се био срѐо On se bio **sreo**	Он би се срѐо On bi se **sreo**
3rd per (F)	Она се срѐла Ona se **srela**	Она се била срѐла Ona se bila **srela**	Она би се срѐла Ona bi se **srela**
3rd per (N)	Оно се срѐло Ono se **srelo**	Оно се било срѐло Ono se bilo **srelo**	Оно би се срѐло Ono bi se **srelo**
1st per pl	Ми смо се срѐли Mi smo se **sreli**	Ми смо се били срѐли Mi smo se bili **sreli**	Ми бисмо се срѐли Mi bismo se **sreli**
2nd per pl	Ви сте се срѐли Vi ste se **sreli**	Ви сте се били срѐли Vi ste se bili **sreli**	Ви бисте се срѐли Vi biste se **sreli**
3rd per pl	Они су се срѐли Oni su se **sreli**	Они су се били срѐли Oni su se bili **sreli**	Они би се срѐли Oni bi se **sreli**

	Imperative (Императив)
2nd per sg	(Ти) срѐтни се (Ti) **sre**tni se
1st per pl	(Ми) срѐтнимо се (Mi) **sre**tnimo se

2nd per pl	(Ви) срѐтните се (Vi) **sret**nite se

Non-finite Forms

Infinitive (Инфинитив)	срѐсти се **sre**sti se
Present Adverbial Participle (Глаголски прилог садашњи)	--
Past Adverbial Participle (Глаголски прилог прошли)	срѐтнувши се **sret**nuvši se

Gender	Active Adjectival Participle (Глаголски придев радни)		Passive Adjectival Participle (Глаголски придев трпни)	
	Singular	Plural	Singular	Plural
Feminine	срѐла **sre**la	срѐле **sre**lo	--	--
Masculine	срѐо **sre**o	срѐли **sre**li	--	--
Neuter	срѐло **sre**lo	срѐла **sre**la	--	--

To Need - трѐбати - trebati

	Present (Презент)	Future I (Футур први)	Future II (Футур други)
1st per	Ja трѐбам	Ja ћу трѐбати/Трѐбаћу	Ja будем трѐбао/трѐбала
2nd per	Ja **treb**am	Ja ću **treb**ati/**Treb**aću	Ja budem **treb**ao/**treb**ala
	Ти трѐбаш	Ти ћеш трѐбати/Трѐбаћеш	Ти будеш трѐбао/трѐбала
3rd per (M)	Ti **treb**aš	Ti ćeš **treb**ati/**Treb**aćeš	Ti budeš **treb**ao/**treb**ala
	Он трѐба	Он ће трѐбати/Трѐбаће	Он буде трѐбао
	On **treb**a	On će **treb**ati/**Treb**aće	On bude **treb**ao
3rd per (F)	Она трѐба	Она ће трѐбати/Трѐбаће	Она буде трѐбала
	Ona **treb**a	Ona će **treb**ati/**Treb**aće	Ona bude **treb**ala
	Оно трѐба	Оно ће трѐбати/Трѐбаће	Оно буде трѐбало
3rd per (N)	Ono **treb**a	Ono će **treb**ati/**Treb**aće	Ono bude **treb**alo
	Ми трѐбамо	Ми ћемо трѐбати/Трѐбаћемо	Ми будемо трѐбали/трѐбале
1st per pl	Mi **treb**amo	Mi ćemo **treb**ati/**Treb**aćemo	Mi budemo **treb**ali/**treb**ale
	Ви трѐбате	Ви ћете трѐбати/Трѐбаћете	Ви будете трѐбали/трѐбале
2nd per pl	Vi **treb**ate	Vi ćete **treb**ati/**Treb**aćete	Vi budete **treb**ali/**treb**ale
	Они/Оне трѐбају	Они/Оне ће трѐбати/Трѐбаће	Они/Оне буду трѐбали/трѐбале
3rd per pl	Oni/One **treb**aju	Oni/One će **treb**ati/**Treb**aće	Oni/One budu **treb**ali/**treb**ale

	Past Tense (Перфект)	Pluperfect (Плусквамперфект)	Conditional (Потенцијал)
1st per	Ja сам трѐбао	Ja сам био трѐбао	Ja бих трѐбао
	Ja sam **treb**ao	Ja sam bio **treb**ao	Ja bih **treb**ao
2nd per	Ти си трѐбао	Ти си био трѐбао	Ти би трѐбао
	Ti si **treb**ao	Ti si bio **treb**ao	Ti bi **treb**ao
3rd per (M)	Он је трѐбао	Он је био трѐбао	Он би трѐбао
	On je **treb**ao	On je bio **treb**ao	On bi **treb**ao
3rd per (F)	Она је трѐбала	Она је била трѐбала	Она би трѐбала
	Ona je **treb**ala	Ona je bila **treb**ala	Ona bi **treb**ala
3rd per (N)	Оно је трѐбало	Оно је било трѐбало	Оно би трѐбало
	Ono je **treb**alo	Ono je bilo **treb**alo	Ono bi **treb**alo
1st per pl	Ми смо трѐбали	Ми смо били трѐбали	Ми бисмо трѐбали
	Mi smo **treb**ali	Mi smo bili **treb**ali	Mi bismo **treb**ali
2nd per pl	Ви сте трѐбали	Ви сте били трѐбали	Ви бисте трѐбали
	Vi ste **treb**ali	Vi ste bili **treb**ali	Vi biste **treb**ali
3rd per pl	Они су трѐбали	Они су били трѐбали	Они би трѐбали
	Oni su **treb**ali	Oni su bili **treb**ali	Oni bi **treb**ali

	Imperative (Императив)
2nd per sg	(Ти) трѐбај
	(Ti) **treb**aj
1st per pl	(Ми) трѐбајмо
	(Mi) **treb**ajmo

2nd per pl	(Ви) трѐбајте
	(Vi) **tre**bajte

Non-finite Forms

Infinitive (Инфинитив)	трѐбати
	trebati
Present Adverbial Participle (Глаголски прилог садашњи)	трѐбајући
	trebajući
Past Adverbial Participle (Глаголски прилог прошли)	--

	Active Adjectival Participle (Глаголски придев радни)		Passive Adjectival Participle (Глаголски придев трпни)	
Gender	Singular	Plural	Singular	Plural
Feminine	трѐбала	трѐбале	--	--
	trebala	**tre**bale		
Masculine	трѐбао	трѐбали	--	--
	trebao	**tre**bali		
Neuter	трѐбало	трѐбала	--	--
	trebalo	**tre**bala		

To Notice - примétити - primetiti

	Present (Презент)	Future I (Футур први)	Future II (Футур други)
1st per	Ja прùметим / Ja **pri**metim	Ja ћу примétити/Примétићу / Ja ću primetiti/Primetiću	Ja будем примéтио/примéтила / Ja budem primetio/primetila
2nd per	Ти прùметиш / Ti **pri**metiš	Ти ћеш примétити/Примétићеш / Ti ćeš primetiti/Primetićeš	Ти будеш примéтио/примéтила / Ti budeš primetio/primetila
3rd per (M)	Он прùмети / On **pri**meti	Он ће примétити/Примétиће / On će primetiti/Primetiće	Он буде примéтио / On bude primetio
3rd per (F)	Она прùмети / Ona **pri**meti	Она ће примétити/Примétиће / Ona će primetiti/Primetiće	Она буде примéтила / Ona bude primetila
3rd per (N)	Оно прùмети / Ono **pri**meti	Оно ће примétити/Примétиће / Ono će primetiti/Primetiće	Оно буде примéтило / Ono bude primetilo
1st per pl	Ми прùметимо / Mi **pri**metimo	Ми ћемо примétити/Примétићемо / Mi ćemo primetiti/Primetićemo	Ми будемо примéтили/примéтиле / Mi budemo primetili/primetile
2nd per pl	Ви прùметите / Vi **pri**metite	Ви ћете примétити/Примétићете / Vi ćete primetiti/Primetićete	Ви будете примéтили/примéтиле / Vi budete primetili/primetile
3rd per pl	Они/Оне прùмете / Oni/One **pri**mete	Они/Оне ће примétити/Примétиће / Oni/One će primetiti/Primetiće	Они/Оне буду примéтили/примéтиле / Oni/One budu primetili/primetile

	Past Tense (Перфект)	Pluperfect (Плусквамперфект)	Conditional (Потенцијал)
1st per	Ja сам примéтио / Ja sam **pri**metio	Ja сам био примéтио / Ja sam bio **pri**metio	Ja бих примéтио / Ja bih **pri**metio
2nd per	Ти си примéтио / Ti si **pri**metio	Ти си био примéтио / Ti si bio **pri**metio	Ти би примéтио / Ti bi **pri**metio
3rd per (M)	Он је примéтио / On je **pri**metio	Он је био примéтио / On je bio **pri**metio	Он би примéтио / On bi **pri**metio
3rd per (F)	Она је примéтила / Ona je **pri**metila	Она је била примéтила / Ona je bila **pri**metila	Она би примéтила / Ona bi **pri**metila
3rd per (N)	Оно је примéтило / Ono je **pri**metilo	Оно је било примéтило / Ono je bilo **pri**metilo	Оно би примéтило / Ono bi **pri**metilo
1st per pl	Ми смо примéтили / Mi smo **pri**metili	Ми смо били примéтили / Mi smo bili **pri**metili	Ми бисмо примéтили / Mi bismo **pri**metili
2nd per pl	Ви сте примéтили / Vi ste **pri**metili	Ви сте били примéтили / Vi ste bili **pri**metili	Ви бисте примéтили / Vi biste **pri**metili
3rd per pl	Они су примéтили / Oni su **pri**metili	Они су били примéтили / Oni su bili **pri**metili	Они би примéтили / Oni bi **pri**metili

	Imperative (Императив)
2nd per sg	(Ти) примéти / (Ti) **pri**meti
1st per pl	(Ми) примéтимо / (Mi) **pri**metimo

2nd per pl	(Ви) приме́тите (Vi) primetite

Non-finite Forms

Infinitive (Инфинитив)	приме́тити primetiti
Present Adverbial Participle (Глаголски прилог садашњи)	--
Past Adverbial Participle (Глаголски прилог прошли)	приме́тивши primetivši

	Active Adjectival Participle (Глаголски придев радни)		Passive Adjectival Participle (Глаголски придев трпни)	
Gender	Singular	Plural	Singular	Plural
Feminine	приме́тила primetila	приме́тиле primetile	приме́ћена primećena	приме́ћене primećene
Masculine	приме́тио primetio	приме́тили primetili	приме́ћен primećen	приме́ћени primećeni
Neuter	приме́тило primetilo	приме́тила primetila	приме́ћено primećeno	приме́ћена primećena

To Open – отво̀рити - otvoriti

	Present (Презент)	Future I (Футур први)	Future II (Футур други)
1st per	Ja о̀творим Ja otvorim	Ja ћу отво̀рити/Отво̀рићу Ja ću otvoriti/Otvoriću	Ja будем отво̀рио/отво̀рила Ja budem otvorio/otvorila
2nd per	Ти о̀твориш Ti otvoriš	Ти ћеш отво̀рити/Отво̀рићеш Ti ćeš otvoriti/Otvorićeš	Ти будеш отво̀рио/отво̀рила Ti budeš otvorio/otvorila
3rd per (M)	Он о̀твори On otvori	Он ће отво̀рити/Отво̀риће On će otvoriti/Otvoriće	Он буде отво̀рио On bude otvorio
3rd per (F)	Она о̀твори Ona otvori	Она ће отво̀рити/Отво̀риће Ona će otvoriti/Otvoriće	Она буде отво̀рила Ona bude otvorila
3rd per (N)	Оно о̀твори Ono otvori	Оно ће отво̀рити/Отво̀риће Ono će otvoriti/Otvoriće	Оно буде отво̀рило Ono bude otvorilo
1st per pl	Ми о̀творимо Mi otvorimo	Ми ћемо отво̀рити/Отво̀рићемо Mi ćemo otvoriti/Otvorićemo	Ми будемо отво̀рили/отво̀риле Mi budemo otvorili/otvorile
2nd per pl	Ви о̀творите Vi otvorite	Ви ћете отво̀рити/Отво̀рићете Vi ćete otvoriti/Otvorićete	Ви будете отво̀рили/отво̀риле Vi budete otvorili/otvorile
3rd per pl	Они/Оне о̀творе Oni/One otvore	Они/Оне ће отво̀рити/Отво̀риће Oni/One će otvoriti/Otvoriće	Они/Оне буду отво̀рили/отво̀риле Oni/One budu otvorili/otvorile

	Past Tense (Перфект)	Pluperfect (Плусквамперфект)	Conditional (Потенцијал)
1st per	Ja сам отво̀рио Ja sam otvorio	Ja сам био отво̀рио Ja sam bio otvorio	Ja бих отво̀рио Ja bih otvorio
2nd per	Ти си отво̀рио Ti si otvorio	Ти си био отво̀рио Ti si bio otvorio	Ти би отво̀рио Ti bi otvorio
3rd per (M)	Он је отво̀рио On je otvorio	Он је био отво̀рио On je bio otvorio	Он би отво̀рио On bi otvorio
3rd per (F)	Она је отво̀рила Ona je otvorila	Она је била отво̀рила Ona je bila otvorila	Она би отво̀рила Ona bi otvorila
3rd per (N)	Оно је отво̀рило Ono je otvorilo	Оно је било отво̀рило Ono je bilo otvorilo	Оно би отво̀рило Ono bi otvorilo
1st per pl	Ми смо отво̀рили Mi smo otvorili	Ми смо били отво̀рили Mi smo bili otvorili	Ми бисмо отво̀рили Mi bismo otvorili
2nd per pl	Ви сте отво̀рили Vi ste otvorili	Ви сте били отво̀рили Vi ste bili otvorili	Ви бисте отво̀рили Vi biste otvorili
3rd per pl	Они су отво̀рили Oni su otvorili	Они су били отво̀рили Oni su bili otvorili	Они би отво̀рили Oni bi otvorili

	Imperative (Императив)
2nd per sg	(Ти) отво̀ри (Ti) otvori
1st per pl	(Ми) отво̀римо (Mi) otvorimo

2nd per pl	(Ви) отвòрите
	(Vi) otvorite

Non-finite Forms

Infinitive (Инфинитив)	отвòрити
	otvoriti
Present Adverbial Participle (Глаголски прилог садашњи)	--
Past Adverbial Participle (Глаголски прилог прошли)	отвòривши
	otvorivši

	Active Adjectival Participle (Глаголски придев радни)		Passive Adjectival Participle (Глаголски придев трпни)	
Gender	Singular	Plural	Singular	Plural
Feminine	отвòрила	отвòриле	òтворена	òтворене
	otvorila	otvorile	otvorena	otvorene
Masculine	отвòрио	отвòрили	òтворен	òтворени
	otvorio	otvorili	otvoren	otvoreni
Neuter	отвòрило	отвòрила	òтворено	òтворена
	otvorilo	otvorila	otvoreno	otvorena

To Play - играти се - igrati se

	Present (Презент)	Future I (Футур први)	Future II (Футур други)
1st per	Ja se играм / Ja se igram	Ja ћу се играти/Играћу се / Ja ću se igrati/Igraću se	Ja se будем играо/играла / Ja se budem igrao/igrala
2nd per	Ти се играш / Ti se igraš	Ти ћеш се играти/Играћеш се / Ti ćeš se igrati/Igraćeš se	Ти се будеш играо/играла / Ti se budeš igrao/igrala
3rd per (M)	Он се игра / On se igra	Он ће се играти/Играће се / On će se igrati/Igraće se	Он се буде играо / On se bude igrao
3rd per (F)	Она се игра / Ona se igra	Она ће се играти/Играће се / Ona će se igrati/Igraće se	Она се буде играла / Ona se bude igrala
3rd per (N)	Оно се игра / Ono se igra	Оно ће се играти/Играће се / Ono će se igrati/Igraće se	Оно се буде играло / Ono se bude igralo
1st per pl	Ми се играмо / Mi se igramo	Ми ћемо се играти/Играћемо се / Mi ćemo se igrati/Igraćemo se	Ми се будемо играли/играле / Mi se budemo igrali/igrale
2nd per pl	Ви се играте / Vi se igrate	Ви ћете се играти/Играћете се / Vi ćete se igrati/Igraćete se	Ви се будете играли/играле / Vi se budete igrali/igrale
3rd per pl	Они/Оне се играју / Oni/One se igraju	Они/Оне ће се играти/Играће се / Oni/One će se igrati/Igraće se	Они/Оне се буду играли/играле / Oni/One se budu igrali/igrale

	Past Tense (Перфект)	Pluperfect (Плусквамперфект)	Conditional (Потенцијал)
1st per	Ja сам се играо / Ja sam se igrao	Ja сам се био играо / Ja sam se bio igrao	Ja бих се играо / Ja bih se igrao
2nd per	Ти си се играо / Ti si se igrao	Ти си се био играо / Ti si se bio igrao	Ти би се играо / Ti bi se igrao
3rd per (M)	Он се играо / On se igrao	Он се био играо / On se bio igrao	Он би се играо / On bi se igrao
3rd per (F)	Она се играла / Ona se igrala	Она се била играла / Ona se bila igrala	Она би се играла / Ona bi se igrala
3rd per (N)	Оно се играло / Ono se igralo	Оно се било играло / Ono se bilo igralo	Оно би се играло / Ono bi se igralo
1st per pl	Ми смо се играли / Mi smo se igrali	Ми смо се били играли / Mi smo se bili igrali	Ми бисмо се играли / Mi bismo se igrali
2nd per pl	Ви сте се играли / Vi ste se igrali	Ви сте се били играли / Vi ste se bili igrali	Ви бисте се играли / Vi biste se igrali
3rd per pl	Они су се играли / Oni su se igrali	Они су се били играли / Oni su se bili igrali	Они би се играли / Oni bi se igrali

	Imperative (Императив)
2nd per sg	(Ти) играј се / (Ti) igraj se
1st per pl	(Ми) играјмо се / (Mi) igrajmo se

2nd per pl	(Ви) йграјте се (Vi) **igrajte se**

Non-finite Forms

Infinitive (Инфинитив)	йграти се **igrati se**
Present Adverbial Participle (Глаголски прилог садашњи)	йграјући се **igrajući se**
Past Adverbial Participle (Глаголски прилог прошли)	йгравши се **igravši se**

	Active Adjectival Participle (Глаголски придев радни)		Passive Adjectival Participle (Глаголски придев трпни)	
Gender	Singular	Plural	Singular	Plural
Feminine	йграла **igrala**	йграле **igrale**	йграна **igrana**	йгране **igrane**
Masculine	йграо **igrao**	йграли **igrali**	йгран **igran**	йграни **igrani**
Neuter	йграло **igralo**	йграла **igrala**	йграно **igrano**	йграна **igrana**

To Put - ста̏вити - staviti

	Present (Презент)	Future I (Футур први)	Future II (Футур други)
1st per	Ja ста̏вим Ja **stav**im	Ja ћу ста̏вити/Ста̏ви̏ћу Ja ću **stav**iti/Sta**vi**ću	Ja бу̏дем ста̏вио/ста̏вила Ja budem **stav**io/**stav**ila
2nd per	Ти ста̏ви̏ш Ti **stav**iš	Ти ћеш ста̏вити/Ста̏ви̏ћеш Ti ćeš **stav**iti/Sta**vi**ćeš	Ти бу̏деш ста̏вио/ста̏вила Ti budeš **stav**io/**stav**ila
3rd per (M)	Он ста̏ви On **stav**i	Он ће ста̏вити/Ста̏ви̏ће On će **stav**iti/Sta**vi**će	Он бу̏де ста̏вио On bude **stav**io
3rd per (F)	Она ста̏ви Ona **stav**i	Она ће ста̏вити/Ста̏ви̏ће Ona će **stav**iti/Sta**vi**će	Она бу̏де ста̏вила Ona bude **stav**ila
3rd per (N)	Оно ста̏ви Ono **stav**i	Оно ће ста̏вити/Ста̏ви̏ће Ono će **stav**iti/Sta**vi**će	Оно бу̏де ста̏вило Ono bude **stav**ilo
1st per pl	Ми ста̏вимо Mi **stav**imo	Ми ћемо ста̏вити/Ста̏ви̏ћемо Mi ćemo **stav**iti/Sta**vi**ćemo	Ми бу̏демо ста̏вили/ста̏виле Mi budemo **stav**ili/**stav**ile
2nd per pl	Ви ста̏вите Vi **stav**ite	Ви ћете ста̏вити/Ста̏ви̏ћете Vi ćete **stav**iti/Sta**vi**ćete	Ви бу̏дете ста̏вили/ста̏виле Vi budete **stav**ili/**stav**ile
3rd per pl	Они/Оне ста̏ве Oni/One **stav**e	Они/Оне ће ста̏вити/Ста̏ви̏ће Oni/One će **stav**iti/Sta**vi**će	Они/Оне бу̏ду ста̏вили/ста̏виле Oni/One budu **stav**ili/**stav**ile

	Past Tense (Перфект)	Pluperfect (Плусквамперфект)	Conditional (Потенцијал)
1st per	Ja сам ста̏вио Ja sam **stav**io	Ja сам био ста̏вио Ja sam bio **stav**io	Ja бих ста̏вио Ja bih **stav**io
2nd per	Ти си ста̏вио Ti si **stav**io	Ти си био ста̏вио Ti si bio **stav**io	Ти би ста̏вио Ti bi **stav**io
3rd per (M)	Он је ста̏вио On je **stav**io	Он је био ста̏вио On je bio **stav**io	Он би ста̏вио On bi **stav**io
3rd per (F)	Она је ста̏вила Ona je **stav**ila	Она је била ста̏вила Ona je bila **stav**ila	Она би ста̏вила Ona bi **stav**ila
3rd per (N)	Оно је ста̏вило Ono je **stav**ilo	Оно је било ста̏вило Ono je bilo **stav**ilo	Оно би ста̏вило Ono bi **stav**ilo
1st per pl	Ми смо ста̏вили Mi smo **stav**ili	Ми смо били ста̏вили Mi smo bili **stav**ili	Ми бисмо ста̏вили Mi bismo **stav**ili
2nd per pl	Ви сте ста̏вили Vi ste **stav**ili	Ви сте били ста̏вили Vi ste bili **stav**ili	Ви бисте ста̏вили Vi biste **stav**ili
3rd per pl	Они су ста̏вили Oni su **stav**ili	Они су били ста̏вили Oni su bili **stav**ili	Они би ста̏вили Oni bi **stav**ili

	Imperative (Императив)
2nd per sg	(Ти) ста̏ви (Ti) **stav**i
1st per pl	(Ми) ста̏вимо (Mi) **stav**imo

137

2nd per pl	(Ви) ста̏вите
	(Vi) **sta**vite

Non-finite Forms

Infinitive (Инфинитив)	ста̏вити
	staviti
Present Adverbial Participle (Глаголски прилог садашњи)	--
Past Adverbial Participle (Глаголски прилог прошли)	ста̏вивши
	stavivši

	Active Adjectival Participle (Глаголски придев радни)		Passive Adjectival Participle (Глаголски придев трпни)	
Gender	Singular	Plural	Singular	Plural
Feminine	ста̏вила	ста̏виле	ста̏вљена	ста̏вљене
	stavila	**sta**vile	**sta**vljena	**sta**vljene
Masculine	ста̏вио	ста̏вили	ста̏вљен	ста̏вљени
	stavio	**sta**vili	**sta**vljen	**sta**vljeni
Neuter	ста̏вило	ста̏вила	ста̏вљено	ста̏вљена
	stavilo	**sta**vila	**sta**vljeno	**sta**vljena

To Read – читати - čitati

	Present (Презент)	Future I (Футур први)	Future II (Футур други)
1st per	Ja читам / Ja čitam	Ja ћу читати/Читаћу / Ja ću čitati/Čitaću	Ja будем читао/читала / Ja budem čitao/čitala
2nd per	Ти читаш / Ti čitaš	Ти ћеш читати/Читаћеш / Ti ćeš čitati/Čitaćeš	Ти будеш читао/читала / Ti budeš čitao/čitala
3rd per (M)	Он чита / On čita	Он ће читати/Читаће / On će čitati/Čitaće	Он буде читао / On bude čitao
3rd per (F)	Она чита / Ona čita	Она ће читати/Читаће / Ona će čitati/Čitaće	Она буде читала / Ona bude čitala
3rd per (N)	Оно чита / Ono čita	Оно ће читати/Читаће / Ono će čitati/Čitaće	Оно буде читало / Ono bude čitalo
1st per pl	Ми читамо / Mi čitamo	Ми ћемо читати/Читаћемо / Mi ćemo čitati/Čitaćemo	Ми будемо читали/читале / Mi budemo čitali/čitale
2nd per pl	Ви читате / Vi čitate	Ви ћете читати/Читаћете / Vi ćete čitati/Čitaćete	Ви будете читали/читале / Vi budete čitali/čitale
3rd per pl	Они/Оне читају / Oni/One čitaju	Они/Оне ће читати/Читаће / Oni/One će čitati/Čitaće	Они/Оне буду читали/читале / Oni/One budu čitali/čitale

	Past Tense (Перфект)	Pluperfect (Плусквамперфект)	Conditional (Потенцијал)
1st per	Ja сам читао / Ja sam čitao	Ja сам био читао / Ja sam bio čitao	Ja бих читао / Ja bih čitao
2nd per	Ти си читао / Ti si čitao	Ти си био читао / Ti si bio čitao	Ти би читао / Ti bi čitao
3rd per (M)	Он је читао / On je čitao	Он је био читао / On je bio čitao	Он би читао / On bi čitao
3rd per (F)	Она је читала / Ona je čitala	Она је била читала / Ona je bila čitala	Она би читала / Ona bi čitala
3rd per (N)	Оно је читало / Ono je čitalo	Оно је било читало / Ono je bilo čitalo	Оно би читало / Ono bi čitalo
1st per pl	Ми смо читали / Mi smo čitali	Ми смо били читали / Mi smo bili čitali	Ми бисмо читали / Mi bismo čitali
2nd per pl	Ви сте читали / Vi ste čitali	Ви сте били читали / Vi ste bili čitali	Ви бисте читали / Vi biste čitali
3rd per pl	Они су читали / Oni su čitali	Они су били читали / Oni su bili čitali	Они би читали / Oni bi čitali

	Imperative (Императив)
2nd per sg	(Ти) читај / (Ti) čitaj
1st per pl	(Ми) читајмо / (Mi) čitajmo

2nd per pl	(Ви) чȕтајте
	(Vi) čȉtajte

Non-finite Forms

Infinitive (Инфинитив)	чȕтати
	čȉtati
Present Adverbial Participle (Глаголски прилог садашњи)	чȕтајући
	čȉtajući
Past Adverbial Participle (Глаголски прилог прошли)	--

	Active Adjectival Participle (Глаголски придев радни)		Passive Adjectival Participle (Глаголски придев трпни)	
Gender	Singular	Plural	Singular	Plural
Feminine	чȕтала	чȕтале	чȕтана	чȕтане
	čȉtala	čȉtale	čȉtana	čȉtane
Masculine	чȕтао	чȕтали	чȕтан	чȕтани
	čȉtao	čȉtali	čȉtan	čȉtane
Neuter	чȕтало	чȕтала	чȕтано	чȕтана
	čȉtalo	čȉtala	čȉtano	čȉtane

To Receive - примити - primiti

	Present (Презент)	Future I (Футур први)	Future II (Футур други)
1st per	Ja примим / Ja primim	Ja ћу примити/Примићу / Ja ću primiti/Primiću	Ja будем примио/примила / Ja budem primio/primila
2nd per	Ти примиш / Ti primiš	Ти ћеш примити/Примићеш / Ti ćeš primiti/Primićeš	Ти будеш примио/примила / Ti budeš primio/primila
3rd per (M)	Он прими / On primi	Он ће примити/Примиће / On će primiti/Primiće	Он буде примио / On bude primio
3rd per (F)	Она прими / Ona primi	Она ће примити/Примиће / Ona će primiti/Primiće	Она буде примила / Ona bude primila
3rd per (N)	Оно прими / Ono primi	Оно ће примити/Примиће / Ono će primiti/Primiće	Оно буде примило / Ono bude primilo
1st per pl	Ми примимо / Mi primimo	Ми ћемо примити/Примићемо / Mi ćemo primiti/Primićemo	Ми будемо примили/примиле / Mi budemo primili/primile
2nd per pl	Ви примите / Vi primite	Ви ћете примити/Примићете / Vi ćete primiti/Primićete	Ви будете примили/примиле / Vi budete primili/primile
3rd per pl	Они/Оне приме / Oni/One prime	Они/Оне ће примити/Примиће / Oni/One će primiti/Primiće	Они/Оне буду примили/примиле / Oni/One budu primili/primile

	Past Tense (Перфект)	Pluperfect (Плусквамперфект)	Conditional (Потенцијал)
1st per	Ja сам примио / Ja sam primio	Ja сам био примио / Ja sam bio primio	Ja бих примио / Ja bih primio
2nd per	Ти си примио / Ti si primio	Ти си био примио / Ti si bio primio	Ти би примио / Ti bi primio
3rd per (M)	Он је примио / On je primio	Он је био примио / On je bio primio	Он би примио / On bi primio
3rd per (F)	Она је примила / Ona je primila	Она је била примила / Ona je bila primila	Она би примила / Ona bi primila
3rd per (N)	Оно је примило / Ono je primilo	Оно је било примило / Ono je bilo primilo	Оно би примило / Ono bi primilo
1st per pl	Ми смо примили / Mi smo primili	Ми смо били примили / Mi smo bili primili	Ми бисмо примили / Mi bismo primili
2nd per pl	Ви сте примили / Vi ste primili	Ви сте били примили / Vi ste bili primili	Ви бисте примили / Vi biste primili
3rd per pl	Они су примили / Oni su primili	Они су били примили / Oni su bili primili	Они би примили / Oni bi primili

	Imperative (Императив)
2nd per sg	(Ти) прими / (Ti) primi
1st per pl	(Ми) примимо / (Mi) primimo

141

2nd per pl	(Ви) при́мите
	(Vi) **pri**mite

Non-finite Forms

Infinitive (Инфинитив)	при́мити
	primiti
Present Adverbial Participle (Глаголски прилог садашњи)	--
Past Adverbial Participle (Глаголски прилог прошли)	при́мивши
	primivši

	Active Adjectival Participle (Глаголски придев радни)		Passive Adjectival Participle (Глаголски придев трпни)	
Gender	Singular	Plural	Singular	Plural
Feminine	при́мила	при́миле	при́мљена	при́мљене
	primila	**pri**mile	**pri**mljena	**pri**mljene
Masculine	при́мио	при́мили	при́мљен	при́мљени
	primio	**pri**mili	**pri**mljen	**pri**mljeni
Neuter	при́мило	при́мила	при́мљено	при́мљена
	primilo	**pri**mila	**pri**mljeno	**pri**mljena

To Remember – сѐћати се - sećati se

	Present (Презент)	Future I (Футур први)	Future II (Футур други)
1st per	Ja se sѐћam Ja se **sećam**	Ja ћу se sѐћati/Sѐћаћу se Ja ću se **sećati**/**Sećaću** se	Ja se будем sѐћao/sѐћala Ja se budem **sećao**/**sećala**
2nd per	Ти se sѐћaш Ti se **sećaš**	Ти ћeш se sѐћati/Sѐћaћeш se Ti ćeš se **sećati**/**Sećaćeš** se	Ти se будеш sѐћao/sѐћala Ti se budeš **sećao**/**sećala**
3rd per (M)	Он se sѐћa On se **sећa**	Он ће se sѐћati/Sѐћaће se On će se **sećati**/**Sećaće** se	Он se буде sѐћao On se bude **sećao**
3rd per (F)	Она se sѐћa Ona se **sећa**	Она ће se sѐћati/Sѐћaће se Ona će se **sećati**/**Sećaće** se	Она se буде sѐћala Ona se bude **sećala**
3rd per (N)	Оно se sѐћa Ono se **seća**	Оно ће se sѐћати/Sѐћaће se Ono će se **sećati**/**Sećaće** se	Оно se буде sѐћало Ono se bude **sećalo**
1st per pl	Ми se sѐћamo Mi se **sećamo**	Ми ћemo se sѐћati/Sѐћaћemo se Mi ćemo se **sećati**/**Sećaćemo** se	Ми se будемо sѐћали/sѐћале Mi se budemo **sećali**/**sećale**
2nd per pl	Ви se sѐћate Vi se **sećate**	Ви ћete se sѐћati/Sѐћaћete se Vi ćete se **sećati**/**Sećaćete** se	Ви se будете sѐћали/sѐћале Vi se budete **sećali**/**sećale**
3rd per pl	Они/Оне se sѐћajу Oni/One se **sećaju**	Они/Оне ће se sѐћati/Sѐћaће se Oni/One će se **sećati**/**Sećaće** se	Они/Оне se буду sѐћали/sѐћале Oni/One se budu **sećali**/**sećale**

	Past Tense (Перфект)	Pluperfect (Плусквамперфект)	Conditional (Потенцијал)
1st per	Ja сам se sѐћao Ja sam se **sećao**	Ja сам se био sѐћao Ja sam se bio **sećao**	Ja бих se sѐћao Ja bih se **sećao**
2nd per	Ти си se sѐћao Ti si se **sećao**	Ти си se био sѐћao Ti si se bio **sećao**	Ти би se sѐћao Ti bi se **sećao**
3rd per (M)	Он se sѐћao On se **sećao**	Он se био sѐћao On se bio **sećao**	Он би se sѐћao On bi se **sećao**
3rd per (F)	Она se sѐћala Ona se **sećala**	Она se била sѐћala Ona se bila **sećala**	Она би se sѐћala Ona bi se **sećala**
3rd per (N)	Оно se sѐћало Ono se **sećalo**	Оно se било sѐћало Ono se bilo **sećalo**	Оно би se sѐћало Ono bi se **sećalo**
1st per pl	Ми смо se sѐћали Mi smo se **sećali**	Ми смо били sѐћали Mi smo bili **sećali**	Ми бисмо se sѐћали Mi bismo se **sećali**
2nd per pl	Ви сте se sѐћали Vi ste se **sećali**	Ви сте se били sѐћали Vi ste se bili **sećali**	Ви бисте se sѐћали Vi biste se **sećali**
3rd per pl	Они су se sѐћали Oni su se **sećali**	Они су se били sѐћали Oni su se bili **sećali**	Они би se sѐћали Oni bi se **sećali**

	Imperative (Императив)
2nd per sg	(Ти) sѐћaj se (Ti) **sećaj** se
1st per pl	(Ми) sѐћajmo se (Mi) **sećajmo** se

143

2nd per pl	(Ви) сѐћајте се
	(Vi) **se**ćajte se

Non-finite Forms

Infinitive (Инфинитив)	сѐћати се
	sećati se
Present Adverbial Participle (Глаголски прилог садашњи)	сѐћајући се
	sećajući se
Past Adverbial Participle (Глаголски прилог прошли)	--

	Active Adjectival Participle (Глаголски придев радни)		Passive Adjectival Participle (Глаголски придев трпни)	
Gender	Singular	Plural	Singular	Plural
Feminine	сѐћала	сѐћале	--	--
	sećala	**se**ćale		
Masculine	сѐћао	сѐћали	--	--
	sećao	**se**ćali		
Neuter	сѐћало	сѐћала	--	--
	sećalo	**se**ćala		

To Repeat – понòвити - ponoviti

	Present (Презент)	Future I (Футур први)	Future II (Футур други)
1st per	Ja пòновим Ja **po**novim	Ja ћу понòвити/Понòвићу Ja ću po**no**viti/Po**no**виću	Ja будем понòвио/понòвила Ja budem po**no**vio/po**no**vila
2nd per	Ти пòновиш Ti **po**noviš	Ти ћеш понòвити/Понòвићеш Ti ćeš po**no**viti/Po**no**vićeš	Ти будеш понòвио/понòвила Ti budeš po**no**vio/po**no**vila
3rd per (M)	Он пòнови On **po**novi	Он ће понòвити/Понòвиће On će po**no**viti/Po**no**viće	Он буде понòвио On bude po**no**vio
3rd per (F)	Она пòнови Ona **po**novi	Она ће понòвити/Понòвиће Ona će po**no**viti/Po**no**viće	Она буде понòвила Ona bude po**no**vila
3rd per (N)	Оно пòнови Ono **po**novi	Оно ће понòвити/Понòвиће Ono će po**no**viti/Po**no**viće	Оно буде понòвило Ono bude po**no**vilo
1st per pl	Ми пòновимо Mi **po**novimo	Ми ћемо понòвити/Понòвићемо Mi ćemo po**no**viti/Po**no**vićemo	Ми будемо понòвили/понòвиле Mi budemo po**no**vili/po**no**vile
2nd per pl	Ви пòновите Vi **po**novite	Ви ћете понòвити/Понòвићете Vi ćete po**no**viti/Po**no**vićete	Ви будете понòвили/понòвиле Vi budete po**no**vili/po**no**vile
3rd per pl	Они/Оне пòнове Oni/One **po**nove	Они/Оне ће понòвити/Понòвиће Oni/One će po**no**viti/Po**no**viće	Они/Оне буду понòвили/понòвиле Oni/One budu po**no**vili/po**no**vile

	Past Tense (Перфект)	Pluperfect (Плусквамперфект)	Conditional (Потенцијал)
1st per	Ja сам понòвио Ja sam po**no**vio	Ja сам био понòвио Ja sam bio po**no**vio	Ja бих понòвио Ja bih po**no**vio
2nd per	Ти си понòвио Ti si po**no**vio	Ти си био понòвио Ti si bio po**no**vio	Ти би понòвио Ti bi po**no**vio
3rd per (M)	Он је понòвио On je po**no**vio	Он је био понòвио On je bio po**no**vio	Он би понòвио On bi po**no**vio
3rd per (F)	Она је понòвила Ona je po**no**vila	Она је била понòвила Ona je bila po**no**vila	Она би понòвила Ona bi po**no**vila
3rd per (N)	Оно је понòвило Ono je po**no**vilo	Оно је било понòвило Ono je bilo po**no**vilo	Оно би понòвило Ono bi po**no**vilo
1st per pl	Ми смо понòвили Mi smo po**no**vili	Ми смо били понòвили Mi smo bili po**no**vili	Ми бисмо понòвили Mi bismo po**no**vili
2nd per pl	Ви сте понòвили Vi ste po**no**vili	Ви сте били понòвили Vi ste bili po**no**vili	Ви бисте понòвили Vi biste po**no**vili
3rd per pl	Они су понòвили Oni su po**no**vili	Они су били понòвили Oni su bili po**no**vili	Они би понòвили Oni bi po**no**vili

	Imperative (Императив)
2nd per sg	(Ти) понòви (Ti) po**no**vi
1st per pl	(Ми) понòвимо (Mi) po**no**vimo

145

2nd per pl	(Ви) поно̀вите
	(Vi) ponovite

Non-finite Forms

Infinitive (Инфинитив)	поно̀вити
	ponoviti
Present Adverbial Participle (Глаголски прилог садашњи)	--
Past Adverbial Participle (Глаголски прилог прошли)	поно̀вивши
	ponovivši

	Active Adjectival Participle (Глаголски придев радни)		Passive Adjectival Participle (Глаголски придев трпни)	
Gender	Singular	Plural	Singular	Plural
Feminine	поно̀вила	поно̀виле	по̀новљена	по̀новљене
	ponovila	ponovile	ponovljena	ponovljene
Masculine	поно̀вио	поно̀вили	по̀новљен	по̀новљени
	ponovio	ponovili	ponovljen	ponovljeni
Neuter	поно̀вило	поно̀вила	по̀новљено	по̀новљена
	ponovilo	ponovila	ponovljeno	ponovljena

To Return - врáтити се – vratiti se

	Present (Презент)	Future I (Футур први)	Future II (Футур други)
1st per	Ja се врáтим Ja se **vra**tim	Ja ћу се врáтити/Врáтићу се Ja ću se **vra**titi/**Vra**tiću se	Ja се будем врáтио/врáтила Ja se budem **vra**tio/**vra**tila
2nd per	Ти се врâтиш Ti se **vra**tiš	Ти ћеш се врáтити/Врáтићеш се Ti ćeš se **vra**titi/**Vra**tićeš se	Ти се будеш врáтио/врáтила Ti se budeš **vra**tio/**vra**tila
3rd per (M)	Он се врâти On se **vra**ti	Он ће се врáтити/Врáтиће се On će se **vra**titi/**Vra**tiće se	Он се буде врáтио On se bude **vra**tio
3rd per (F)	Она се врâти Ona se **vra**ti	Она ће се врáтити/Врáтиће се Ona će se **vra**titi/**Vra**tiće se	Она се буде врáтила Ona se bude **vra**tila
3rd per (N)	Оно се врâти Ono se **vra**ti	Оно ће се врáтити/Врáтиће се Ono će se **vra**titi/**Vra**tiće se	Оно се буде врáтило Ono se bude **vra**tilo
1st per pl	Ми се врáтимо Mi se **vra**timo	Ми ћемо се врáтити/Врáтићемо се Mi ćemo se **vra**titi/**Vra**tićemo se	Ми се будемо врáтили/врáтиле Mi se budemo **vra**tili/**vra**tile
2nd per pl	Ви се врâтите Vi se **vra**tite	Ви ћете се врáтити/Врáтићете се Vi ćete se **vra**titi/**Vra**tićete se	Ви се будете врáтили/врáтиле Vi se budete **vra**tili/**vra**tile
3rd per pl	Они/Оне се врâте Oni/One se **vra**te	Они/Оне ће се врáтити/Врáтиће се Oni/One će se **vra**titi/**Vra**tiće se	Они/Оне се буду врáтили/врáтиле Oni/One se budu **vra**tili/**vra**tile

	Past Tense (Перфект)	Pluperfect (Плусквамперфект)	Conditional (Потенцијал)
1st per	Ja сам се врáтио Ja sam se **vra**tio	Ja сам се био врáтио Ja sam se bio **vra**tio	Ja бих се врáтио Ja bih se **vra**tio
2nd per	Ти си се врáтио Ti si se **vra**tio	Ти си се био врáтио Ti si se bio **vra**tio	Ти би се врáтио Ti bi se **vra**tio
3rd per (M)	Он се врáтио On se **vra**tio	Он се био врáтио On se bio **vra**tio	Он би се врáтио On bi se **vra**tio
3rd per (F)	Она се врáтила Ona se **vra**tila	Она се била врáтила Ona se bila **vra**tila	Она би се врáтила Ona bi se **vra**tila
3rd per (N)	Оно се врáтило Ono se **vra**tilo	Оно се било врáтило Ono se bilo **vra**tilo	Оно би се врáтило Ono bi se **vra**tilo
1st per pl	Ми смо се врáтили Mi smo se **vra**tili	Ми смо се били врáтили Mi smo se bili **vra**tili	Ми бисмо се врáтили Mi bismo se **vra**tili
2nd per pl	Ви сте се врáтили Vi ste se **vra**tili	Ви сте се били врáтили Vi ste se bili **vra**tili	Ви бисте се врáтили Vi biste se **vra**tili
3rd per pl	Они су се врáтили Oni su se **vra**tili	Они су се били врáтили Oni su se bili **vra**tili	Они би се врáтили Oni bi se **vra**tili

	Imperative (Императив)
2nd per sg	(Ти) врáти се (Ti) **vra**ti se
1st per pl	(Ми) врáтимо се (Mi) **vra**timo se

2nd per pl	(Ви) вра́тите се (Vi) **vra**tite se

Non-finite Forms

Infinitive (Инфинитив)	вра́тити се **vra**titi se
Present Adverbial Participle (Глаголски прилог садашњи)	--
Past Adverbial Participle (Глаголски прилог прошли)	вра́тивши се **vra**tivši se

Gender	Active Adjectival Participle (Глаголски придев радни)		Passive Adjectival Participle (Глаголски придев трпни)	
	Singular	Plural	Singular	Plural
Feminine	вра́тила **vra**tila	вра́тиле **vra**tile	вра́ћена **vra**ćena	вра́ћене **vra**ćene
Masculine	вра́тио **vra**tio	вра́тили **vra**tili	вра́ћен **vra**ćen	вра́ћени **vra**ćeni
Neuter	вра́тило **vra**tilo	вра́тила **vra**tila	вра́ћено **vra**ćeno	вра́ћена **vra**ćena

To Run – тр̏чати - trčati

	Present (Презент)	Future I (Футур први)	Future II (Футур други)
1st per	Ja тр̏чим Ja **trčim**	Ja ћу тр̏чати/Тр̏чаћу Ja ću **trčati/Trčaću**	Ja будем тр̏чао/тр̏чала Ja budem **trčao/trčala**
2nd per	Ти тр̏чиш Ti **trčiš**	Ти ћеш тр̏чати/Тр̏чаћеш Ti ćeš **trčati/Trčaćeš**	Ти будеш тр̏чао/тр̏чала Ti budeš **trčao/trčala**
3rd per (M)	Он тр̏чи On **trči**	Он ће тр̏чати/Тр̏чаће On će **trčati/Trčaće**	Он буде тр̏чао On bude **trčao**
3rd per (F)	Она тр̏чи Ona **trči**	Она ће тр̏чати/Тр̏чаће Ona će **trčati/Trčaće**	Она буде тр̏чала Ona bude **trčala**
3rd per (N)	Оно тр̏чи Ono **trči**	Оно ће тр̏чати/Тр̏чаће Ono će **trčati/Trčaće**	Оно буде тр̏чало Ono bude **trčalo**
1st per pl	Ми тр̏чимо Mi **trčimo**	Ми ћемо тр̏чати/Тр̏чаћемо Mi ćemo **trčati/Trčaćemo**	Ми будемо тр̏чали/тр̏чале Mi budemo **trčali/trčale**
2nd per pl	Ви тр̏чите Vi **trčite**	Ви ћете тр̏чати/Тр̏чаћете Vi ćete **trčati/Trčaćete**	Ви будете тр̏чали/тр̏чале Vi budete **trčali/trčale**
3rd per pl	Они/Оне тр̏че Oni/One **trče**	Они/Оне ће тр̏чати/Тр̏чаће Oni/One će **trčati/Trčaće**	Они/Оне буду тр̏чали/тр̏чале Oni/One budu **trčali/trčale**

	Past Tense (Перфект)	Pluperfect (Плусквамперфект)	Conditional (Потенцијал)
1st per	Ja сам тр̏чао Ja sam **trčao**	Ja сам био тр̏чао Ja sam bio **trčao**	Ja бих тр̏чао Ja bih **trčao**
2nd per	Ти си тр̏чао Ti si **trčao**	Ти си био тр̏чао Ti si bio **trčao**	Ти би тр̏чао Ti bi **trčao**
3rd per (M)	Он је тр̏чао On je **trčao**	Он је био тр̏чао On je bio **trčao**	Он би тр̏чао On bi **trčao**
3rd per (F)	Она је тр̏чала Ona je **trčala**	Она је била тр̏чала Ona je bila **trčala**	Она би тр̏чала Ona bi **trčala**
3rd per (N)	Оно је тр̏чало Ono je **trčalo**	Оно је било тр̏чало Ono je bilo **trčalo**	Оно би тр̏чало Ono bi **trčalo**
1st per pl	Ми смо тр̏чали Mi smo **trčali**	Ми смо били тр̏чали Mi smo bili **trčali**	Ми бисмо тр̏чали Mi bismo **trčali**
2nd per pl	Ви сте тр̏чали Vi ste **trčali**	Ви сте били тр̏чали Vi ste bili **trčali**	Ви бисте тр̏чали Vi biste **trčali**
3rd per pl	Они су тр̏чали Oni su **trčali**	Они су били тр̏чали Oni su bili **trčali**	Они би тр̏чали Oni bi **trčali**

	Imperative (Императив)
2nd per sg	(Ти) тр̏чи (Ti) **trči**
1st per pl	(Ми) тр̏чимо (Mi) **trčimo**

2nd per pl	(Ви) тр̏чите
	(Vi) **tr**čite

Non-finite Forms

Infinitive (Инфинитив)	тр̏чати
	trčati
Present Adverbial Participle (Глаголски прилог садашњи)	тр̏чећи
	trčeći
Past Adverbial Participle (Глаголски прилог прошли)	--

	Active Adjectival Participle (Глаголски придев радни)		Passive Adjectival Participle (Глаголски придев трпни)	
Gender	Singular	Plural	Singular	Plural
Feminine	тр̏чала	тр̏чале	тр̏чана	тр̏чане
	trčala	**tr**čale	**tr**čana	**tr**čane
Masculine	тр̏чао	тр̏чали	тр̏чан	тр̏чани
	trčao	**tr**čali	**tr**čan	**tr**čani
Neuter	тр̏чало	тр̏чала	тр̏чано	тр̏чана
	trčalo	**tr**čala	**tr**čano	**tr**čana

To Say – рѐћи - reći

	Present (Презент)	Future I (Футур први)	Future II (Футур други)
1st per	--	Ja ћу рѐћи/Рѐћи ћу Ja ću reći/Reći ću	Ja будем рѐкао/рѐкла Ja budem rekao/rekla
2nd per		Ти ћеш рѐћи/Рѐћи ћеш Ti ćeš reći/Reći ćeš	Ти будеш рѐкао/рѐкла Ti budeš rekao/rekla
3rd per (M)		Он ће рѐћи/Рѐћи ће On će reći/Reći će	Он буде рѐкао On bude rekao
3rd per (F)		Она ће рѐћи/Рѐћи ће Ona će reći/Reći će	Она буде рѐкла Ona bude rekla
3rd per (N)		Оно ће рѐћи/Рѐћи ће Ono će reći/Reći će	Оно буде рѐкло Ono bude reklo
1st per pl		Ми ћемо рѐћи/Рѐћи ћемо Mi ćemo reći/Reći ćemo	Ми будемо рѐкли/рѐкле Mi budemo rekli/rekle
2nd per pl		Ви ћете рѐћи/Рѐћи ћете Vi ćete reći/Reći ćete	Ви будете рѐкли/рѐкле Vi budete rekli/rekle
3rd per pl		Они/Оне ће рѐћи/Рѐћи ће Oni/One će reći/Reći će	Они/Оне буду рѐкли/рѐкле Oni/One budu rekli/rekle

	Past Tense (Перфект)	Pluperfect (Плусквамперфект)	Conditional (Потенцијал)
1st per	Ja сам рѐкао Ja sam rekao	Ja сам био рѐкао Ja sam bio rekao	Ja бих рѐкао Ja bih rekao
2nd per	Ти си рѐкао Ti si rekao	Ти си био рѐкао Ti si bio rekao	Ти би рѐкао Ti bi rekao
3rd per (M)	Он је рѐкао On je rekao	Он је био рѐкао On je bio rekao	Он би рѐкао On bi rekao
3rd per (F)	Она је рѐкла Ona je rekla	Она је била рѐкла Ona je bila rekla	Она би рѐкла Ona bi rekla
3rd per (N)	Оно је рѐкло Ono je reklo	Оно је било рѐкло Ono je bilo reklo	Оно би рѐкло Ono bi reklo
1st per pl	Ми смо рѐкли Mi smo rekli	Ми смо били рѐкли Mi smo bili rekli	Ми бисмо рѐкли Mi bismo rekli
2nd per pl	Ви сте рѐкли Vi ste rekli	Ви сте били рѐкли Vi ste bili rekli	Ви бисте рѐкли Vi biste rekli
3rd per pl	Они су рѐкли Oni su rekli	Они су били рѐкли Oni su bili rekli	Они би рѐкли Oni bi rekli

	Imperative (Императив)
2nd per sg	(Ти) рѐци (Ti) reci
1st per pl	(Ми) рѐцимо (Mi) recimo
2nd per pl	(Ви) рѐците (Vi) recite

Non-finite Forms

Infinitive (Инфинитив)	рѐћи **re**ći
Present Adverbial Participle (Глаголски прилог садашњи)	--
Past Adverbial Participle (Глаголски прилог прошли)	рѐкавши **re**kavši

	Active Adjectival Participle (Глаголски придев радни)		Passive Adjectival Participle (Глаголски придев трпни)	
Gender	Singular	Plural	Singular	Plural
Feminine	рѐкла **re**kla	рѐкле **re**kle	речѐна re**č**ena	речѐне re**č**ene
Masculine	рѐкао **re**kao	рѐкли **re**kli	речѐн re**č**en	речѐни re**č**eni
Neuter	рѐкло **re**klo	рѐкла **re**kla	речѐно re**č**eno	речѐна re**č**ena

To Scream - ври́снути - vrisnuti

	Present (Презент)	Future I (Футур први)	Future II (Футур други)
1st per	Ja ври́снем Ja vrisnem	Ja ћу ври́снути/Ври́снућу Ja ću vrisnuti/Vrisnuću	Ja будем ври́снуо/ври́снула Ja budem vrisnuo/vrisnula
2nd per	Ти ври́снеш Ti vrisneš	Ти ћеш ври́снути/Ври́снућеш Ti ćeš vrisnuti/Vrisnućeš	Ти будеш ври́снуо/ври́снула Ti budeš vrisnuo/vrisnula
3rd per (M)	Он ври́сне On vrisne	Он ће ври́снути/Ври́снуће On će vrisnuti/Vrisnuće	Он буде ври́снуо On bude vrisnuo
3rd per (F)	Она ври́сне Ona vrisne	Она ће ври́снути/Ври́снуће Ona će vrisnuti/Vrisnuće	Она буде ври́снула Ona bude vrisnula
3rd per (N)	Оно ври́сне Ono vrisne	Оно ће ври́снути/Ври́снуће Ono će vrisnuti/Vrisnuće	Оно буде ври́снуло Ono bude vrisnulo
1st per pl	Ми ври́снемо Mi vrisnemo	Ми ћемо ври́снути/Ври́снућемо Mi ćemo vrisnuti/Vrisnućemo	Ми будемо ври́снули/ври́снуле Mi budemo vrisnuli/vrisnule
2nd per pl	Ви ври́снете Vi vrisnete	Ви ћете ври́снути/Ври́снућете Vi ćete vrisnuti/Vrisnućete	Ви будете ври́снули/ври́снуле Vi budete vrisnuli/vrisnule
3rd per pl	Они/Оне ври́сну Oni/One vrisnu	Они/Оне ће ври́снути/Ври́снуће Oni/One će vrisnuti/Vrisnuće	Они/Оне буду ври́снули/ври́снуле Oni/One budu vrisnuli/vrisnule

	Past Tense (Перфект)	Pluperfect (Плусквамперфект)	Conditional (Потенцијал)
1st per	Ja сам ври́снуо Ja sam vrisnuo	Ja сам био ври́снуо Ja sam bio vrisnuo	Ja бих ври́снуо Ja bih vrisnuo
2nd per	Ти си ври́снуо Ti si vrisnuo	Ти си био ври́снуо Ti si bio vrisnuo	Ти би ври́снуо Ti bi vrisnuo
3rd per (M)	Он је ври́снуо On je vrisnuo	Он је био ври́снуо On je bio vrisnuo	Он би ври́снуо On bi vrisnuo
3rd per (F)	Она је ври́снула Ona je vrisnula	Она је била ври́снула Ona je bila vrisnula	Она би ври́снула Ona bi vrisnula
3rd per (N)	Оно је ври́снуло Ono je vrisnulo	Оно је било ври́снуло Ono je bilo vrisnulo	Оно би ври́снуло Ono bi vrisnulo
1st per pl	Ми смо ври́снули Mi smo vrisnuli	Ми смо били ври́снули Mi smo bili vrisnuli	Ми бисмо ври́снули Mi bismo vrisnuli
2nd per pl	Ви сте ври́снули Vi ste vrisnuli	Ви сте били ври́снули Vi ste bili vrisnuli	Ви бисте ври́снули Vi biste vrisnuli
3rd per pl	Они су ври́снули Oni su vrisnuli	Они су били ври́снули Oni su bili vrisnuli	Они би ври́снули Oni bi vrisnuli

Imperative (Императив)

2nd per sg	(Ти) ври́сни (Ti) vrisni
1st per pl	(Ми) ври́снимо (Mi) vrisnimo

153

2nd per pl	(Ви) ври́сните (Vi) **vri**snite

Non-finite Forms

Infinitive (Инфинитив)	ври́снути **vri**snuti
Present Adverbial Participle (Глаголски прилог садашњи)	--
Past Adverbial Participle (Глаголски прилог прошли)	ври́снувши **vri**snuvši

	Active Adjectival Participle (Глаголски придев радни)		Passive Adjectival Participle (Глаголски придев трпни)	
Gender	Singular	Plural	Singular	Plural
Feminine	ври́снула **vri**snula	ври́снуле **vri**snule	--	--
Masculine	ври́снуо **vri**snuo	ври́снули **vri**snuli	--	--
Neuter	ври́снуло **vri**snulo	ври́снула **vri**snula	--	--

To See - вѝдети - videti

	Present (Презент)	Future I (Футур први)	Future II (Футур други)
1st per	Ja вѝдим Ja vidim	Ja ћу вѝдети/Вѝдећу Ja ću videti/Videću	Ja будем вѝдео/вѝдела Ja budem video/videla
2nd per	Ти вѝдиш Ti vidiš	Ти ћеш вѝдети/Вѝдећеш Ti ćeš videti/Videćeš	Ти будеш вѝдео/вѝдела Ti budeš video/videla
3rd per (M)	Он вѝди On vidi	Он ће вѝдети/Вѝдеће On će videti/Videće	Он буде вѝдео On bude video
3rd per (F)	Она вѝди Ona vidi	Она ће вѝдети/Вѝдеће Ona će videti/Videće	Она буде вѝдела Ona bude videla
3rd per (N)	Оно вѝди Ono vidi	Оно ће вѝдети/Вѝдеће Ono će videti/Videće	Оно буде вѝдело Ono bude videlo
1st per pl	Ми вѝдимо Mi vidimo	Ми ћемо вѝдети/Вѝдећемо Mi ćemo videti/Videćemo	Ми будемо вѝдели/вѝделе Mi budemo videli/videle
2nd per pl	Ви вѝдите Vi vidite	Ви ћете вѝдети/Вѝдећете Vi ćete videti/Videćete	Ви будете вѝдели/вѝделе Vi budete videli/videle
3rd per pl	Они/Оне вѝде Oni/One vide	Они/Оне ће вѝдети/Вѝдеће Oni/One će videti/Videće	Они/Оне буду вѝдели/вѝделе Oni/One budu videli/videle

	Past Tense (Перфект)	Pluperfect (Плусквамперфект)	Conditional (Потенцијал)
1st per	Ja сам вѝдео Ja sam video	Ja сам био вѝдео Ja sam bio video	Ja бих вѝдео Ja bih video
2nd per	Ти си вѝдео Ti si video	Ти си био вѝдео Ti si bio video	Ти би вѝдео Ti bi video
3rd per (M)	Он је вѝдео On je video	Он је био вѝдео On je bio video	Он би вѝдео On bi video
3rd per (F)	Она је вѝдела Ona je videla	Она је била вѝдела Ona je bila videla	Она би вѝдела Ona bi videla
3rd per (N)	Оно је вѝдело Ono je videlo	Оно је било вѝдело Ono je bilo videlo	Оно би вѝдело Ono bi videlo
1st per pl	Ми смо вѝдели Mi smo videli	Ми смо били вѝдели Mi smo bili videli	Ми бисмо вѝдели Mi bismo videli
2nd per pl	Ви сте вѝдели Vi ste videli	Ви сте били вѝдели Vi ste bili videli	Ви бисте вѝдели Vi biste videli
3rd per pl	Они су вѝдели Oni su videli	Они су били вѝдели Oni su bili videli	Они би вѝдели Oni bi videli

	Imperative (Императив)
2nd per sg	(Ти) вѝди (Ti) vidi
1st per pl	(Ми) вѝдимо (Mi) vidimo

155

2nd per pl	(Ви) вйдите
	(Vi) **vi**dite

Non-finite Forms

Infinitive (Инфинитив)	вйдети
	videti
Present Adverbial Participle (Глаголски прилог садашњи)	вйдећи
	vidеći
Past Adverbial Participle (Глаголски прилог прошли)	вйдевши
	videvši

	Active Adjectival Participle (Глаголски придев радни)		Passive Adjectival Participle (Глаголски придев трпни)	
Gender	Singular	Plural	Singular	Plural
Feminine	вйдела	вйделе	вйђена	вйђене
	videla	**vi**dele	**vi**đena	**vi**đene
Masculine	вйдео	вйдели	вйђен	вйђени
	video	**vi**deli	**vi**đen	**vi**đeni
Neuter	вйдело	вйдела	вйђено	вйђена
	videlo	**vi**dela	**vi**đeno	**vi**đena

To Seem – чйнити се - činiti se

	Present (Презент)	Future I (Футур први)	Future II (Футур други)
1st per	Ja se чйним / Ja se činim	Ja ћу се чйнити/Чйнићу се / Ja ću se činiti/Činiću se	Ja se будем чйнио/чйнила / Ja se budem činio/činila
2nd per	Ти се чйниш / Ti se činiš	Ти ћеш се чйнити/Чйнићеш се / Ti ćeš se činiti/Činićeš se	Ти се будеш чйнио/чйнила / Ti se budeš činio/činila
3rd per (M)	Он се чйни / On se čini	Он ће се чйнити/Чйниће се / On će se činiti/Činiće se	Он се буде чйнио / On se bude činio
3rd per (F)	Она се чйни / Ona se čini	Она ће се чйнити/Чйниће се / Ona će se činiti/Činiće se	Она се буде чйнила / Ona se bude činila
3rd per (N)	Оно се чйни / Ono se čini	Оно ће се чйнити/Чйниће се / Ono će se činiti/Činiće se	Оно се буде чйнило / Ono se bude činilo
1st per pl	Ми се чйнимо / Mi se činimo	Ми ћемо се чйнити/Чйнићемо се / Mi ćemo se činiti/Činićemo se	Ми се будемо чйнили/чйниле / Mi se budemo činili/činile
2nd per pl	Ви се чйните / Vi se činite	Ви ћете се чйнити/Чйнићете се / Vi ćete se činiti/Činićete se	Ви се будете чйнили/чйниле / Vi se budete činili/činile
3rd per pl	Они/Оне се чйне / Oni/One se čine	Они/Оне ће се чйнити/Чйниће се / Oni/One će se činiti/Činiće se	Они/Оне се буду чйнили/чйниле / Oni/One se budu činili/činile

	Past Tense (Перфект)	Pluperfect (Плусквамперфект)	Conditional (Потенцијал)
1st per	Ja сам се чйнио / Ja sam se činio	Ja сам се био чйнио / Ja sam se bio činio	Ja бих се чйнио / Ja bih se činio
2nd per	Ти си се чйнио / Ti si se činio	Ти си се био чйнио / Ti si se bio činio	Ти би се чйнио / Ti bi se činio
3rd per (M)	Он се чйнио / On se činio	Он се био чйнио / On se bio činio	Он би се чйнио / On bi se činio
3rd per (F)	Она се чйнила / Ona se činila	Она се била чйнила / Ona se bila činila	Она би се чйнила / Ona bi se činila
3rd per (N)	Оно се чйнило / Ono se činilo	Оно се било чйнило / Ono se bilo činilo	Оно би се чйнило / Ono bi se činilo
1st per pl	Ми смо се чйнили / Mi smo se činili	Ми смо се били чйнили / Mi smo se bili činili	Ми бисмо се чйнили / Mi bismo se činili
2nd per pl	Ви сте се чйнили / Vi ste se činili	Ви сте се били чйнили / Vi ste se bili činili	Ви бисте се чйнили / Vi biste se činili
3rd per pl	Они су се чйнили / Oni su se činili	Они су се били чйнили / Oni su se bili činili	Они би се чйнили / Oni bi se činili

	Imperative (Императив)
2nd per sg	(Ти) чйни се / (Ti) čini se
1st per pl	(Ми) чйнимо се / (Mi) činimo se

157

2ⁿᵈ per pl	(Ви) чи̏ните се (Vi) **či**nite se

Non-finite Forms

Infinitive (Инфинитив)	чи̏нити се **či**niti se
Present Adverbial Participle (Глаголски прилог садашњи)	чи̏нећи се **či**neći se
Past Adverbial Participle (Глаголски прилог прошли)	--

	Active Adjectival Participle (Глаголски придев радни)		Passive Adjectival Participle (Глаголски придев трпни)	
Gender	Singular	Plural	Singular	Plural
Feminine	чи̏нила **či**nila	чи̏ниле **či**nile	--	--
Masculine	чи̏нио **či**nio	чи̏нили **či**nili	--	--
Neuter	чи̏нило **či**nilo	чи̏нила **či**nila	--	--

To Sell – прѐдати - prodati

	Present (Презент)	Future I (Футур први)	Future II (Футур други)
1st per	Ja прѐдам Ja **pro**dam	Ja ћу прѐдати/Прѐдаћу Ja ću **pro**dati/**Pro**daću	Ja будем прѐдао/прѐдала Ja budem **pro**dao/**pro**dala
2nd per	Ти прѐдаш Ti **pro**daš	Ти ћеш прѐдати/Прѐдаћеш Ti ćeš **pro**dati/**Pro**daćeš	Ти будеш прѐдао/прѐдала Ti budeš **pro**dao/**pro**dala
3rd per (M)	Он прѐда On **pro**da	Он ће прѐдати/Прѐдаће On će **pro**dati/**Pro**daće	Он буде прѐдао On bude **pro**dao
3rd per (F) 3rd per (N)	Она прѐда Ona **pro**da Оно прѐда Ono **pro**da	Она ће прѐдати/Прѐдаће Ona će **pro**dati/**Pro**daće Оно ће прѐдати/Прѐдаће Ono će **pro**dati/**Pro**daće	Она буде прѐдала Ona bude **pro**dala Оно буде прѐдало Ono bude **pro**dalo
1st per pl	Ми прѐдамо Mi **pro**damo	Ми ћемо прѐдати/Прѐдаћемо Mi ćemo **pro**dati/**Pro**daćemo	Ми будемо прѐдали/прѐдале Mi budemo **pro**dali/**pro**dale
2nd per pl	Ви прѐдате Vi **pro**date	Ви ћете прѐдати/Прѐдаћете Vi ćete **pro**dati/**Pro**daćete	Ви будете прѐдали/прѐдале Vi budete **pro**dali/**pro**dale
3rd per pl	Они/Оне прѐдају Oni/One **pro**daju	Они/Оне ће прѐдати/Прѐдаће Oni/One će **pro**dati/**Pro**daće	Они/Оне буду прѐдали/прѐдале Oni/One budu **pro**dali/**pro**dale

	Past Tense (Перфект)	Pluperfect (Плусквамперфект)	Conditional (Потенцијал)
1st per	Ja сам прѐдао Ja sam **pro**dao	Ja сам био прѐдао Ja sam bio **pro**dao	Ja бих прѐдао Ja bih **pro**dao
2nd per	Ти си прѐдао Ti si **pro**dao	Ти си био прѐдао Ti si bio **pro**dao	Ти би прѐдао Ti bi **pro**dao
3rd per (M)	Он је прѐдао On je **pro**dao	Он је био прѐдао On je bio **pro**dao	Он би прѐдао On bi **pro**dao
3rd per (F) 3rd per (N)	Она је прѐдала Ona je **pro**dala Оно је прѐдало Ono je **pro**dalo	Она је била прѐдала Ona je bila **pro**dala Оно је било прѐдало Ono je bilo **pro**dalo	Она би прѐдала Ona bi **pro**dala Оно би прѐдало Ono bi **pro**dalo
1st per pl	Ми смо прѐдали Mi smo **pro**dali	Ми смо били прѐдали Mi smo bili **pro**dali	Ми бисмо прѐдали Mi bismo **pro**dali
2nd per pl	Ви сте прѐдали Vi ste **pro**dali	Ви сте били прѐдали Vi ste bili **pro**dali	Ви бисте прѐдали Vi biste **pro**dali
3rd per pl	Они су прѐдали Oni su **pro**dali	Они су били прѐдали Oni su bili **pro**dali	Они би прѐдали Oni bi **pro**dali

	Imperative (Императив)
2nd per sg	(Ти) прѐдај (Ti) **pro**daj
1st per pl	(Ми) прѐдајмо (Mi) **pro**dajmo

2nd per pl	(Ви) прòдајте (Vi) **pro**dajte

Non-finite Forms

Infinitive (Инфинитив)	прòдати **pro**dati
Present Adverbial Participle (Глаголски прилог садашњи)	--
Past Adverbial Participle (Глаголски прилог прошли)	прòдавши **pro**davši

	Active Adjectival Participle (Глаголски придев радни)		Passive Adjectival Participle (Глаголски придев трпни)	
Gender	Singular	Plural	Singular	Plural
Feminine	прòдала **pro**dala	прòдале **pro**dale	прòдана **pro**dana	прòдане **pro**dane
Masculine	прòдао **pro**dao	прòдали **pro**dali	прòдан **pro**dan	прòдани **pro**dani
Neuter	прòдало **pro**dalo	прòдала **pro**dala	прòдано **pro**dano	прòдана **pro**dana

To Send – пòслати - poslati

	Present (Презент)	Future I (Футур први)	Future II (Футур други)
1st per	Ja пòшаљем	Ja ћу пòслати/Пòслаћу	Ja будем пòслао/пòслала
	Ja pošaljem	Ja ću poslati/Poslaću	Ja budem poslao/poslala
2nd per	Ти пòшаљеш	Ти ћеш пòслати/Пòслаћеш	Ти будеш пòслао/пòслала
	Ti pošalješ	Ti ćeš poslati/Poslaćeš	Ti budeš poslao/poslala
3rd per (M)	Он пòшаље	Он ће пòслати/Пòслаће	Он буде пòслао
	On pošalje	On će poslati/Poslaće	On bude poslao
3rd per (F)	Она пòшаље	Она ће пòслати/Пòслаће	Она буде пòслала
	Ona pošalje	Ona će poslati/Poslaće	Ona bude poslala
3rd per (N)	Оно пòшаље	Оно ће пòслати/Пòслаће	Оно буде пòслало
	Ono pošalje	Ono će poslati/Poslaće	Ono bude poslalo
1st per pl	Ми пòшаљемо	Ми ћемо пòслати/Пòслаћемо	Ми будемо пòслали/пòслале
	Mi pošaljemo	Mi ćemo poslati/Poslaćemo	Mi budemo poslali/poslale
2nd per pl	Ви пòшаљете	Ви ћете пòслати/Пòслаћете	Ви будете пòслали/пòслале
	Vi pošaljete	Vi ćete poslati/Poslaćete	Vi budete poslali/poslale
3rd per pl	Они/Оне пòшаљу	Они/Оне ће пòслати/Пòслаће	Они/Оне буду пòслали/пòслале
	Oni/One pošalju	Oni/One će poslati/Poslaće	Oni/One budu poslali/poslale

	Past Tense (Перфект)	Pluperfect (Плусквамперфект)	Conditional (Потенцијал)
1st per	Ja сам пòслао	Ja сам био пòслао	Ja бих пòслао
	Ja sam poslao	Ja sam bio poslao	Ja bih poslao
2nd per	Ти си пòслао	Ти си био пòслао	Ти би пòслао
	Ti si poslao	Ti si bio poslao	Ti bi poslao
3rd per (M)	Он је пòслао	Он је био пòслао	Он би пòслао
	On je poslao	On je bio poslao	On bi poslao
3rd per (F)	Она је пòслала	Она је била пòслала	Она би пòслала
	Ona je poslala	Ona je bila poslala	Ona bi poslala
3rd per (N)	Оно је пòслало	Оно је било пòслало	Оно би пòслало
	Ono je poslalo	Ono je bilo poslalo	Ono bi poslalo
1st per pl	Ми смо пòслали	Ми смо били пòслали	Ми бисмо пòслали
	Mi smo poslali	Mi smo bili poslali	Mi bismo poslali
2nd per pl	Ви сте пòслали	Ви сте били пòслали	Ви бисте пòслали
	Vi ste poslali	Vi ste bili poslali	Vi biste poslali
3rd per pl	Они су пòслали	Они су били пòслали	Они би пòслали
	Oni su poslali	Oni su bili poslali	Oni bi poslali

	Imperative (Императив)
2nd per sg	(Ти) пòшаљи
	(Ti) pošalji
1st per pl	(Ми) пòшаљимо
	(Mi) pošaljimo

2nd per pl	(Ви) по̀ша̀љите
	(Vi) pošaljite

Non-finite Forms

Infinitive (Инфинитив)	по̀слати
	poslati
Present Adverbial Participle (Глаголски прилог садашњи)	--
Past Adverbial Participle (Глаголски прилог прошли)	по̀славши
	poslavši

	Active Adjectival Participle (Глаголски придев радни)		Passive Adjectival Participle (Глаголски придев трпни)	
Gender	Singular	Plural	Singular	Plural
Feminine	по̀слала	по̀слале	по̀слата	по̀слате
	poslala	poslale	poslata	poslate
Masculine	по̀слао	по̀слали	по̀слат	по̀слати
	poslao	poslali	poslat	poslati
Neuter	по̀слало	по̀слала	по̀слато	по̀слата
	poslalo	poslala	poslato	poslata

To Show - показати – pokazati

	Present (Презент)	Future I (Футур први)	Future II (Футур други)
1st per	Ja пóкажем / Ja **po**kažem	Ja ћу покáзати/Покáзаћу / Ja ću pokazati/Pokazaću	Ja будем покáзао/покáзала / Ja budem pokazao/pokazala
2nd per	Ти пóкажеш / Ti **po**kažeš	Ти ћеш покáзати/Покáзаћеш / Ti ćeš pokazati/Pokazaćeš	Ти будеш покáзао/покáзала / Ti budeš pokazao/pokazala
3rd per (M)	Он пóкаже / On **po**kaže	Он ће покáзати/Покáзаће / On će pokazati/Pokazaće	Он буде покáзао / On bude pokazao
3rd per (F)	Она пóкаже / Ona **po**kaže	Она ће покáзати/Покáзаће / Ona će pokazati/Pokazaće	Она буде покáзала / Ona bude pokazala
3rd per (N)	Оно пóкаже / Ono **po**kaže	Оно ће покáзати/Покáзаће / Ono će pokazati/Pokazaće	Оно буде покáзало / Ono bude pokazalo
1st per pl	Ми пóкажемо / Mi **po**kažemo	Ми ћемо покáзати/Покáзаћемо / Mi ćemo pokazati/Pokazaćemo	Ми будемо покáзали/покáзале / Mi budemo pokazali/pokazale
2nd per pl	Ви пóкажете / Vi **po**kažete	Ви ћете покáзати/Покáзаћете / Vi ćete pokazati/Pokazaćete	Ви будете покáзали/покáзале / Vi budete pokazali/pokazale
3rd per pl	Они/Оне пóкажу / Oni/One **po**kažu	Они/Оне ће покáзати/Покáзаће / Oni/One će pokazati/Pokazaće	Они/Оне буду покáзали/покáзале / Oni/One budu pokazali/pokazale

	Past Tense (Перфект)	Pluperfect (Плусквамперфект)	Conditional (Потенцијал)
1st per	Ja сам покáзао / Ja sam po**ka**zao	Ja сам био покáзао / Ja sam bio po**ka**zao	Ja бих покáзао / Ja bih po**ka**zao
2nd per	Ти си покáзао / Ti si po**ka**zao	Ти си био покáзао / Ti si bio po**ka**zao	Ти би покáзао / Ti bi po**ka**zao
3rd per (M)	Он је покáзао / On je po**ka**zao	Он је био покáзао / On je bio po**ka**zao	Он би покáзао / On bi po**ka**zao
3rd per (F)	Она је покáзала / Ona je po**ka**zala	Она је била покáзала / Ona je bila po**ka**zala	Она би покáзала / Ona bi po**ka**zala
3rd per (N)	Оно је покáзало / Ono je po**ka**zalo	Оно је било покáзало / Ono je bilo po**ka**zalo	Оно би покáзало / Ono bi po**ka**zalo
1st per pl	Ми смо покáзали / Mi smo po**ka**zali	Ми смо били покáзали / Mi smo bili po**ka**zali	Ми бисмо покáзали / Mi bismo po**ka**zali
2nd per pl	Ви сте покáзали / Vi ste po**ka**zali	Ви сте били покáзали / Vi ste bili po**ka**zali	Ви бисте покáзали / Vi biste po**ka**zali
3rd per pl	Они су покáзали / Oni su po**ka**zali	Они су били покáзали / Oni su bili po**ka**zali	Они би покáзали / Oni bi po**ka**zali

	Imperative (Императив)
2nd per sg	(Ти) покáжи / (Ti) po**ka**ži
1st per pl	(Ми) покáжимо / (Mi) po**ka**žimo

163

2ⁿᵈ per pl	(Ви) пока́жите (Vi) poka**ž**ite

Non-finite Forms

Infinitive (Инфинитив)	пока́зати poka**z**ati
Present Adverbial Participle (Глаголски прилог садашњи)	--
Past Adverbial Participle (Глаголски прилог прошли)	пока́завши poka**z**avši

	Active Adjectival Participle (Глаголски придев радни)		Passive Adjectival Participle (Глаголски придев трпни)	
Gender	Singular	Plural	Singular	Plural
Feminine	пока́зала poka**z**ala	пока́зале poka**z**ale	по̀казана **po**ka**z**ana	по̀казане **po**ka**z**ane
Masculine	пока́зао poka**z**ao	пока́зали poka**z**ali	по̀казан **po**ka**z**an	по̀казани **po**ka**z**ani
Neuter	пока́зало poka**z**alo	пока́зала poka**z**ala	по̀казано **po**ka**z**ano	по̀казана **po**ka**z**ana

To Sing - пѐвати - pevati

	Present (Презент)	Future I (Футур први)	Future II (Футур други)
1st per	Ja пѐвам / Ja pevam	Ja ћу пѐвати/Пѐваћу / Ja ću pevati/Pevaću	Ja будем пѐвао/пѐвала / Ja budem pevao/pevala
2nd per	Ти пѐваш / Ti pevaš	Ти ћеш пѐвати/Пѐваћеш / Ti ćeš pevati/Pevaćeš	Ти будеш пѐвао/пѐвала / Ti budeš pevao/pevala
3rd per (M)	Он пѐва / On peva	Он ће пѐвати/Пѐваће / On će pevati/Pevaće	Он буде пѐвао / On bude pevao
3rd per (F)	Она пѐва / Ona peva	Она ће пѐвати/Пѐваће / Ona će pevati/Pevaće	Она буде пѐвала / Ona bude pevala
3rd per (N)	Оно пѐва / Ono peva	Оно ће пѐвати/Пѐваће / Ono će pevati/Pevaće	Оно буде пѐвало / Ono bude pevalo
1st per pl	Ми пѐвамо / Mi pevamo	Ми ћемо пѐвати/Пѐваћемо / Mi ćemo pevati/Pevaćemo	Ми будемо пѐвали/пѐвале / Mi budemo pevali/pevale
2nd per pl	Ви пѐвате / Vi pevate	Ви ћете пѐвати/Пѐваћете / Vi ćete pevati/Pevaćete	Ви будете пѐвали/пѐвале / Vi budete pevali/pevale
3rd per pl	Они/Оне пѐвају / Oni/One pevaju	Они/Оне ће пѐвати/Пѐваће / Oni/One će pevati/Pevaće	Они/Оне буду пѐвали/пѐвале / Oni/One budu pevali/pevale

	Past Tense (Перфект)	Pluperfect (Плусквамперфект)	Conditional (Потенцијал)
1st per	Ja сам пѐвао / Ja sam pevao	Ja сам био пѐвао / Ja sam bio pevao	Ja бих пѐвао / Ja bih pevao
2nd per	Ти си пѐвао / Ti si pevao	Ти си био пѐвао / Ti si bio pevao	Ти би пѐвао / Ti bi pevao
3rd per (M)	Он је пѐвао / On je pevao	Он је био пѐвао / On je bio pevao	Он би пѐвао / On bi pevao
3rd per (F)	Она је пѐвала / Ona je pevala	Она је била пѐвала / Ona je bila pevala	Она би пѐвала / Ona bi pevala
3rd per (N)	Оно је пѐвало / Ono je pevalo	Оно је било пѐвало / Ono je bilo pevalo	Оно би пѐвало / Ono bi pevalo
1st per pl	Ми смо пѐвао / Mi smo pevali	Ми смо били пѐвали / Mi smo bili pevali	Ми бисмо пѐвали / Mi bismo pevali
2nd per pl	Ви сте пѐвали / Vi ste pevali	Ви сте били пѐвали / Vi ste bili pevali	Ви бисте пѐвали / Vi biste pevali
3rd per pl	Они су пѐвали / Oni su pevali	Они су били пѐвали / Oni su bili pevali	Они би пѐвали / Oni bi pevali

	Imperative (Императив)
2nd per sg	(Ти) пѐвај / (Ti) pevaj
1st per pl	(Ми) пѐвајмо / (Mi) pevajmo

2nd per pl	(Ви) пѐвајте (Vi) **pe**vajte

Non-finite Forms

Infinitive (Инфинитив)	пѐвати **pe**vati
Present Adverbial Participle (Глаголски прилог садашњи)	пѐвајући **pe**vajući
Past Adverbial Participle (Глаголски прилог прошли)	--

	Active Adjectival Participle (Глаголски придев радни)		Passive Adjectival Participle (Глаголски придев трпни)	
Gender	Singular	Plural	Singular	Plural
Feminine	пѐвала **pe**vala	пѐвале **pe**vale	пѐвана **pe**vana	пѐване **pe**vane
Masculine	пѐвао **pe**vao	пѐвали **pe**vali	пѐван **pe**van	пѐвани **pe**vani
Neuter	пѐвало **pe**valo	пѐвала **pe**vala	пѐвано **pe**vano	пѐвана **pe**vana

To Sit Down - сѐсти - sesti

	Present (Презент)	Future I (Футур први)	Future II (Футур други)
1st per	Ја сѐднем Ja sednem	Ја ћу сѐсти/Сѐшћу Ja ću sesti/Sešću	Ја будем сѐо/сѐла Ja budem seo/sela
2nd per	Ти сѐднеш Ti sedneš	Ти ћеш сѐсти/Сѐшћеш Ti ćeš sesti/Sešćeš	Ти будеш сѐо/сѐла Ti budeš seo/sela
3rd per (M)	Он сѐдне On sedne	Он ће сѐсти/Сѐшће On će sesti/Sešće	Он буде сѐо On bude seo
3rd per (F)	Она сѐдне Ona sedne	Она ће сѐсти/Сѐшће Ona će sesti/Sešće	Она буде сѐла Ona bude sela
3rd per (N)	Оно сѐдне Ono sedne	Оно ће сѐсти/Сѐшће Ono će sesti/Sešće	Оно буде сѐло Ono bude selo
1st per pl	Ми сѐднемо Mi sednemo	Ми ћемо сѐсти/Сѐшћемо Mi ćemo sesti/Sešćemo	Ми будемо сѐли/сѐле Mi budemo seli/sele
2nd per pl	Ви сѐднете Vi sednete	Ви ћете сѐсти/Сѐшћете Vi ćete sesti/Sešćete	Ви будете сѐли/сѐле Vi budete seli/sele
3rd per pl	Они/Оне сѐдну Oni/One sednu	Они/Оне ће сѐсти/Сѐшће Oni/One će sesti/Sešće	Они/Оне буду сѐли/сѐле Oni/One budu seli/sele

	Past Tense (Перфект)	Pluperfect (Плусквамперфект)	Conditional (Потенцијал)
1st per	Ја сам сѐо Ja sam seo	Ја сам био сѐо Ja sam bio seo	Ја бих сѐо Ja bih seo
2nd per	Ти си сѐо Ti si seo	Ти си био сѐо Ti si bio seo	Ти би сѐо Ti bi seo
3rd per (M)	Он је сѐо On je seo	Он је био сѐо On je bio seo	Он би сѐо On bi seo
3rd per (F)	Она је сѐла Ona je sela	Она је била сѐла Ona je bila sela	Она би сѐла Ona bi sela
3rd per (N)	Оно је сѐло Ono je selo	Оно је било сѐло Ono je bilo selo	Оно би сѐло Ono bi selo
1st per pl	Ми смо сѐли Mi smo seli	Ми смо били сѐли Mi smo bili seli	Ми бисмо сѐли Mi bismo seli
2nd per pl	Ви сте сѐли Vi ste seli	Ви сте били сѐли Vi ste bili seli	Ви бисте сѐли Vi biste seli
3rd per pl	Они су сѐли Oni su seli	Они су били сѐли Oni su bili seli	Они би сѐли Oni bi seli

	Imperative (Императив)
2nd per sg	(Ти) сѐди (Ti) sedi
1st per pl	(Ми) сѐдимо (Mi) sedimo

167

2nd per pl	(Ви) сѐдите
	(Vi) **se**dite

Non-finite Forms

Infinitive (Инфинитив)	сѐсти
	sesti
Present Adverbial Participle (Глаголски прилог садашњи)	--
Past Adverbial Participle (Глаголски прилог прошли)	сѐднувши
	sednuvši

	Active Adjectival Participle (Глаголски придев радни)		Passive Adjectival Participle (Глаголски придев трпни)	
Gender	Singular	Plural	Singular	Plural
Feminine	сѐла	сѐле	--	--
	sela	**se**le		
Masculine	сѐо	сѐли	--	--
	seo	**se**li		
Neuter	сѐло	сѐла	--	--
	selo	**se**la		

To Sleep - спа́вати - spavati

	Present (Презент)	Future I (Футур први)	Future II (Футур други)
1st per	Ja спа̑вам Ja **spa**vam	Ja ћу спа́вати/Спа́ваћу Ja ću **spa**vati/**Spa**vaću	Ja будем спа́вао/спа́вала Ja budem **spa**vao/**spa**vala
2nd per	Ти спа̑ваш Ti **spa**vaš	Ти ћеш спа́вати/Спа́ваћеш Ti ćeš **spa**vati/**Spa**vaćeš	Ти будеш спа́вао/спа́вала Ti budeš **spa**vao/**spa**vala
3rd per (M)	Он спа̑ва On **spa**va	Он ће спа́вати/Спа́ваће On će **spa**vati/**Spa**vaće	Он буде спа́вао On bude **spa**vao
3rd per (F)	Она спа̑ва Ona **spa**va	Она ће спа́вати/Спа́ваће Ona će **spa**vati/**Spa**vaće	Она буде спа́вала Ona bude **spa**vala
3rd per (N)	Оно спа̑ва Ono **spa**va	Оно ће спа́вати/Спа́ваће Ono će **spa**vati/**Spa**vaće	Оно буде спа́вало Ono bude **spa**valo
1st per pl	Ми спа̑вамо Mi **spa**vamo	Ми ћемо спа́вати/Спа́ваћемо Mi ćemo **spa**vati/**Spa**vaćemo	Ми будемо спа́вали/спа́вале Mi budemo **spa**vali/**spa**vale
2nd per pl	Ви спа̑вате Vi **spa**vate	Ви ћете спа́вати/Спа́ваћете Vi ćete **spa**vati/**Spa**vaćete	Ви будете спа́вали/спа́вале Vi budete **spa**vali/**spa**vale
3rd per pl	Они/Оне спа̑вају Oni/One **spa**vaju	Они/Оне ће спа́вати/Спа́ваће Oni/One će **spa**vati/**Spa**vaće	Они/Оне буду спа́вали/спа́вале Oni/One budu **spa**vali/**spa**vale

	Past Tense (Перфект)	Pluperfect (Плусквамперфект)	Conditional (Потенцијал)
1st per	Ja сам спа́вао Ja sam **spa**vao	Ja сам био спа́вао Ja sam bio **spa**vao	Ja бих спа́вао Ja bih **spa**vao
2nd per	Ти си спа́вао Ti si **spa**vao	Ти си био спа́вао Ti si bio **spa**vao	Ти би спа́вао Ti bi **spa**vao
3rd per (M)	Он је спа́вао On je **spa**vao	Он је био спа́вао On je bio **spa**vao	Он би спа́вао On bi **spa**vao
3rd per (F)	Она је спа́вала Ona je **spa**vala	Она је била спа́вала Ona je bila **spa**vala	Она би спа́вала Ona bi **spa**vala
3rd per (N)	Оно је спа́вало Ono je **spa**valo	Оно је било спа́вало Ono je bilo **spa**valo	Оно би спа́вало Ono bi **spa**valo
1st per pl	Ми смо спа́вали Mi smo **spa**vali	Ми смо били спа́вали Mi smo bili **spa**vali	Ми бисмо спа́вали Mi bismo **spa**vali
2nd per pl	Ви сте спа́вали Vi ste **spa**vali	Ви сте били спа́вали Vi ste bili **spa**vali	Ви бисте спа́вали Vi biste **spa**vali
3rd per pl	Они су спа́вали Oni su **spa**vali	Они су били спа́вали Oni su bili **spa**vali	Они би спа́вали Oni bi **spa**vali

	Imperative (Императив)
2nd per sg	(Ти) спа̑вај (Ti) **spa**vaj
1st per pl	(Ми) спа̑вајмо (Ti) **spa**vajmo

SERBIAN LANGUAGE: 101 SERBIAN VERBS

2nd per pl	(Ви) спа̂вајте (Vi) **spa**vajte

Non-finite Forms

Infinitive (Инфинитив)	спа́вати **spa**vati
Present Adverbial Participle (Глаголски прилог садашњи)	спа́вајући **spa**vajući
Past Adverbial Participle (Глаголски прилог прошли)	--

	Active Adjectival Participle (Глаголски придев радни)		Passive Adjectival Participle (Глаголски придев трпни)	
Gender	Singular	Plural	Singular	Plural
Feminine	спа́вала **spa**vala	спа́вале **spa**vale	--	--
Masculine	спа́вао **spa**vao	спа́вали **spa**vali	--	--
Neuter	спа́вало **spa**valo	спа́вала **spa**vala	--	--

To Smile - осмéхнути се – osmehnuti se

	Present (Презент)	Future I (Футур први)	Future II (Футур други)
1st per	Ja се òсмехнем / Ja se **os**mehnem	Ja ћу се осмéхнути/Осмéхнућу се / Ja ću se osmehnuti/Osmehnuću se	Ja се будем осмéхнуо/осмéхнула / Ja se budem osmehnuo/osmehnula
2nd per	Ти се òсмехнеш / Ti se **os**mehneš	Ти ћеш се осмéхнути/Осмéхнућеш се / Ti ćeš se osmehnuti/Osmehnućeš se	Ти се будеш осмéхнуо/осмéхнула / Ti se budeš osmehnuo/osmehnula
3rd per (M)	Он се òсмехне / On se **os**mehne	Он ће се осмéхнути/Осмéхнуће се / On će se osmehnuti/Osmehnuće se	Он се буде осмéхнуо / On se bude osmehnuo
3rd per (F)	Она се òсмехне / Ona se **os**mehne	Она ће се осмéхнути/Осмéхнуће се / Ona će se osmehnuti/Osmehnuće se	Она се буде осмéхнула / Ona se bude osmehnula
3rd per (N)	Оно се òсмехне / Ono se **os**mehne	Оно ће се осмéхнути/Осмéхнуће се / Ono će se osmehnuti/Osmehnuće se	Оно се буде осмéхнуло / Ono se bude osmehnulo
1st per pl	Ми се òсмехнемо / Mi se **os**mehnemo	Ми ћемо се осмéхнути/Осмéхнућемо се / Mi ćemo se osmehnuti/Osmehnućemo se	Ми се будемо осмéхнули/ осмéхнуле / Mi se budemo osmehnuli/ osmehnule
2nd per pl	Ви се òсмехнете / Vi se **os**mehnete	Ви ћете се осмéхнути/Осмéхнућете се / Vi ćete se osmehnuti/Osmehnućete se	Ви се будете осмéхнули/ осмéхнуле / Vi se budete osmehnuli/ osmehnule
3rd per pl	Они/Оне се òсмехну / Oni/One se **os**mehnu	Они/Оне ће се осмéхнути/Осмéхнуће се / Oni/One će se osmehnuti/Osmehnuće se	Они/Оне се буду осмéхнули/ осмéхнуле / Oni/One se budu osmehnuli/ osmehnule

	Past Tense (Перфект)	Pluperfect (Плусквамперфект)	Conditional (Потенцијал)
1st per	Ja сам се осмéхнуо / Ja sam se **os**mehnuo	Ja сам се био осмéхнуо / Ja sam se bio **os**mehnuo	Ja бих се осмéхнуо / Ja bih se **os**mehnuo
2nd per	Ти си се осмéхнуо / Ti si se **os**mehnuo	Ти си се био осмéхнуо / Ja sam se bio **os**mehnuo	Ти би се осмéхнуо / Ti bi se **os**mehnuo
3rd per (M)	Он се осмéхнуо / On se **os**mehnuo	Он се био осмéхнуо / On se bio **os**mehnuo	Он би се осмéхнуо / On bi se **os**mehnuo
3rd per (F)	Она се осмéхнула / Ona se **os**mehnula	Она се била осмéхнула / Ona se bila **os**mehnula	Она би се осмéхнула / Ona bi se **os**mehnula
3rd per (N)	Оно се осмéхнуло / Ono se **os**mehnulo	Оно се било осмéхнуло / Ono se bilo **os**mehnulo	Оно би се осмéхнуло / Ono bi se **os**mehnulo
1st per pl	Ми смо се осмéхнули / Mi smo se **os**mehnuli	Ми смо се били осмéхнули / Mi smo se bili **os**mehnuli	Ми бисмо се осмéхнули / Mi bismo se **os**mehnuli
2nd per pl	Ви сте се осмéхнули / Vi ste se **os**mehnuli	Ви сте се били осмéхнули / Vi ste se bili **os**mehnuli	Ви бисте се осмéхнули / Vi biste se **os**mehnuli
3rd per pl	Они су се осмéхнули / Oni su se **os**mehnuli	Они су се били осмéхнули / Oni su se bili **os**mehnuli	Они би се осмéхнули / Oni bi se **os**mehnuli

	Imperative (Императив)
2nd per sg	(Ти) осме́хни се (Ti) osmehni se
1st per pl	(Ми) осме́хнимо се (Mi) osmehnimo se
2nd per pl	(Ви) осме́хните се (Vi) osmehnite se

Non-finite Forms

Infinitive (Инфинитив)	осме́хнути се osmehnuti se
Present Adverbial Participle (Глаголски прилог садашњи)	--
Past Adverbial Participle (Глаголски прилог прошли)	осме́хнувши се osmehnuvši se

Gender	Active Adjectival Participle (Глаголски придев радни)		Passive Adjectival Participle (Глаголски придев трпни)	
	Singular	Plural	Singular	Plural
Feminine	осме́хнула osmehnula	осме́хнуле osmehnule	--	--
Masculine	осме́хнуо osmehnuo	осме́хнули osmehnuli	--	--
Neuter	осме́хнуло osmehnulo	осме́хнула osmehnula	--	--

To Speak - причати - pričati

	Present (Презент)	Future I (Футур први)	Future II (Футур други)
1st per	Ja причам / Ja **pri**čam	Ja ћу причати/Причаћу / Ja ću **pri**čati/**Pri**čaću	Ja будем причао/причала / Ja budem **pri**čao/**pri**čala
2nd per	Ти причаш / Ti **pri**čaš	Ти ћеш причати/Причаћеш / Ti ćeš **pri**čati/**Pri**čaćeš	Ти будеш причао/причала / Ti budeš **pri**čao/**pri**čala
3rd per (M)	Он прича / On **pri**ča	Он ће причати/Причаће / On će **pri**čati/**Pri**čaće	Он буде причао / On bude **pri**čao
3rd per (F)	Она прича / Ona **pri**ča	Она ће причати/Причаће / Ona će **pri**čati/**Pri**čaće	Она буде причала / Ona bude **pri**čala
3rd per (N)	Оно прича / Ono **pri**ča	Оно ће причати/Причаће / Ono će **pri**čati/**Pri**čaće	Оно буде причало / Ono bude **pri**čalo
1st per pl	Ми причамо / Mi **pri**čamo	Ми ћемо причати/Причаћемо / Mi ćemo **pri**čati/**Pri**čaćemo	Ми будемо причали/причале / Mi budemo **pri**čali/**pri**čale
2nd per pl	Ви причате / Vi **pri**čate	Ви ћете причати/Причаћете / Vi ćete **pri**čati/**Pri**čaćete	Ви будете причали/причале / Vi budete **pri**čali/**pri**čale
3rd per pl	Они/Оне причају / Oni/One **pri**čaju	Они/Оне ће причати/Причаће / Oni/One će **pri**čati/**Pri**čaće	Они/Оне буду причали/причале / Oni/One budu **pri**čali/**pri**čale

	Past Tense (Перфект)	Pluperfect (Плусквамперфект)	Conditional (Потенцијал)
1st per	Ja сам причао / Ja sam **pri**čao	Ja сам био причао / Ja sam bio **pri**čao	Ja бих причао / Ja bih **pri**čao
2nd per	Ти си причао / Ti si **pri**čao	Ти си био причао / Ti si bio **pri**čao	Ти би причао / Ti bi **pri**čao
3rd per (M)	Он је причао / On je **pri**čao	Он је био причао / On je bio **pri**čao	Он би причао / On bi **pri**čao
3rd per (F)	Она је причала / Ona je **pri**čala	Она је била причала / Ona je bila **pri**čala	Она би причала / Ona bi **pri**čala
3rd per (N)	Оно је причало / Ono je **pri**čalo	Оно је било причало / Ono je bilo **pri**čalo	Оно би причало / Ono bi **pri**čalo
1st per pl	Ми смо причали / Mi smo **pri**čali	Ми смо били причали / Mi smo bili **pri**čali	Ми бисмо причали / Mi bismo **pri**čali
2nd per pl	Ви сте причали / Vi ste **pri**čali	Ви сте били причали / Vi ste bili **pri**čali	Ви бисте причали / Vi biste **pri**čali
3rd per pl	Они су причали / Oni su **pri**čali	Они су били причали / Oni su bili **pri**čali	Они би причали / Oni bi **pri**čali

	Imperative (Императив)
2nd per sg	(Ти) причај / (Ti) **pri**čaj
1st per pl	(Ми) причајмо / (Mi) **pri**čajmo

173

2nd per pl	(Ви) при́чајте (Vi) **pri**čajte

Non-finite Forms

Infinitive (Инфинитив)	при́чати **pri**čati
Present Adverbial Participle (Глаголски прилог садашњи)	при́чајући **pri**čajući
Past Adverbial Participle (Глаголски прилог прошли)	--

	Active Adjectival Participle (Глаголски придев радни)		Passive Adjectival Participle (Глаголски придев трпни)	
Gender	Singular	Plural	Singular	Plural
Feminine	при́чала **pri**čala	при́чале **pri**čale	при́чана **pri**čana	при́чане **pri**čane
Masculine	при́чао **pri**čao	при́чали **pri**čali	при́чан **pri**čan	при́чани **pri**čani
Neuter	при́чало **pri**čalo	при́чала **pri**čala	при́чано **pri**čano	при́чана **pri**čana

To Stand – сто̀јати – stojati

	Present (Презент)	Future I (Футур први)	Future II (Футур други)
1st per	Ja сто̀јим / Ja stojim	Ja ћу сто̀јати/Сто̀јаћу / Ja ћу stojati/Stojaћу	Ja будем сто̀јао/сто̀јала / Ja budem stojao/stojala
2nd per	Ти сто̀јиш / Ti stojiš	Ти ћеш сто̀јати/Сто̀јаћеш / Ti ћeš stojati/Stojaћeš	Ти будеш сто̀јао/сто̀јала / Ti budeš stojao/stojala
3rd per (M)	Он сто̀ји / On stoji	Он ће сто̀јати/ Сто̀јаће / On ће stojati/ Stojaће	Он буде сто̀јао / On bude stojao
3rd per (F)	Она сто̀ји / Ona stoji	Она ће сто̀јати/Сто̀јаће / Ona ће stojati/Stojaће	Она буде сто̀јала / Ona bude stojala
3rd per (N)	Оно сто̀ји / Ono stoji	Оно ће сто̀јати/Сто̀јаће / Ono ће stojati/Stojaће	Оно буде сто̀јало / Ono bude stojalo
1st per pl	Ми сто̀јимо / Mi stojimo	Ми ћемо сто̀јати/Сто̀јаћемо / Mi ћemo stojati/Stojaћemo	Ми будемо сто̀јали/сто̀јале / Mi budemo stojali/stojale
2nd per pl	Ви сто̀јите / Vi stojite	Ви ћете сто̀јати/Сто̀јаћете / Vi ћete stojati/Stojaћete	Ви будете сто̀јали/сто̀јале / Vi budete stojali/stojale
3rd per pl	Они/Оне сто̀је / Oni/One stoje	Они/Оне ће сто̀јати/Сто̀јаће / Oni/One ће stojati/Stojaће	Они/Оне буду сто̀јали/сто̀јале / Oni/One budu stojali/stojale

	Past Tense (Перфект)	Pluperfect (Плусквамперфект)	Conditional (Потенцијал)
1st per	Ja сам сто̀јао / Ja sam stojao	Ja сам био сто̀јао / Ja sam bio stojao	Ja бих сто̀јао / Ja bih stojao
2nd per	Ти си сто̀јао / Ti si stojao	Ти си био сто̀јао / Ti si bio stojao	Ти би сто̀јао / Ti bi stojao
3rd per (M)	Он је сто̀јао / On je stojao	Он је био сто̀јао / On je bio stojao	Он би сто̀јао / On bi stojao
3rd per (F)	Она је сто̀јала / Ona je stojala	Она је била сто̀јала / Ona je bila stojala	Она би сто̀јала / Ona bi stojala
3rd per (N)	Оно је сто̀јало / Ono je stojalo	Оно је било сто̀јало / Ono je bilo stojalo	Оно би сто̀јало / Ono bi stojalo
1st per pl	Ми смо сто̀јали / Mi smo stojali	Ми смо били сто̀јали / Mi smo bili stojali	Ми бисмо сто̀јали / Mi bismo stojali
2nd per pl	Ви сте сто̀јали / Vi ste stojali	Ви сте били сто̀јали / Vi ste bili stojali	Ви бисте сто̀јали / Vi biste stojali
3rd per pl	Они су сто̀јали / Oni su stojali	Они су били сто̀јали / Oni su bili stojali	Они би сто̀јали / Oni bi stojali

	Imperative (Императив)
2nd per sg	(Ти) сто̀ј / (Ti) stoj
1st per pl	(Ми) сто̀јмо / (Mi) stojmo

2nd per pl	(Ви) ст**ȍ**jтe
	(Vi) **sto**jte

Non-finite Forms

Infinitive (Инфинитив)	ст**ȍ**jати
	stojati
Present Adverbial Participle (Глаголски прилог садашњи)	ст**ȍ**jeћи
	stojeći
Past Adverbial Participle (Глаголски прилог прошли)	--

	Active Adjectival Participle (Глаголски придев радни)		Passive Adjectival Participle (Глаголски придев трпни)	
Gender	Singular	Plural	Singular	Plural
Feminine	ст**ȍ**jала	ст**ȍ**jале	--	--
	stojala	**sto**jale		
Masculine	ст**ȍ**jao	ст**ȍ**jали	--	--
	stojao	**sto**jali		
Neuter	ст**ȍ**jало	ст**ȍ**jала	--	--
	stojalo	**sto**jala		

To Start – запо̀чети - zapòčeti

	Present (Презент)	Future I (Футур први)	Future II (Футур други)
1st per	Ja за̀почнем Ja zapòčnem	Ja ћу за̀почети/Запо̀чећу Ja ću zapòčeti/Zapòčeću	Ja будем за̀почео/за̀почела Ja budem zapòčeo/zapòčela
2nd per	Ти за̀почнеш Ti zapòčneš	Ти ћеш за̀почети/Запо̀чећеш Ti ćeš zapòčeti/Zapòčećeš	Ти будеш за̀почео/за̀почела Ti budeš zapòčeo/zapòčela
3rd per (M)	Он за̀почне On zapòčne	Он ће за̀почети/ Запо̀чеће On će zapòčeti/ Zapòčeće	Он буде за̀почео On bude zapòčeo
3rd per (F)	Она за̀почне Ona zapòčne	Она ће за̀почети/Запо̀чеће Ona će zapòčeti/Zapòčeće	Она буде за̀почела Ona bude zapòčela
3rd per (N)	Оно за̀почне Ono zapòčne	Оно ће за̀почети/ Запо̀чеће Ono će zapòčeti/ Zapòčeće	Оно буде за̀почело Ono bude zapòčelo
1st per pl	Ми за̀почнемо Mi zapòčnemo	Ми ћемо за̀почети/Запо̀чећемо Mi ćemo zapòčeti/Zapòčećemo	Ми будемо за̀почели/за̀почел Mi budemo zapòčeli/zapòčele
2nd per pl	Ви за̀почнете Vi zapòčnete	Ви ћете за̀почети/Запо̀чећете Vi ćete zapòčeti/Zapòčećete	Ви будете за̀почели/за̀почеле Vi budete zapòčeli/zapòčele
3rd per pl	Они/Оне за̀почну Oni/One zapòčnu	Они/Оне ће за̀почети/Запо̀чеће Oni/One će zapòčeti/Zapòčeće	Они/Оне буду за̀почели/за̀почеле Oni/One budu zapòčeli/zapòčele

	Past Tense (Перфект)	Pluperfect (Плусквамперфект)	Conditional (Потенцијал)
1st per	Ja сам за̀почео Ja sam zapòčeo	Ja сам био за̀почео Ja sam bio zapòčeo	Ja бих за̀почео Ja bih zapòčeo
2nd per	Ти си за̀почео Ti si zapòčeo	Ти си био за̀почео Ti si bio zapòčeo	Ти би за̀почео Ti bi zapòčeo
3rd per (M)	Он је за̀почео On je zapòčeo	Он је био за̀почео On je bio zapòčeo	Он би за̀почео On bi zapòčeo
3rd per (F)	Она је за̀почела Ona je zapòčela	Она је била за̀почела Ona je bila zapòčela	Она би за̀почела Ona bi zapòčela
3rd per (N)	Оно је за̀почело Ono je zapòčelo	Оно је било за̀почело Ono je bilo zapòčelo	Оно би за̀почело Ono bi zapòčelo
1st per pl	Ми смо за̀почели Mi smo zapòčeli	Ми смо били за̀почели Mi smo bili zapòčeli	Ми бисмо за̀почели Mi bismo zapòčeli
2nd per pl	Ви сте за̀почели Vi ste zapòčeli	Ви сте били за̀почели Vi ste bili zapòčeli	Ви бисте за̀почели Vi biste zapòčeli
3rd per pl	Они су за̀почели Oni su zapòčeli	Они су били за̀почели Oni su bili zapòčeli	Они би за̀почели Oni bi zapòčeli

	Imperative (Императив)
2nd per sg	(Ти) запо̀чни (Ti) zapòčni
1st per pl	(Ми) запо̀чнимо (Mi) zapòčnimo

2nd per pl	(Ви) запо̀чните
	(Vi) za**po**čnite

Non-finite Forms

Infinitive (Инфинитив)	запо̀чети
	za**po**četi
Present Adverbial Participle (Глаголски прилог садашњи)	--
Past Adverbial Participle (Глаголски прилог прошли)	запо̀чевши
	za**po**čevši

	Active Adjectival Participle (Глаголски придев радни)		Passive Adjectival Participle (Глаголски придев трпни)	
Gender	Singular	Plural	Singular	Plural
Feminine	за̏почела	за̏почеле	за̏почета	за̏почете
	za**po**čela	za**po**čele	za**po**četa	za**po**čete
Masculine	за̏почео	за̏почели	за̏почет	за̏почети
	za**po**čeo	za**po**čeli	za**po**čet	za**po**četi
Neuter	за̏почело	за̏почела	за̏почето	за̏почета
	za**po**čelo	za**po**čela	za**po**četo	za**po**četa

To Stay – òстати - ostati

	Present (Презент)	Future I (Футур први)	Future II (Футур други)
1st per	Ja òстанем Ja ostanem	Ja ħу òстати/Òстаħу Ja ću ostati/Ostaću	Ja будем òстао/òстала Ja budem ostao/ostala
2nd per	Ти òстанеш Ti ostaneš	Ти ħеш òстати/Òстаħеш Ti ćeš ostati/Ostaćeš	Ти будеш òстао/òстала Ti budeš ostao/ostala
3rd per (M)	Он òстане On ostane	Он ħе òстати/Òстаħе On će ostati/Ostaće	Он буде òстао On bude ostao
3rd per (F)	Она òстане Ona ostane	Она ħе òстати/Òстаħе Ona će ostati/Ostaće	Она буде òстала Ona bude ostala
3rd per (N)	Оно òстане Ono ostane	Оно ħе òстати/Òстаħе Ono će ostati/Ostaće	Оно буде òстало Ono bude ostalo
1st per pl	Ми òстанемо Mi ostanemo	Ми ħемо òстати/Òстаħемо Mi ćemo ostati/Ostaćemo	Ми будемо òстали/òстале Mi budemo ostali/ostale
2nd per pl	Ви òстанете Vi ostanete	Ви ħете òстати/Òстаħете Vi ćete ostati/Ostaćete	Ви будете òстали/òстале Vi budete ostali/ostale
3rd per pl	Они/Оне òстану Oni/One ostanu	Они/Оне ħе òстати/Òстаħе Oni/One će ostati/Ostaće	Они/Оне буду òстали/òстале Oni/One budu ostali/ostale

	Past Tense (Перфект)	Pluperfect (Плусквамперфект)	Conditional (Потенцијал)
1st per	Ja сам òстао Ja sam ostao	Ja сам био òстао Ja sam bio ostao	Ja бих òстао Ja bih ostao
2nd per	Ти си òстао Ti si ostao	Ти си био òстао Ti si bio ostao	Ти би òстао Ti bi ostao
3rd per (M)	Он је òстао On je ostao	Он је био òстао On je bio ostao	Он би òстао On bi ostao
3rd per (F)	Она је òстала Ona je ostala	Она је била òстала Ona je bila ostala	Она би òстала Ona bi ostala
3rd per (N)	Оно је òстало Ono je ostalo	Оно је било òстало Ono je bilo ostalo	Оно би òстало Ono bi ostalo
1st per pl	Ми смо òстали Mi smo ostali	Ми смо били òстали Mi smo bili ostali	Ми бисмо òстали Mi bismo ostali
2nd per pl	Ви сте òстали Vi ste ostali	Ви сте били òстали Vi ste bili ostali	Ви бисте òстали Vi biste ostali
3rd per pl	Они су òстали Oni su ostali	Они су били òстали Oni su bili ostali	Они би òстали Oni bi ostali

	Imperative (Императив)
2nd per sg	(Ти) òстани (Ti) ostani
1st per pl	(Ми) òстанимо (Mi) ostanimo

2nd per pl	(Ви) о̀станите
	(Vi) **os**tanite

Non-finite Forms

Infinitive (Инфинитив)	о̀стати
	ostati
Present Adverbial Participle (Глаголски прилог садашњи)	--
Past Adverbial Participle (Глаголски прилог прошли)	о̀ставши
	ostavši

Gender	Active Adjectival Participle (Глаголски придев радни)		Passive Adjectival Participle (Глаголски придев трпни)	
	Singular	Plural	Singular	Plural
Feminine	о̀стала	о̀стале	--	--
	ostala	**os**tale		
Masculine	о̀стао	о̀стали	--	--
	ostao	**os**tali		
Neuter	о̀стало	о̀стала	--	--
	ostalo	**os**tala		

To Take – у̀зети - uzeti

	Present (Презент)	Future I (Футур први)	Future II (Футур други)
1st per	Ja у̀змем Ja uzmem	Ja ћу у̀зети/У̀зећу Ja ću uzeti/Uzeću	Ja будем у̀зео/у̀зела Ja budem uzeo/uzela
2nd per	Ти у̀змеш Ti uzmeš	Ти ћеш у̀зети/У̀зећеш Ti ćeš uzeti/Uzećeš	Ти будеш у̀зео/у̀зела Ti budeš uzeo/uzela
3rd per (M)	Он у̀зме On uzme	Он ће у̀зети/У̀зеће On će uzeti/Uzeće	Он буде у̀зео On bude uzeo
3rd per (F)	Она у̀зме Ona uzme	Она ће у̀зети/У̀зеће Ona će uzeti/Uzeće	Она буде у̀зела Ona bude uzela
3rd per (N)	Оно у̀зме Ono uzme	Оно ће у̀зети/У̀зеће Ono će uzeti/Uzeće	Оно буде у̀зело Ono bude uzelo
1st per pl	Ми у̀змемо Mi uzmemo	Ми ћемо у̀зети/У̀зећемо Mi ćemo uzeti/Uzećemo	Ми будемо у̀зели/у̀зеле Mi budemo uzeli/uzele
2nd per pl	Ви у̀змете Vi uzmete	Ви ћете у̀зети/У̀зећете Vi ćete uzeti/Uzećete	Ви будете у̀зели/у̀зеле Vi budete uzeli/uzele
3rd per pl	Они/Оне у̀зму Oni/One uzmu	Они/Оне ће у̀зети/У̀зеће Oni/One će uzeti/Uzeće	Они/Оне буду у̀зели/у̀зеле Oni/One budu uzeli/uzele

	Past Tense (Перфект)	Pluperfect (Плусквамперфект)	Conditional (Потенцијал)
1st per	Ja сам у̀зео Ja sam uzeo	Ja сам био у̀зео Ja sam bio uzeo	Ja бих у̀зео Ja bih uzeo
2nd per	Ти си у̀зео Ti si uzeo	Ти си био у̀зео Ti si bio uzeo	Ти би у̀зео Ti bi uzeo
3rd per (M)	Он је у̀зео On je uzeo	Он је био у̀зео On je bio uzeo	Он би у̀зео On bi uzeo
3rd per (F)	Она је у̀зела Ona je uzela	Она је била у̀зела Ona je bila uzela	Она би у̀зела Ona bi uzela
3rd per (N)	Оно је у̀зело Ono je uzelo	Оно је било у̀зело Ono je bilo uzelo	Оно би у̀зело Ono bi uzelo
1st per pl	Ми смо у̀зели Mi smo uzeli	Ми смо били у̀зели Mi smo bili uzeli	Ми бисмо у̀зели Mi bismo uzeli
2nd per pl	Ви сте у̀зели Vi ste uzeli	Ви сте били у̀зели Vi ste bili uzeli	Ви бисте у̀зели Vi biste uzeli
3rd per pl	Они су у̀зели Oni su uzeli	Они су били у̀зели Oni su bili uzeli	Они би у̀зели Oni bi uzeli

	Imperative (Императив)
2nd per sg	(Ти) у̀зми (Ti) uzmi
1st per pl	(Ми) у̀змимо (Mi) uzmimo

2ⁿᵈ per pl	(Ви) у̀змите (Vi) **u**zmite

Non-finite Forms

Infinitive (Инфинитив)	у̀зети **u**zeti
Present Adverbial Participle (Глаголски прилог садашњи)	--
Past Adverbial Participle (Глаголски прилог прошли)	у̀зевши **u**zevši

Gender	Active Adjectival Participle (Глаголски придев радни)		Passive Adjectival Participle (Глаголски придев трпни)	
	Singular	Plural	Singular	Plural
Feminine	у̀зела **u**zela	у̀зеле **u**zele	у̀зета **u**zeta	у̀зете **u**zete
Masculine	у̀зео **u**zeo	у̀зели **u**zeli	у̀зет **u**zet	у̀зети **u**zeti
Neuter	у̀зело **u**zelo	у̀зела **u**zela	у̀зето **u**zeto	у̀зета **u**zeta

To Talk – говòрити - govoriti

	Present (Презент)	Future I (Футур први)	Future II (Футур други)
1st per	Ja гòворим / Ja **go**vorim	Ja ћу говòрити/Говòрићу / Ja ću go**vo**riti/Go**vo**riću	Ja будем говòрио/говòрила / Ja budem go**vo**rio/go**vo**rila
2nd per	Ти гòвориш / Ti **go**voriš	Ти ћеш говòрити/Говòрићеш / Ti ćeš go**vo**riti/Go**vo**ričeš	Ти будеш говòрио/говòрила / Ti budeš go**vo**rio/go**vo**rila
3rd per (M)	Он гòвори / On **go**vori	Он ће говòрити/Говòриће / On će go**vo**riti/Go**vo**riće	Он буде говòрио / On bude go**vo**rio
3rd per (F)	Она гòвори / Ona **go**vori	Она ће говòрити/Говòриће / Ona će go**vo**riti/Go**vo**riće	Она буде говòрила / Ona bude go**vo**rila
3rd per (N)	Оно гòвори / Ono **go**vori	Оно ће говòрити/Говòриће / Ono će go**vo**riti/Go**vo**riće	Оно буде говòрило / Ono bude go**vo**rilo
1st per pl	Ми гòворимо / Mi **go**vorimo	Ми ћемо говòрити/Говòрићемо / Mi ćemo go**vo**riti/Go**vo**rićemo	Ми будемо говòрили/говòриле / Mi budemo go**vo**rili/go**vo**rile
2nd per pl	Ви гòворите / Vi **go**vorite	Ви ћете говòрити/Говòрићете / Vi ćete go**vo**riti/Go**vo**rićete	Ви будете говòрили/говòриле / Vi budete go**vo**rili/go**vo**rile
3rd per pl	Они/Оне гòворе / Oni/One **go**vore	Они/Оне ће говòрити/Говòриће / Oni/One će go**vo**riti/Go**vo**riće	Они/Оне буду говòрили/говòриле / Oni/One budu go**vo**rili/go**vo**rile

	Past Tense (Перфект)	Pluperfect (Плусквамперфект)	Conditional (Потенцијал)
1st per	Ja сам говòрио / Ja sam go**vo**rio	Ja сам био говòрио / Ja sam bio go**vo**rio	Ja бих говòрио / Ja bih go**vo**rio
2nd per	Ти си говòрио / Ti si go**vo**rio	Ти си био говòрио / Ti si bio go**vo**rio	Ти би говòрио / Ti bi go**vo**rio
3rd per (M)	Он је говòрио / On je go**vo**rio	Он је био говòрио / On je bio go**vo**rio	Он би говòрио / On bi go**vo**rio
3rd per (F)	Она је говòрила / Ona je go**vo**rila	Она је била говòрила / Ona je bila go**vo**rila	Она би говòрила / Ona bi go**vo**rila
3rd per (N)	Оно је говòрило / Ono je go**vo**rilo	Оно је било говòрило / Ono je bilo go**vo**rilo	Оно би говòрило / Ono bi go**vo**rilo
1st per pl	Ми смо говòрили / Mi smo go**vo**rili	Ми смо били говòрили / Mi smo bili go**vo**rili	Ми бисмо говòрили / Mi bismo go**vo**rili
2nd per pl	Ви сте говòрили / Vi ste go**vo**rili	Ви сте били говòрили / Vi ste bili go**vo**rili	Ви бисте говòрили / Vi biste go**vo**rili
3rd per pl	Они су говòрили / Oni su go**vo**rili	Они су били говòрили / Oni su bili go**vo**rili	Они би говòрили / Oni bi go**vo**rili

	Imperative (Императив)
2nd per sg	(Ти) говòри / (Ti) go**vo**ri
1st per pl	(Ми) говòримо / (Mi) go**vo**rimo

2nd per pl	(Ви) гово̀рите
	(Vi) go**vo**rite

Non-finite Forms

Infinitive (Инфинитив)	гово̀рити
	go**vo**riti
Present Adverbial Participle (Глаголски прилог садашњи)	гово̀рећи
	go**vo**reći
Past Adverbial Participle (Глаголски прилог прошли)	--

	Active Adjectival Participle (Глаголски придев радни)		Passive Adjectival Participle (Глаголски придев трпни)	
Gender	Singular	Plural	Singular	Plural
Feminine	гово̀рила	гово̀риле	--	--
	go**vo**rila	go**vo**rile		
Masculine	гово̀рио	гово̀рили	--	--
	go**vo**rio	go**vo**rili		
Neuter	гово̀рило	гово̀рила	--	--
	go**vo**rilo	go**vo**rila		

To Teach - подучáвати - podučavati

	Present (Презент)	Future I (Футур први)	Future II (Футур други)
1st per	Ja подỳчавам Ja podučavam	Ja ћу подучáвати/Подучáваћу Ja ću podučavati/Podučavaću	Ja будем подучáвао/подучáвала Ja budem podučavao/podučavala
2nd per	Ти подỳчаваш Ti podučavaš	Ти ћеш подучáвати/Подучáваћеш Ti ćeš podučavati/Podučavaćeš	Ти будеш подучáвао/подучáвала Ti budeš podučavao/podučavala
3rd per (M)	Он подỳчава On podučava	Он ће подучáвати/Подучáваће On će podučavati/Podučavaće	Он буде подучáвао On bude podučavao
3rd per (F)	Она подỳчава Ona podučava	Она ће подучáвати/Подучáваће Ona će podučavati/Podučavaće	Она буде подучáвала Ona bude podučavala
3rd per (N)	Оно подỳчава Ono podučava	Оно ће подучáвати/Подучáваће Ono će podučavati/Podučavaće	Оно буде подучáвало Ono bude podučavalo
1st per pl	Ми подỳчавамо Mi podučavamo	Ми ћемо подучáвати/Подучáваћемо Mi ćemo podučavati/Podučavaćemo	Ми будемо подучáвали/ подучáвале Mi budemo podučavali/ podučavale
2nd per pl	Ви подỳчавате Vi podučavate	Ви ћете подучáвати/Подучáваћете Vi ćete podučavati/Podučavaćete	Ви будете подучáвали/подучáвале Vi budete podučavali/podučavale
3rd per pl	Они/Оне подучáвају Oni/One podučavaju	Они/Оне ће подучáвати/Подучáваће Oni/One će podučavati/Podučavaće	Они/Оне буду подучáвали/подучáвале Oni/One budu podučavali/podučavale

	Past Tense (Перфект)	Pluperfect (Плусквамперфект)	Conditional (Потенцијал)
1st per	Ja сам подучáвао Ja sam podučavao	Ja сам био подучáвао Ja sam bio podučavao	Ja бих подучáвао Ja bih podučavao
2nd per	Ти си подучáвао Ti si podučavao	Ти си био подучáвао Ti si bio podučavao	Ти би подучáвао Ti bi podučavao
3rd per (M)	Он је подучáвао On je podučavao	Он је био подучáвао On je bio podučavao	Он би подучáвао On bi podučavao
3rd per (F)	Она је подучáвала Ona je podučavala	Она је била подучáвала Ona je bila podučavala	Она би подучáвала Ona bi podučavala
3rd per (N)	Оно је подучáвало Ono je podučavalo	Оно је било подучáвало Ono je bilo podučavalo	Оно би подучáвало Ono bi podučavalo
1st per pl	Ми смо подучáвали Mi smo podučavali	Ми смо били подучáвали Mi smo bili podučavali	Ми бисмо подучáвали Mi bismo podučavali
2nd per pl	Ви сте подучáвали Vi ste podučavali	Ви сте били подучáвали Vi ste bili podučavali	Ви бисте подучáвали Vi biste podučavali
3rd per pl	Они су подучáвали Oni su podučavali	Они су били подучáвали Oni su bili podučavali	Они би подучáвали Oni bi podučavali

	Imperative (Императив)
2nd per sg	(Ти) подỳчавај (Ti) podučavaj
1st per pl	(Ми) подỳчавајмо (Mi) podučavajmo

2nd per pl	(Ви) поду̀чавајте
	(Vi) podučavajte

Non-finite Forms

Infinitive (Инфинитив)	подуча́вати
	podučavati
Present Adverbial Participle (Глаголски прилог садашњи)	подуча́вајући
	podučavajući
Past Adverbial Participle (Глаголски прилог прошли)	--

	Active Adjectival Participle (Глаголски придев радни)		Passive Adjectival Participle (Глаголски придев трпни)	
Gender	Singular	Plural	Singular	Plural
Feminine	подуча́вала	подуча́вале	поду̀чавана	поду̀чаване
	podučavala	podučavale	podučavana	podučavane
Masculine	подуча́вао	подуча́вали	поду̀чаван	поду̀чавани
	podučavao	podučavali	podučavan	podučavani
Neuter	подуча́вало	подуча́вала	поду̀чавано	поду̀чавана
	podučavalo	podučavala	podučavano	podučavana

To Think - мѝслити - misliti

	Present (Презент)	Future I (Футур први)	Future II (Футур други)
1st per	Ja мѝслим Ja mislim	Ja ћу мѝслити/Мѝслићу Ja ću misliti/Misliću	Ja будем мѝслио/мѝслила Ja budem mislio/mislila
2nd per	Ти мѝслиш Ti misliš	Ти ћеш мѝслити/Мѝслићеш Ti ćeš misliti/Mislićeš	Ти будеш мѝслио/мѝслила Ti budeš mislio/mislila
3rd per (M)	Он мѝсли On misli	Он ће мѝслити/Мѝслиће On će misliti/Misliće	Он буде мѝслио On bude mislio
3rd per (F)	Она мѝсли Ona misli	Она ће мѝслити/Мѝслиће Ona će misliti/Misliće	Она буде мѝслила Ona bude mislila
3rd per (N)	Оно мѝсли Ono misli	Оно ће мѝслити/Мѝслиће Ono će misliti/Misliće	Оно буде мѝслило Ono bude mislilo
1st per pl	Ми мѝслимо Mi mislimo	Ми ћемо мѝслити/Мѝслићемо Mi ćemo misliti/Mislićemo	Ми будемо мѝслили/мѝслиле Mi budemo mislili/mislile
2nd per pl	Ви мѝслите Vi mislite	Ви ћете мѝслити/Мѝслићете Vi ćete misliti/Mislićete	Ви будете мѝслили/мѝслиле Vi budete mislili/mislile
3rd per pl	Они/Оне мѝсле Oni/One misle	Они/Оне ће мѝслити/Мѝслиће Oni/One će misliti/Misliće	Они/Оне буду мѝслили/мѝслиле Oni/One budu mislili/mislile

	Past Tense (Перфект)	Pluperfect (Плусквамперфект)	Conditional (Потенцијал)
1st per	Ja сам мѝслио Ja sam mislio	Ja сам био мѝслио Ja sam bio mislio	Ja бих мѝслио Ja bih mislio
2nd per	Ти си мѝслио Ti si mislio	Ти си био мѝслио Ti si bio mislio	Ти би мѝслио Ti bi mislio
3rd per (M)	Он је мѝслио On je mislio	Он је био мѝслио On je bio mislio	Он би мѝслио On bi mislio
3rd per (F)	Она је мѝслила Ona je mislila	Она је била мѝслила Ona je bila mislila	Она би мѝслила Ona bi mislila
3rd per (N)	Оно је мѝслило Ono je mislilo	Оно је било мѝслило Ono je bilo mislilo	Оно би мѝслило Ono bi mislilo
1st per pl	Ми смо мѝслили Mi smo mislili	Ми смо били мѝслили Mi smo bili mislili	Ми бисмо мѝслили Mi bismo mislili
2nd per pl	Ви сте мѝслили Vi ste mislili	Ви сте били мѝслили Vi ste bili mislili	Ви бисте мѝслили Vi biste mislili
3rd per pl	Они су мѝслили Oni su mislili	Они су били мѝслили Oni su bili mislili	Они би мѝслили Oni bi mislili

	Imperative (Императив)
2nd per sg	(Ти) мѝсли (Ti) misli
1st per pl	(Ми) мѝслимо (Mi) mislimo

187

2nd per pl	(Ви) мӣслите (Vi) **mi**slite

Non-finite Forms

Infinitive (Инфинитив)	мӣслити **mi**sliti
Present Adverbial Participle (Глаголски прилог садашњи)	мӣслећи **mi**sleći
Past Adverbial Participle (Глаголски прилог прошли)	--

	Active Adjectival Participle (Глаголски придев радни)		Passive Adjectival Participle (Глаголски придев трпни)	
Gender	Singular	Plural	Singular	Plural
Feminine	мӣслила **mi**slila	мӣслиле **mi**slile	--	--
Masculine	мӣслио **mi**slio	мӣслили **mi**slili	--	--
Neuter	мӣслило **mi**slilo	мӣслила **mi**slila	--	--

To Touch – дотàћи - dotaći

	Present (Презент)	Future I (Футур први)	Future II (Футур други)
1st per	Ja дòтакнем	Ja ћу дотàћи/Дотàћи ћу	Ja будем дòтакао/дòтакла
	Ja dotaknem	Ja ću dotaći/Dotaći ću	Ja budem dotakao/dotakla
2nd per	Ти дòтакнеш	Ти ћеш дотàћи/Дотàћи ћеш	Ти будеш дòтакао/дòтакла
	Ti dotakneš	Ti ćeš dotaći/Dotaći ćeš	Ti budeš dotakao/dotakla
3rd per (M)	Он дòтакне	Он ће дотàћи/Дотàћи ће	Он буде дòтакао
	On dotakne	On će dotaći/Dotaći će	On bude dotakao
3rd per (F)	Она дòтакне	Она ће дотàћи/Дотàћи ће	Она буде дòтакла
	Ona dotakne	Ona će dotaći/Dotaći će	Ona bude dotakla
3rd per (N)	Оно дòтакне	Оно ће дотàћи/Дотàћи ће	Оно буде дòтакло
	Ono dotakne	Ono će dotaći/Dotaći će	Ono bude dotaklo
1st per pl	Ми дòтакнемо	Ми ћемо дотàћи/Дотàћи ћемо	Ми будемо дòтакли/дòтакле
	Mi dotaknemo	Mi ćemo dotaći/Dotaći ćemo	Mi budemo dotakli/dotakle
2nd per pl	Ви дòтакнете	Ви ћете дотàћи/Дотàћи ћете	Ви будете дòтакли/дòтакле
	Vi dotaknete	Vi ćete dotaći/Dotaći ćete	Vi budete dotakli/dotakle
3rd per pl	Они/Оне дòтакну	Они/Оне ће дотàћи/Дотàћи ће	Они/Оне буду дòтакли/дòтакле
	Oni/One dotaknu	Oni/One će dotaći/Dotaći će	Oni/One budu dotakli/dotakle

	Past Tense (Перфект)	Pluperfect (Плусквамперфект)	Conditional (Потенцијал)
1st per	Ja сам дòтакао	Ja сам био дòтакао	Ja бих дòтакао
	Ja sam dotakao	Ja sam bio dotakao	Ja bih dotakao
2nd per	Ти си дòтакао	Ти си био дòтакао	Ти би дòтакао
	Ti si dotakao	Ti si bio dotakao	Ti bi dotakao
3rd per (M)	Он је дòтакао	Он је био дòтакао	Он би дòтакао
	On je dotakao	On je bio dotakao	On bi dotakao
3rd per (F)	Она је дòтакла	Она је била дòтакла	Она би дòтакла
	Ona je dotakla	Ona je bila dotakla	Ona bi dotakla
3rd per (N)	Оно је дòтакло	Оно је било дòтакло	Оно би дòтакло
	Ono je dotaklo	Ono je bilo dotaklo	Ono bi dotaklo
1st per pl	Ми смо дòтакли	Ми смо били дòтакли	Ми бисмо дòтакли
	Mi smo dotakli	Mi smo bili dotakli	Mi bismo dotakli
2nd per pl	Ви сте дòтакли	Ви сте били дòтакли	Ви бисте дòтакли
	Vi ste dotakli	Vi ste bili dotakli	Vi biste dotakli
3rd per pl	Они су дòтакли	Они су били дòтакли	Они би дòтакли
	Oni su dotakli	Oni su bili dotakli	Oni bi dotakli

	Imperative (Императив)
2nd per sg	(Ти) дòтакни
	(Ti) dotakni
1st per pl	(Ми) дòтакнимо
	(Mi) dotaknimo

2nd per pl	(Ви) до̀такните
	(Vi) **do**taknite

Non-finite Forms

Infinitive (Инфинитив)	дота̀ћи
	dotaći
Present Adverbial Participle (Глаголски прилог садашњи)	--
Past Adverbial Participle (Глаголски прилог прошли)	до̀такнувши
	dotaknuvši

	Active Adjectival Participle (Глаголски придев радни)		Passive Adjectival Participle (Глаголски придев трпни)	
Gender	Singular	Plural	Singular	Plural
Feminine	до̀такла	до̀такле	до̀такнута	до̀такнуте
	dotakla	**do**takle	**do**taknuta	**do**taknute
Masculine	до̀такао	до̀такли	до̀такнут	до̀такнути
	dotakao	**do**takli	**do**taknut	**do**taknuti
Neuter	до̀такло	до̀такла	до̀такнуто	до̀такнута
	dotaklo	**do**takla	**do**taknuto	**do**taknuta

To Travel – путòвати - putovati

	Present (Презент)	Future I (Футур први)	Future II (Футур други)
1st per	Ja пу̀тујем Ja **pu**tujem	Ja ћу путòвати/Путòва̀ћу Ja ću pu**to**vati/Pu**to**vaću	Ja будем пу̏товао/пу̏товала Ja budem **pu**tovao/**pu**tovala
2nd per	Ти пу̀тујеш Ti **pu**tuješ	Ти ћеш путòвати/Путòва̀ћеш Ti ćeš pu**to**vati/Pu**to**vaćeš	Ти будеш пу̏товао/пу̏товала Ti budeš **pu**tovao/**pu**tovala
3rd per (M)	Он пу̀тује On **pu**tuje	Он ће путòвати/Путòва̀ће On će pu**to**vati/Pu**to**vaće	Он буде пу̏товао On bude **pu**tovao
3rd per (F)	Она пу̀тује Ona **pu**tuje	Она ће путòвати/Путòва̀ће Ona će pu**to**vati/Pu**to**vaće	Она буде пу̏товала Ona bude **pu**tovala
3rd per (N)	Оно пу̀тује Ono **pu**tuje	Оно ће путòвати/Путòва̀ће Ono će pu**to**vati/Pu**to**vaće	Оно буде пу̏товало Ono bude **pu**tovalo
1st per pl	Ми пу̀тујемо Mi **pu**tujemo	Ми ћемо путòвати/Путòва̀ћемо Mi ćemo pu**to**vati/Pu**to**vaćemo	Ми будемо пу̏товали/пу̏товале Mi budemo **pu**tovali/**pu**tovale
2nd per pl	Ви пу̀тујете Vi **pu**tujete	Ви ћете путòвати/Путòва̀ћете Vi ćete pu**to**vati/Pu**to**vaćete	Ви будете пу̏товали/пу̏товале Vi budete **pu**tovali/**pu**tovale
3rd per pl	Они/Оне пу̀тују Oni/One **pu**tuju	Они/Оне ће путòвати/Путòва̀ће Oni/One će pu**to**vati/Pu**to**vaće	Они/Оне буду пу̏товали/пу̏товале Oni/One budu **pu**tovali/**pu**tovale

	Past Tense (Перфект)	Pluperfect (Плусквамперфект)	Conditional (Потенцијал)
1st per	Ja сам пу̏товао Ja sam **pu**tovao	Ja сам био пу̏товао Ja sam bio **pu**tovao	Ja бих пу̏товао Ja bih **pu**tovao
2nd per	Ти си пу̏товао Ti si **pu**tovao	Ти си био пу̏товао Ti si bio **pu**tovao	Ти би пу̏товао Ti bi **pu**tovao
3rd per (M)	Он је пу̏товао On je **pu**tovao	Он је био пу̏товао On je bio **pu**tovao	Он би пу̏товао On bi **pu**tovao
3rd per (F)	Она је пу̏товала Ona je **pu**tovala	Она је била пу̏товала Ona je bila **pu**tovala	Она би пу̏товала Ona bi **pu**tovala
3rd per (N)	Оно је пу̏товало Ono je **pu**tovalo	Оно је било пу̏товало Ono je bilo **pu**tovalo	Оно би пу̏товало Ono bi **pu**tovalo
1st per pl	Ми смо пу̏товали Mi smo **pu**tovali	Ми смо били пу̏товали Mi smo bili **pu**tovali	Ми бисмо пу̏товали Mi bismo **pu**tovali
2nd per pl	Ви сте пу̏товали Vi ste **pu**tovali	Ви сте били пу̏товали Vi ste bili **pu**tovali	Ви бисте пу̏товали Vi biste **pu**tovali
3rd per pl	Они су пу̏товали Oni su **pu**tovali	Они су били пу̏товали Oni su bili **pu**tovali	Они би пу̏товали Oni bi **pu**tovali

	Imperative (Императив)
2nd per sg	(Ти) пу̏туј (Ti) **pu**tuj
1st per pl	(Ми) пу̏тујмо (Mi) **pu**tujmo

2ⁿᵈ per pl	(Ви) пу̏тӯјте
	(Vi) **pu**tujte

Non-finite Forms

Infinitive (Инфинитив)	пу̀то̀вати
	putovati
Present Adverbial Participle (Глаголски прилог садашњи)	пу̏тӯјући
	putujući
Past Adverbial Participle (Глаголски прилог прошли)	--

	Active Adjectival Participle (Глаголски придев радни)		Passive Adjectival Participle (Глаголски придев трпни)	
Gender	Singular	Plural	Singular	Plural
Feminine	пу̏товала	пу̏товале	--	--
	putovala	**pu**tovale		
Masculine	пу̏товао	пу̏товали	--	--
	putovao	**pu**tovali		
Neuter	пу̏товало	пу̏товала	--	--
	putovalo	**pu**tovala		

To Understand – разу̀мети – razumeti

	Present (Презент)	Future I (Футур први)	Future II (Футур други)
1st per	Ja разу̀мем / Ja razumem	Ja ћу разу̀мети/Разу̀мећу / Ja ću razumeti/Razumećи	Ja бу̀дем разу̀мео/разу̀мела / Ja budem razumeo/razumela
2nd per	Ти разу̀меш / Ti razumeš	Ти ћеш разу̀мети/Разу̀мећеш / Ti ćeš razumeti/Razumećeš	Ти бу̀деш разу̀мео/разу̀мела / Ti budeš razumeo/razumela
3rd per (M)	Он разу̀ме / On razume	Он ће разу̀мети/Разу̀меће / On će razumeti/Razumeće	Он бу̀де разу̀мео / On bude razumeo
3rd per (F)	Она разу̀ме / Ona razume	Она ће разу̀мети/Разу̀меће / Ona će razumeti/Razumeće	Она бу̀де разу̀мела / Ona bude razumela
3rd per (N)	Оно разу̀ме / Ono razume	Оно ће разу̀мети/Разу̀меће / Ono će razumeti/Razumeće	Оно бу̀де разу̀мело / Ono bude razumelo
1st per pl	Ми разу̀мемо / Mi razumemo	Ми ћемо разу̀мети/Разу̀мећемо / Mi ćemo razumeti/Razumećemo	Ми бу̀демо разу̀мели/разу̀меле / Mi budemo razumeli/razumele
2nd per pl	Ви разу̀мете / Vi razumete	Ви ћете разу̀мети/Разу̀мећете / Vi ćete razumeti/Razumećete	Ви бу̀дете разу̀мели/разу̀меле / Vi budete razumeli/razumele
3rd per pl	Они/Оне разу̀мејy / Oni/One razumeju	Они/Оне ће разу̀мети/Разу̀меће / Oni/One će razumeti/Razumeće	Они/Оне бу̀ду разу̀мели/разу̀меле / Oni/One budu razumeli/razumele

	Past Tense (Перфект)	Pluperfect (Плусквамперфект)	Conditional (Потенцијал)
1st per	Ja сам разу̀мео / Ja sam razumeo	Ja сам био разу̀мео / Ja sam bio razumeo	Ja бих разу̀мео / Ja bih razumeo
2nd per	Ти си разу̀мео / Ti si razumeo	Ти си био разу̀мео / Ti si bio razumeo	Ти би разу̀мео / Ti bi razumeo
3rd per (M)	Он је разу̀мео / On je razumeo	Он је био разу̀мео / On je bio razumeo	Он би разу̀мео / On bi razumeo
3rd per (F)	Она је разу̀мела / Ona je razumela	Она је била разу̀мела / Ona je bila razumela	Она би разу̀мела / Ona bi razumela
3rd per (N)	Оно је разу̀мело / Ono je razumelo	Оно је било разу̀мело / Ono je bilo razumelo	Оно би разу̀мело / Ono bi razumelo
1st per pl	Ми смо разу̀мели / Mi smo razumeli	Ми смо били разу̀мели / Mi smo bili razumeli	Ми бисмо разу̀мели / Mi bismo razumeli
2nd per pl	Ви сте разу̀мели / Vi ste razumeli	Ви сте били разу̀мели / Vi ste bili razumeli	Ви бисте разу̀мели / Vi biste razumeli
3rd per pl	Они су разу̀мели / Oni su razumeli	Они су били разу̀мели / Oni su bili razumeli	Они би разу̀мели / Oni bi razumeli

	Imperative (Императив)
2nd per sg	(Ти) разу̀ми / (Ti) razumi
1st per pl	(Ми) разу̀мимо / (Mi) razumimo

2nd per pl	(Ви) разу̀мите (Vi) razumite

Non-finite Forms

Infinitive (Инфинитив)	разу̀мети razumeti
Present Adverbial Participle (Глаголски прилог садашњи)	--
Past Adverbial Participle (Глаголски прилог прошли)	разу̀мевши razumevši

Gender	Active Adjectival Participle (Глаголски придев радни)		Passive Adjectival Participle (Глаголски придев трпни)	
	Singular	Plural	Singular	Plural
Feminine	разу̀мела razumela	разу̀меле razumele	--	--
Masculine	разу̀мео razumeo	разу̀мели razumeli	--	--
Neuter	разу̀мело razumelo	разу̀мела razumela	--	--

To Use - кори́стити - koristiti

	Present (Презент)	Future I (Футур први)	Future II (Футур други)
1st per	Ja ко̀ристим Ja **ko**ristim	Ja ћу кори́стити/Кори́стићу Ja ću koristiti/Koristiću	Ja бу́дем кори́стио/кори́стила Ja budem koristio/koristila
2nd per	Ти ко̀ристиш Ti **ko**ristiš	Ти ћеш кори́стити/Кори́стићеш Ti ćeš koristiti/Koristićeš	Ти бу́деш кори́стио/кори́стила Ti budeš koristio/koristila
3rd per (M)	Он ко̀ристи On **ko**risti	Он ће кори́стити/Кори́стиће On će koristiti/Koristiće	Он буде кори́стио On bude koristio
3rd per (F)	Она ко̀ристи Ona **ko**risti	Она ће кори́стити/Кори́стиће Ona će koristiti/Koristiće	Она буде кори́стила Ona bude koristila
3rd per (N)	Оно ко̀ристи Ono **ko**risti	Оно ће кори́стити/Кори́стиће Ono će koristiti/Koristiće	Оно буде кори́стило Ono bude koristilo
1st per pl	Ми ко̀ристимо Mi **ko**ristimo	Ми ћемо кори́стити/Кори́стићемо Mi ćemo koristiti/Koristićemo	Ми будемо кори́стили/кори́стиле Mi budemo koristili/koristile
2nd per pl	Ви ко̀ристите Vi **ko**ristite	Ви ћете кори́стити/Кори́стићете Vi ćete koristiti/Koristićete	Ви будете кори́стили/кори́стиле Vi budete koristili/koristile
3rd per pl	Они/Оне ко̀ристе Oni/One **ko**riste	Они/Оне ће кори́стити/Кори́стиће Oni/One će koristiti/Koristiće	Они/Оне буду кори́стили/кори́стиле Oni/One budu koristili/koristile

	Past Tense (Перфект)	Pluperfect (Плусквамперфект)	Conditional (Потенцијал)
1st per	Ja сам кори́стио Ja sam koristio	Ja сам био кори́стио Ja sam bio koristio	Ja бих кори́стио Ja bih koristio
2nd per	Ти си кори́стио Ti si koristio	Ти си био кори́стио Ti si bio koristio	Ти би кори́стио Ti bi koristio
3rd per (M)	Он је кори́стио On je koristio	Он је био кори́стио On je bio koristio	Он би кори́стио On bi koristio
3rd per (F)	Она је кори́стила Ona je koristila	Она је била кори́стила Ona je bila koristila	Она би кори́стила Ona bi koristila
3rd per (N)	Оно је кори́стило Ono je koristilo	Оно је било кори́стило Ono je bilo koristilo	Оно би кори́стило Ono bi koristilo
1st per pl	Ми смо кори́стили Mi smo koristili	Ми смо били кори́стили Mi smo bili koristili	Ми бисмо кори́стили Mi bismo koristili
2nd per pl	Ви сте кори́стили Vi ste koristili	Ви сте били кори́стили Vi ste bili koristili	Ви бисте кори́стили Vi biste koristili
3rd per pl	Они су кори́стили Oni su koristili	Они су били кори́стили Oni su bili koristili	Они би кори́стили Oni bi koristili

	Imperative (Императив)
2nd per sg	(Ти) кори́сти (Ti) **ko**risti
1st per pl	(Ми) кори́стимо (Mi) **ko**ristimo

2nd per pl	(Ви) кори́стите (Vi) koristite

Non-finite Forms

Infinitive (Инфинитив)	кори́стити koristiti
Present Adverbial Participle (Глаголски прилог садашњи)	кори́стећи koristeći
Past Adverbial Participle (Глаголски прилог прошли)	кори́стивши koristivši

Gender	Active Adjectival Participle (Глаголски придев радни)		Passive Adjectival Participle (Глаголски придев трпни)	
	Singular	Plural	Singular	Plural
Feminine	кори́стила koristila	кори́стиле koristile	кòриштена korištena	кòриштене korištene
Masculine	кори́стио koristio	кори́стили koristili	кòриштен korišten	кòриштени korišteni
Neuter	кори́стило koristilo	кори́стила koristila	кòриштено korišteno	кòриштена korištena

To Wait - чѐкати - čekati

	Present (Презент)	Future I (Футур први)	Future II (Футур други)
1st per	Ja чѐкам / Ja čekam	Ja ћу чѐкати/Чѐкаћу / Ja ću čekati/**Čekaću**	Ja будем чѐкао/чѐкала / Ja budem čekao/čekala
2nd per	Ти чѐкаш / Ti čekaš	Ти ћеш чѐкати/Чѐкаћеш / Ti ćeš čekati/**Čekaćeš**	Ти будеш чѐкао/чѐкала / Ti budeš čekao/čekala
3rd per (M)	Он чѐка / On čeka	Он ће чѐкати/Чѐкаће / On će čekati/**Čekaće**	Он буде чѐкао / On bude čekao
3rd per (F)	Она чѐка / Ona čeka	Она ће чѐкати/Чѐкаће / Ona će čekati/**Čekaće**	Она буде чѐкала / Ona bude čekala
3rd per (N)	Оно чѐка / Ono čeka	Оно ће чѐкати/Чѐкаће / Ono će čekati/**Čekaće**	Оно буде чѐкало / Ono bude čekalo
1st per pl	Ми чѐкамо / Mi čekamo	Ми ћемо чѐкати/Чѐкаћемо / Mi ćemo čekati/**Čekaćemo**	Ми будемо чѐкали/чѐкале / Mi budemo čekali/čekale
2nd per pl	Ви чѐкате / Vi čekate	Ви ћете чѐкати/Чѐкаћете / Vi ćete čekati/**Čekaćete**	Ви будете чѐкали/чѐкале / Vi budete čekali/čekale
3rd per pl	Они/Оне чѐкају / Oni/One čekaju	Они/Оне ће чѐкати/Чѐкаће / Oni će čekati/**Čekaće**	Они/Оне буду чѐкали/чѐкале / Oni/One budu čekali/čekale

	Past Tense (Перфект)	Pluperfect (Плусквамперфект)	Conditional (Потенцијал)
1st per	Ja сам чѐкао / Ja sam čekao	Ja сам био чѐкао / Ja sam bio **čekao**	Ja бих чѐкао / Ja bih **čekao**
2nd per	Ти си чѐкао / Ti si čekao	Ти си био чѐкао / Ti si bio čekao	Ти би чѐкао / Ti bi čekao
3rd per (M)	Он је чѐкао / On je čekao	Он је био чѐкао / On je bio **čekao**	Он би чѐкао / On bi čekao
3rd per (F)	Она је чѐкала / Ona je čekala	Она је била чѐкала / Ona je bila **čekala**	Она би чѐкала / Ona bi čekala
3rd per (N)	Оно је чѐкало / Ono je čekalo	Оно је било чѐкало / Ono je bilo čekalo	Оно би чѐкало / Ono bi čekalo
1st per pl	Ми смо чѐкали / Mi smo čekali	Ми смо били чѐкали / Mi smo bili **čekali**	Ми бисмо чѐкали / Mi bismo čekali
2nd per pl	Ви сте чѐкали / Vi ste čekali	Ви сте били чѐкали / Vi ste bili **čekali**	Ви бисте чѐкали / Vi biste čekali
3rd per pl	Они су чѐкали / Oni su čekali	Они су били чѐкали / Oni su bili **čekali**	Они би чѐкали / Oni bi čekali

	Imperative (Императив)
2nd per sg	(Ти) чѐкај / (Ti) **čekaj**
1st per pl	(Ми) чѐкајте / (Mi) **čekajte**

197

2nd per pl	(Ви) чѐкајмо
	(Vi) **če**kajmo

Non-finite Forms

Infinitive (Инфинитив)	чѐкати
	čekati
Present Adverbial Participle (Глаголски прилог садашњи)	чѐкајући
	čekajući
Past Adverbial Participle (Глаголски прилог прошли)	чѐкавши
	čekavši

	Active Adjectival Participle (Глаголски придев радни)		Passive Adjectival Participle (Глаголски придев трпни)	
Gender	Singular	Plural	Singular	Plural
Feminine	чѐкала	чѐкале	--	--
	čekala	**če**kale		
Masculine	чѐкао	чѐкали	--	--
	čekao	**če**kali		
Neuter	чѐкало	чѐкала	--	--
	čekalo	**če**kala		

To Walk - шётати - šetati

	Present (Презент)	Future I (Футур први)	Future II (Футур други)
1st per	Ja шётам / Ja šetam	Ja ħу шётати/Шётаħу / Ja ću šetati/**Šeta**ću	Ja будем шётао/шётала / Ja budem šetao/šetala
2nd per	Ти шёташ / Ti šetaš	Ти ħеш шётати/Шётаħеш / Ti ćeš šetati/**Šeta**ćeš	Ти будеш шётао/шётала / Ti budeš šetao/šetala
3rd per (M)	Он шёта / On šeta	Он ħе шётати/Шётаħе / On će šetati/**Šeta**će	Он буде шётао / On bude šetao
3rd per (F)	Она шёта / Ona šeta	Она ħе шётати/Шётаħе / Ona će šetati/**Šeta**će	Она буде шётала / Ona bude šetala
3rd per (N)	Оно шёта / Ono šeta	Оно ħе шётати/Шётаħе / Ono će šetati/**Šeta**će	Оно буде шётало / Ono bude šetalo
1st per pl	Ми шётамо / Mi šetamo	Ми ħемо шётати/Шётаħемо / Mi ćemo šetati/**Šeta**ćemo	Ми будемо шётали/шётале / Mi budemo šetali/šetale
2nd per pl	Ви шётате / Vi šetate	Ви ħете шётати/Шётаħете / Vi ćete šetati/**Šeta**ćete	Ви будете шётали/шётале / Vi budete šetali/šetale
3rd per pl	Они/Оне шётају / Oni/One šetaju	Они/Оне ħе шётати/Шётаħе / Oni/One će šetati/**Šeta**će	Они/Оне буду шётали/шётале / Oni/One budu šetali/šetale

	Past Tense (Перфект)	Pluperfect (Плусквамперфект)	Conditional (Потенцијал)
1st per	Ja сам шётао / Ja sam šetao	Ja сам био шётао / Ja sam bio šetao	Ja бих шётао / Ja bih šetao
2nd per	Ти си шётао / Ti si šetao	Ти си био шётао / Ti si bio šetao	Ти би шётао / Ti bi šetao
3rd per (M)	Он је шётао / On je šetao	Он је био шётао / On je bio šetao	Он би шётао / On bi šetao
3rd per (F)	Она је шётала / Ona je šetala	Она је била шётала / Ona je bila šetala	Она би шётала / Ona bi šetala
3rd per (N)	Оно је шётало / Ono je šetalo	Оно је било шётало / Ono je bilo šetalo	Оно би шётало / Ono bi šetalo
1st per pl	Ми смо шётали / Mi smo šetali	Ми смо били шётали / Mi smo bili šetali	Ми бисмо шётали / Mi bismo šetali
2nd per pl	Ви сте шётали / Vi ste šetali	Ви сте били шётали / Vi ste bili šetali	Ви бисте шётали / Vi biste šetali
3rd per pl	Они су шётали / Oni su šetali	Они су били шётали / Oni su bili šetali	Они би шётали / Oni bi šetali

	Imperative (Императив)
2nd per sg	(Ти) шётај / (Ti) šetaj
1st per pl	(Ми) шётајмо / (Mi) šetajmo

2nd per pl	(Ви) шȇтајте
	(Vi) **še**tajte

Non-finite Forms

Infinitive (Инфинитив)	шȇтати
	šetati
Present Adverbial Participle (Глаголски прилог садашњи)	шȇтајући
	šetajući
Past Adverbial Participle (Глаголски прилог прошли)	--

	Active Adjectival Participle (Глаголски придев радни)		Passive Adjectival Participle (Глаголски придев трпни)	
Gender	Singular	Plural	Singular	Plural
Feminine	шȇтала	шȇтале	шȇтана	шȇтане
	šetala	**še**tale	**še**tana	**še**tane
Masculine	шȇтао	шȇтали	шȇтан	шȇтани
	šetao	**še**tali	**še**tan	**še**tani
Neuter	шȇтало	шȇтала	шȇтано	шȇтана
	šetalo	**še**tala	**še**tano	**še**tana

To Want – жѐлети - želeti

	Present (Презент)	Future I (Футур први)	Future II (Футур други)
1st per	Ja жѐлим / Ja želim	Ja ħy жѐлети/Жѐлеħу / Ja ću želeti/Želeću	Ja будем жѐлео/жѐлела / Ja budem želeo/želela
2nd per	Ти жѐлиш / Ti želiš	Ти ħеш жѐлети/Жѐлеħеш / Ti ćeš želeti/Želećeš	Ти будеш жѐлео/жѐлела / Ti budeš želeo/želela
3rd per (M)	Он жѐли / On želi	Он ħе жѐлети/Жѐлеħе / On će želeti/Želeće	Он буде жѐлео / On bude želeo
3rd per (F)	Она жѐли / Ona želi	Она ħе жѐлети/Жѐлеħе / Ona će želeti/Želeće	Она буде жѐлела / Ona bude želela
3rd per (N)	Оно жѐли / Ono želi	Оно ħе жѐлети/Жѐлеħе / Ono će želeti/Želeće	Оно буде жѐлело / Ono bude želelo
1st per pl	Ми жѐлимо / Mi želimo	Ми ħемо жѐлети/Жѐлеħемо / Mi ćemo želeti/Želećemo	Ми будемо жѐлели/жѐлеле / Mi budemo želeli/želele
2nd per pl	Ви жѐлите / Vi želite	Ви ħете жѐлети/Жѐлеħете / Vi ćete želeti/Želećete	Ви будете жѐлели/жѐлеле / Vi budete želeli/želele
3rd per pl	Они/Оне жѐле / Oni/One žele	Они/Оне ħе жѐлети/Жѐлеħе / Oni/One će želeti/Želeće	Они/Оне буду жѐлели/жѐлеле / Oni/One budu želeli/želele

	Past Tense (Перфект)	Pluperfect (Плусквамперфект)	Conditional (Потенцијал)
1st per	Ja сам жѐлео / Ja sam želeo	Ja сам био жѐлео / Ja sam bio želeo	Ja бих жѐлео / Ja bih želeo
2nd per	Ти си жѐлео / Ti si želeo	Ти си био жѐлео / Ti si bio želeo	Ти би жѐлео / Ti bi želeo
3rd per (M)	Он је жѐлео / On je želeo	Он је био жѐлео / On je bio želeo	Он би жѐлео / On bi želeo
3rd per (F)	Она је жѐлела / Ona je želela	Она је била жѐлела / Ona je bila želela	Она би жѐлела / Ona bi želela
3rd per (N)	Оно је жѐлело / Ono je želelo	Оно је било жѐлело / Ono je bilo želelo	Оно би жѐлело / Ono bi želelo
1st per pl	Ми смо жѐлели / Mi smo želeli	Ми смо били жѐлели / Mi smo bili želeli	Ми бисмо жѐлели / Mi bismo želeli
2nd per pl	Ви сте жѐлели / Vi ste želeli	Ви сте били жѐлели / Vi ste bili želeli	Ви бисте жѐлели / Vi biste želeli
3rd per pl	Они су жѐлели / Oni su želeli	Они су били жѐлели / Oni su bili želeli	Они би жѐлели / Oni bi želeli

	Imperative (Императив)
2nd per sg	(Ти) жѐли / (Ti) želi
1st per pl	(Ми) жѐлимо / (Mi) želimo

2nd per pl	(Ви) жѐлите
	(Vi) **ž**elite

Non-finite Forms

Infinitive (Инфинитив)	жѐлети
	želeti
Present Adverbial Participle (Глаголски прилог садашњи)	жѐлећи
	želeći
Past Adverbial Participle (Глаголски прилог прошли)	--

	Active Adjectival Participle (Глаголски придев радни)		Passive Adjectival Participle (Глаголски придев трпни)	
Gender	Singular	Plural	Singular	Plural
Feminine	жѐлела	жѐлеле	жѐљена	жѐљене
	želela	**ž**elele	**ž**eljena	**ž**eljene
Masculine	жѐлео	жѐлели	жѐљен	жѐљени
	želeo	**ž**eleli	**ž**eljen	**ž**eljeni
Neuter	жѐлело	жѐлела	жѐљено	жѐљена
	želelo	**ž**elela	**ž**eljeno	**ž**eljena

To Watch - глѐдати - gledati

	Present (Презент)	Future I (Футур први)	Future II (Футур други)
1st per	Ja глѐдам Ja **gled**am	Ja ћу глѐдати/Глѐдаћу Ja ću **gled**ati/**Gled**aću	Ja будем глѐдао/глѐдала Ja budem **gled**ao/**gled**ala
2nd per	Ти глѐдаш Ti **gled**aš	Ти ћеш глѐдати/Глѐдаћеш Ti ćeš **gled**ati/**Gled**aćeš	Ти будеш глѐдао/глѐдала Ti budeš **gled**ao/**gled**ala
3rd per (M)	Он глѐда On **gled**a	Он ће глѐдати/Глѐдаће On će **gled**ati/**Gled**aće	Он буде глѐдао On bude **gled**ao
3rd per (F)	Она глѐда Ona **gled**a	Она ће глѐдати/Глѐдаће Ona će **gled**ati/**Gled**aće	Она буде глѐдала Ona bude **gled**ala
3rd per (N)	Оно глѐда Ono **gled**a	Оно ће глѐдати/Глѐдаће Ono će **gled**ati/**Gled**aće	Оно буде глѐдало Ono bude **gled**alo
1st per pl	Ми глѐдамо Mi **gled**amo	Ми ћемо глѐдати/Глѐдаћемо Mi ćemo **gled**ati/**Gled**aćemo	Ми будемо глѐдали/глѐдале Mi budemo **gled**ali/**gled**ale
2nd per pl	Ви глѐдате Vi **gled**ate	Ви ћете глѐдати/Глѐдаћете Vi ćete **gled**ati/**Gled**aćete	Ви будете глѐдали/глѐдале Vi budete **gled**ali/**gled**ale
3rd per pl	Они/Оне глѐдају Oni/One **gled**aju	Они/Оне ће глѐдати/Глѐдаће Oni/One će **gled**ati/**Gled**aće	Они/Оне буду глѐдали/глѐдале Oni/One budu **gled**ali/**gled**ale

	Past Tense (Перфект)	Pluperfect (Плусквамперфект)	Conditional (Потенцијал)
1st per	Ja сам глѐдао Ja sam **gled**ao	Ja сам био глѐдао Ja sam bio **gled**ao	Ja бих глѐдао Ja bih **gled**ao
2nd per	Ти си глѐдао Ti si **gled**ao	Ти си био глѐдао Ti si bio **gled**ao	Ти би глѐдао Ti bi **gled**ao
3rd per (M)	Он је глѐдао On je **gled**ao	Он је био глѐдао On je bio **gled**ao	Он би глѐдао On bi **gled**ao
3rd per (F)	Она је глѐдала Ona je **gled**ala	Она је била глѐдала Ona je bila **gled**ala	Она би глѐдала Ona bi **gled**ala
3rd per (N)	Оно је глѐдало Ono je **gled**alo	Оно је било глѐдало Ono je bilo **gled**alo	Оно би глѐдало Ono bi **gled**alo
1st per pl	Ми смо глѐдали Mi smo **gled**ali	Ми смо били глѐдали Mi smo bili **gled**ali	Ми бисмо глѐдали Mi bismo **gled**ali
2nd per pl	Ви сте глѐдали Vi ste **gled**ali	Ви сте били глѐдали Vi ste bili **gled**ali	Ви бисте глѐдали Vi biste **gled**ali
3rd per pl	Они су глѐдали Oni su **gled**ali	Они су били глѐдали Oni su bili **gled**ali	Они би глѐдали Oni bi **gled**ali

	Imperative (Императив)
2nd per sg	(Ти) глѐдај (Ti) **gled**aj
1st per pl	(Ми) глѐдајмо (Mi) **gled**ajmo

2nd per pl	(Ви) глȅдајте (Vi) **gle**dajte

Non-finite Forms

Infinitive (Инфинитив)	глȅдати **gle**dati
Present Adverbial Participle (Глаголски прилог садашњи)	глȅдајући **gle**dajući
Past Adverbial Participle (Глаголски прилог прошли)	--

	Active Adjectival Participle (Глаголски придев радни)		Passive Adjectival Participle (Глаголски придев трпни)	
Gender	Singular	Plural	Singular	Plural
Feminine	глȅдала **gle**dala	глȅдале **gle**dale	глȅдана **gle**dana	глȅдане **gle**dane
Masculine	глȅдао **gle**dao	глȅдали **gle**dali	глȅдан **gle**dan	глȅдани **gle**dani
Neuter	глȅдало **gle**dalo	глȅдала **gle**dala	глȅдано **gle**dano	глȅдана **gle**dana

To Win - побéдити - pobediti

	Present (Презент)	Future I (Футур први)	Future II (Футур други)
1st per	Ja пòбедим / Ja pobedim	Ja ћу побéдити/Побéдићу / Ja ću pobediti/Pobediću	Ja будем побéдио/побéдила / Ja budem pobedio/pobedila
2nd per	Ти пòбедиш / Ti pobediš	Ти ћеш побéдити/Побéдићеш / Ti ćeš pobediti/Pobedićeš	Ти будеш побéдио/побéдила / Ti budeš pobedio/pobedila
3rd per (M)	Он пòбеди / On pobedi	Он ће побéдити/Побéдиће / On će pobediti/Pobediće	Он буде побéдио / On bude pobedio
3rd per (F)	Она пòбеди / Ona pobedi	Она ће побéдити/Побéдиће / Ona će pobediti/Pobediće	Она буде побéдила / Ona bude pobedila
3rd per (N)	Оно пòбеди / Ono pobedi	Оно ће побéдити/Побéдиће / Ono će pobediti/Pobediće	Оно буде побéдило / Ono bude pobedilo
1st per pl	Ми пòбедимо / Mi pobedimo	Ми ћемо побéдити/Побéдићемо / Mi ćemo pobediti/Pobedićemo	Ми будемо побéдили/побéдиле / Mi budemo pobedili/pobedile
2nd per pl	Ви пòбедите / Vi pobedite	Ви ћете побéдити/Побéдићете / Vi ćete pobediti/Pobedićete	Ви будете побéдили/побéдиле / Vi budete pobedili/pobedile
3rd per pl	Они/Оне пòбеде / Oni/One pobede	Они/Оне ће побéдити/Побéдиће / Oni/One će pobediti/Pobediće	Они/Оне буду побéдили/побéдиле / Oni/One budu pobedili/pobedile

	Past Tense (Перфект)	Pluperfect (Плусквамперфект)	Conditional (Потенцијал)
1st per	Ja сам побéдио / Ja sam pobedio	Ja сам био побéдио / Ja sam bio pobedio	Ja бих побéдио / Ja bih pobedio
2nd per	Ти си побéдио / Ti si pobedio	Ти си био побéдио / Ti si bio pobedio	Ти би побéдио / Ti bi pobedio
3rd per (M)	Он је побéдио / On je pobedio	Он је био побéдио / On je bio pobedio	Он би побéдио / On bi pobedio
3rd per (F)	Она је побéдила / Ona je pobedila	Она је била побéдила / Ona je bila pobedila	Она би побéдила / Ona bi pobedila
3rd per (N)	Оно је побéдило / Ono je pobedilo	Оно је било побéдило / Ono je bilo pobedilo	Оно би побéдило / Ono bi pobedilo
1st per pl	Ми смо побéдили / Mi smo pobedili	Ми смо били побéдили / Mi smo bili pobedili	Ми бисмо побéдили / Mi bismo pobedili
2nd per pl	Ви сте побéдили / Vi ste pobedili	Ви сте били побéдили / Vi ste bili pobedili	Ви бисте побéдили / Vi biste pobedili
3rd per pl	Они су побéдили / Oni su pobedili	Они су били побéдили / Oni su bili pobedili	Они би побéдили / Oni bi pobedili

	Imperative (Императив)
2nd per sg	(Ти) побéди / (Ti) pobedi
1st per pl	(Ми) побéдимо / (Mi) pobedimo

2nd per pl	(Ви) побéдите (Vi) po**be**dite

Non-finite Forms

Infinitive (Инфинитив)	побéдити po**be**diti
Present Adverbial Participle (Глаголски прилог садашњи)	--
Past Adverbial Participle (Глаголски прилог прошли)	побéдивши po**be**divši

Gender	Active Adjectival Participle (Глаголски придев радни)		Passive Adjectival Participle (Глаголски придев трпни)	
	Singular	Plural	Singular	Plural
Feminine	побéдила po**be**dila	побéдиле po**be**dile	пòбеђена po**be**đena	пòбеђене po**be**đene
Masculine	побéдио po**be**dio	побéдили po**be**dili	пòбеђен po**be**đen	пòбеђени po**be**đeni
Neuter	побéдило po**be**dilo	побéдила po**be**dila	пòбеђено po**be**đeno	пòбеђена po**be**đena

To Work - ра́дити - raditi

	Present (Презент)	Future I (Футур први)	Future II (Футур други)
1st per	Ja ра́дим / Ja radim	Ja ћу ра́дити/Ра́дићу / Ja ću raditi/Radiću	Ja будем ра́дио/ра́дила / Ja budem radio/radila
2nd per	Ти ра̂диш / Ti radiš	Ти ћеш ра́дити/Ра́дићеш / Ti ćeš raditi/Radićeš	Ти будеш ра́дио/ра́дила / Ti budeš radio/radila
3rd per (M)	Он ра̂ди / On radi	Он ће ра́дити/Ра́диће / On će raditi/Radiće	Он буде ра́дио / On bude radio
3rd per (F)	Она ра̂ди / Ona radi	Она ће ра́дити/Ра́диће / Ona će raditi/Radiće	Она буде ра́дила / Ona bude radila
3rd per (N)	Оно ра̂ди / Ono radi	Оно ће ра́дити/Ра́диће / Ono će raditi/Radiće	Оно буде ра́дило / Ono bude radilo
1st per pl	Ми ра̂димо / Mi radimo	Ми ћемо ра́дити/Ра́дићемо / Mi ćemo raditi/Radićemo	Ми будемо ра́дили/ра́диле / Mi budemo radili/radile
2nd per pl	Ви ра̂дите / Vi radite	Ви ћете ра́дити/Ра́дићете / Vi ćete raditi/Radićete	Ви будете ра́дили/ра́диле / Vi budete radili/radile
3rd per pl	Они/Оне ра̂де / Oni/One rade	Они/Оне ће ра́дити/Ра́диће / Oni/One će raditi/Radiće	Они/Оне буду ра́дили/ра́диле / Oni/One budu radili/radile

	Past Tense (Перфект)	Pluperfect (Плусквамперфект)	Conditional (Потенцијал)
1st per	Ja сам ра́дио / Ja sam radio	Ja сам био ра́дио / Ja sam bio radio	Ja бих ра́дио / Ja bih radio
2nd per	Ти си ра́дио / Ti si radio	Ти си био ра́дио / Ti si bio radio	Ти би ра́дио / Ti bi radio
3rd per (M)	Он је ра́дио / On je radio	Он је био ра́дио / On je bio radio	Он би ра́дио / On bi radio
3rd per (F)	Она је ра́дила / Ona je radila	Она је била ра́дила / Ona je bila radila	Она би ра́дила / Ona bi radila
3rd per (N)	Оно је ра́дило / Ono je radilo	Оно је било ра́дило / Ono je bilo radilo	Оно би ра́дило / Ono bi radilo
1st per pl	Ми смо ра́дили / Mi smo radili	Ми смо били ра́дили / Mi smo bili radili	Ми бисмо ра́дили / Mi bismo radili
2nd per pl	Ви сте ра́дили / Vi ste radili	Ви сте били ра́дили / Vi ste bili radili	Ви бисте ра́дили / Vi biste radili
3rd per pl	Они су ра́дили / Oni su radili	Они су били ра́дили / Oni su bili radili	Они би ра́дили / Oni bi radili

	Imperative (Императив)
2nd per sg	(Ти) ра́ди / (Ti) radi
1st per pl	(Ми) ра́димо / (Mi) radimo

207

2nd per pl	(Ви) ра́дите
	(Vi) **ra**dite

Non-finite Forms

Infinitive (Инфинитив)	ра́дити
	raditi
Present Adverbial Participle (Глаголски прилог садашњи)	ра́дећи
	radeći
Past Adverbial Participle (Глаголски прилог прошли)	ра́дивши
	radivši

	Active Adjectival Participle (Глаголски придев радни)		Passive Adjectival Participle (Глаголски придев трпни)	
Gender	Singular	Plural	Singular	Plural
Feminine	ра́дила	ра́диле	ра̂ђена	ра̂ђене
	radila	**ra**dile	**ra**đena	**ra**đene
Masculine	ра́дио	ра́дили	ра̂ђен	ра̂ђени
	radio	**ra**dili	**ra**đen	**ra**đeni
Neuter	ра́дило	ра́дила	ра̂ђено	ра̂ђена
	radilo	**ra**dila	**ra**đeno	**ra**đena

To Write - писати - pisati

	Present (Презент)	Future I (Футур први)	Future II (Футур други)
1st per	Ja пишем Ja **pišem**	Ja ћу писати /Писаћу Ja ću **pisati** /**Pisaću**	Ja будем писао/писала Ja budem **pisao/pisala**
2nd per	Ти пишеш Ti **pišeš**	Ти ћеш писати/Писаћеш Ti ćeš **pisati**/**Pisaćeš**	Ти будеш писао/писала Ti budeš **pisao/pisala**
3rd per (M)	Он пише On **piše**	Он ће писати /Писаће On će **pisati** /**Pisaće**	Он буде писао On bude **pisao**
3rd per (F)	Она пише Ona **piše**	Она ће писати /Писаће Ona će **pisati** /**Pisaće**	Она буде писала Ona bude **pisala**
3rd per (N)	Оно пише Ono **piše**	Оно ће писати/Писаће Ono će **pisati**/**Pisaće**	Оно буде писало Ono bude **pisalo**
1st per pl	Ми пишемо Mi **pišemo**	Ми ћемо писати/Писаћемо Mi ćemo **pisati**/**Pisaćemo**	Ми будемо писали/писале Mi budemo **pisali/pisale**
2nd per pl	Ви пишете Vi **pišete**	Ви ћете писати/Писаћете Vi ćete **pisati**/**Pisaćete**	Ви будете писали/писале Vi budete **pisali/pisale**
3rd per pl	Они/Оне пишу Oni/One **pišu**	Они/Оне ће писати/Писаће Oni/One će **pisati**/**Pisaće**	Они/Оне буду писали/писале Oni/One budu **pisali/pisale**

	Past Tense (Перфект)	Pluperfect (Плусквамперфект)	Conditional (Потенцијал)
1st per	Ja сам писао Ja sam **pisao**	Ja сам био писао Ja sam bio **pisao**	Ja бих писао Ja bih **pisao**
2nd per	Ти си писао Ti si **pisao**	Ти си био писао Ti si bio **pisao**	Ти би писао Ti bi **pisao**
3rd per (M)	Он је писао On je **pisao**	Он је био писао On je bio **pisao**	Он би писао On bi **pisao**
3rd per (F)	Она је писала Ona je **pisala**	Она је била писала Ona je bila **pisala**	Она би писала Ona bi **pisala**
3rd per (N)	Оно је писало Ono je **pisalo**	Оно је било писало Ono je bilo **pisalo**	Оно би писало Ono bi **pisalo**
1st per pl	Ми смо писали Mi smo **pisali**	Ми смо били писали Mi smo bili **pisali**	Ми бисмо писали Mi bismo **pisali**
2nd per pl	Ви сте писали Vi ste **pisali**	Ви сте били писали Vi ste bili **pisali**	Ви бисте писали Vi biste **pisali**
3rd per pl	Они су писали Oni su **pisali**	Они су били писали Oni su bili **pisali**	Они би писали Oni bi **pisali**

	Imperative (Императив)
2nd per sg	(Ти) пиши (Ti) **piši**
1st per pl	(Ми) пишимо (Mi) **pišimo**

2nd per pl	(Ви) пишите (Vi) **pi**šite

Non-finite Forms

Infinitive (Инфинитив)	писати **pi**sati
Present Adverbial Participle (Глаголски прилог садашњи)	пишући **pi**šući
Past Adverbial Participle (Глаголски прилог прошли)	писавши **pi**savši

	Active Adjectival Participle (Глаголски придев радни)		Passive Adjectival Participle (Глаголски придев трпни)	
Gender	Singular	Plural	Singular	Plural
Feminine	писала **pi**sala	писале **pi**sale	писана **pi**sana	писане **pi**sane
Masculine	писао **pi**sao	писали **pi**sali	писан **pi**san	писани **pi**sani
Neuter	писало **pi**salo	писала **pi**sala	писано **pi**sano	писана **pi**sana